A TOUR OF FRENCH HISTORY

*From a Province of Rome
to the Kingdom of France*

PIERRE D. BOGNON

To Leigh, with our hope that this book will help our children and grandchildren continue their exploration and love of France

Contents

"Lieu de Mémoire":
Basilica of Saint Denis

Solitary tower of Basilica of Saint Denis

On the way from Charles de Gaulle Airport to the City of Light on the A1, and on the opposite side of the solidly anchored Stade de France, a solitary square tower can be glimpsed. It is that of the Basilica of Saint Denis. Up until the middle of the nineteenth century, the Basilica had a second tower with an elegant spire piercing the sky. There are great expectations that they will be seen again after 2019 (see page 180).

Saint Denis is the necropolis of the French monarchy and the first Gothic religious building in the world. It holds a special place in France's collective memory, it is a true *lieu de memoire.*

Bishop Denis and his Legend (250 A.D.)

Circa 250 A.D. Bishop Denis begged his superior the bishop of Rome, Fabian, to allow him to leave Rome and evangelize. His wish was granted, at last, when he was sent to preach the gospel in Gaul, a northern province of the Roman Empire. Denis and two companions, Rusticus, a priest, and Eleutherius, a deacon, travelled to Lutetia, the imperial Roman city, later to be known as the Gallic city of Paris.

The zeal of the envoys of Rome in spreading the word about the one God and the resurrection of His son made them a threat. The Roman authorities did not mind adding the God of the Christians to their pantheon, but the Christians preferred to die rather than concede that their God was not the one and only. This growing tribe of believers was putting the social order at risk. Sisinnius Fescenninus, the representative of Rome, reacted swiftly and expeditiously when news of the three missionaries reached him. They were arrested and decapitated.

The action took place on the Mons Martyrum, the Mountain of Martyrs, known today as *Montmartre.* The favorite legend of Denis says that he then picked up his head and walked to the site of the current basilica, on the top of a hill north of the city. His body was later buried there, and his tomb became a popular destination for converts to the new Church. Denis would eventually be honored as Saint Denis.

This is one of the four or five versions of the life and death of Denis. In each of them, he is sent to Gaul to evangelize and is decapitated somewhere north of today's Paris; who he was, when his martyrdom took place and what happened after he was decapitated vary from one version to the next. Wherever the truth lies, the lasting image of a decapitated Denis carrying his head is the most enduring construct of his myth.

Statue of Denis at left portal of Notre Dame

Genevieve's Miracle

Two centuries later, in 451, Attila and his Huns reached the outskirts of Lutetia. The barbarian army had a fearsome reputation and the town would have surrendered had it not been for a young woman from a great Gallo-Roman family, Genevieve, France's first Joan of Arc. Earlier in her life she had become a nun and had devoted her life to charity. When Lutetia faced the threat of Attila she proclaimed her faith in the God of the Christians and her belief that He would protect the city. The besieged heard her exhortations, mustered their courage to rise and resist the barbarians and, *mirabile dictu*, Attila skirted their town. The people of Lutetia convinced they had been saved by Genevieve's heroic bearing and her prayers, thought of no better way to be thankful than to honor her God and build a modest place of worship on the site of Denis' mausoleum.

The stories of Denis carrying his head and of the miracle performed by Genevieve belong with the numerous mysteries and legends of the history of proto-France. Similar stories of events that took place in Late Antiquity and the Early Middle Ages always seem to draw their inspiration as much from legend as reality.

During the last years of Genevieve's life, Gaul became the Kingdom of the Franks. About a hundred years later, Dagobert, one of the kings of the first French dynasty, the Merovingian, who much admired Saint Denis, enlarged Genevieve's church. He also gathered the remains of the Saint and his two companions and entrusted his goldsmith Eloi with the honorific task of building a richly adorned reliquary. Nothing remains of this fine work and it is left to our imagination to picture it made of gold, silver and precious stones. Dagobert was the first French king to be buried in Saint Denis in 639 where he was given a place of honor next to the altar.

Meticulous archeological excavations undertaken in Saint Denis in the late 1970's have uncovered the remains of an abbey next to the church built in honor of Genevieve. The monks must have settled there to watch over the relics of Denis and welcome the pilgrims who came in great numbers to seek the blessing of the martyr. It is reasonable to assume that the monastery dates from the middle of the seventh century.

The Basilica and the Kingdom of the Franks

In 754, Pope Stephen II came to Saint Denis to anoint the first king of the second dynasty, the Carolingian Pepin le Bref, and his son, the future Charlemagne. The rite was rich in regal and religious symbolism and would become ever more elaborate during the High Middle Ages.

Saint Denis by then symbolized the alliance of the Church of Rome and the Kingdom of the Franks. It had retained the modest proportions of the Merovingian church built at the time of Dagobert and would be enlarged between 754 and 775 under the direction of Abbot Fulrad.

Louis le Pieux, son of Charlemagne, and all future French kings with few exceptions would be anointed and crowned in the cathedral of Reims not at Saint Denis. Hincmar, who became archbishop of Reims in 845, had made a convincing argument: the *sacred oil* used to baptize Clovis, the first king of the Franks, had been kept in the cathedral of Reims and consequently the anointing and crowning of Frankish kings should take place in that cathedral.

Saint Denis did keep a role in the coronation proceedings, in the shadow of Reims. In the twelfth century, at the time of Louis VI, the Abbey was entrusted with safeguarding the regalia, the tunic adorned with the heraldic emblem of the French kings called fleur de lis, the ring, the scepter and the crown. The Abbot would take them to Reims in great solemnity before each coronation.

One of the symbols of royalty still on display in the basilica is a replica of the *oriflamme*, the battle standard of the king of France. Before going to war, the kings would make a pilgrimage to Saint Denis and be handed the oriflamme. On the battlefield, it would be a great honor for the knight entrusted with the banner to ride at the side of the king.

Oriflamme de Saint-Denis

Oriflamme of Saint Denis

First Gothic Cathedral in the World

Saint Denis became undeniably one of France's most significant *lieu de mémoire* when the eighth century Romanesque building was transformed into the first Gothic church in the world. It became the inspiration for Chartres, Notre Dame in Paris and other masterpieces which to this day are the glory of French architecture. The mastermind of this new architectural style was Abbot Suger. The son of a serf, this very capable and intelligent man who would become adviser to two kings was abbot of Saint Denis. He was convinced that seeing is believing, that the new church needed to be a testimony to the glory of God; he wanted rose windows allowing light to filter freely inside the basilica, *lux continua*. Light, for Suger, elevated the soul to the kingdom of God. How much he actually contributed to the new style is open to debate but he was undoubtedly the spirit behind the transformation of Saint Denis and was certainly blessed with extraordinary architects and stonemasons.

Suger understood the important political role that his new church could play. It was crucial to show strong ties between the Church and the king, important for the king of France to be seen as chosen by God. The abbot-politician-architect gave the tomb of Dagobert a place of honor, facing the relics of Saint Denis, and the consecration of the new Gothic apse in June 1144 was a splendid affair presided by King Louis VII and Queen Alienor.

Among his many contributions to Saint Denis, Suger encouraged historian monks to document the Capetian monarchy. The monk in charge became one of the main dignitaries of the abbey and several left works of great importance, which are still referenced. Rigord, who died in 1209, is remembered for his *Gesta Philippi Augusti,* the life of King Philippe II. The work covers the first twenty-eight years of the reign and in its prologue the king is referred to for the first time as *Auguste.* In Rigord's eyes the king had added so much land to the kingdom that he deserved the title given to Roman emperors. Philippe II would hence be known as Philippe Auguste. One hundred and fifty years later, Richard Lescot, another Saint Denis historian-monk, made his mark when researching succession rights to the throne of France. Lescot uncovered a Code dating from Clovis, the first king of the Franks at the very end of the fifth century, known as *Salic law.* His biased interpretation of article 62 of this Code would be referenced after the middle of the fourteenth century to substantiate male-only succession rights to the crown.

The chroniclers of the abbey were in such high regard that in 1437 they were acknowledged as the official historians of the kings of France.

Royal Necropolis

In the thirteenth century Saint Denis became the royal necropolis and, as such, is truly the candidate of choice to introduce *A Tour of French History, from a Province of Rome to the Kingdom of France*. It had been the burial place for members of the royal family starting with the descendants of Clovis; the tomb of Dagobert, in particular, had been prominently displayed. Five kings of the second dynasty, the Carolingian, had then been buried in the basilica as had most of the early kings of the third dynasty, the Capetian. The abbots had not given the royal tombs the place of honor they deserved when, in 1231, Abbot Eudes Clement and King Louis IX, Saint Louis, commissioned the sculpting of the gisants of sixteen kings and queens who had preceded the saintly king.

Gisants at Saint Denis

A *gisant* is a funeral statue representing a recumbent person and the word is derived from ci-git, that is, here lies. These gisants were meant to portray idealized men and women in their prime. They were displayed in the transept of the basilica, facing east, the rising sun, peacefully awaiting their resurrection; the members of the Merovingian and the Carolingian dynasties were placed on the south side, the Capetians on the north and Louis VIII and Philippe Auguste, the father and grandfather of Saint Louis, in the middle. This, Saint Louis thought, would impress

7

upon the feudal lords the continuity of the royal dynasties and support his claim that his lineage went back to the first kings of the Franks (it was a questionable claim unless the notion of lineage was broadened to descendants through marriage). The king also proclaimed that kings and queens must be buried at Saint Denis making it the *necropolis of kings* as a chronicler wrote at the time.

After generations of leaders who at the time of their death showed humility and acknowledged divine power, the Renaissance kings in the fifteenth century, sought glorification and wanted to be remembered for their deeds. Their tombs at Saint Denis are a testimony to this new spirit. They are richly decorated monuments, standing in sharp contrast to the austere gisants at their feet.

Funerals of kings had become elaborate affairs, rich in symbolism. There could not be two kings at the same time and so, while the preparations for the burial were slowly proceeding, the successor had to stay in hiding. Francois I's son did not appear in the public eye until eight weeks after the death of his father. The perennity of the monarchy was affirmed by an effigy of the dead king wearing the full regalia, with a head carved in wood or wax, and paraded, wined and dined up to the time the dead king was entombed. After 1610, an effigy would no longer be used, and continuity of the royal dignity would only be affirmed by the heralding in the basilica of "the king is dead, long live the king," which had been first heard in 1515 at the death of Louis XII.

The importance of Saint Denis waned during the last French dynasty, the Bourbons. Henri IV, the first king of that dynasty, crowned in 1594, and his successors, did not need the aura of Saint Denis to legitimize their titles. Kings by then gave more weight to highly visible and majestic equestrian statues on public places than to massive tombs in a necropolis. Henri IV was buried in a lead and wood casket, simply left on trestles in the crypt of Saint Denis, where he would be joined in great simplicity by the other Bourbons.

The basilica had lost its emblematic role and the abbey was no longer an important intellectual center for the monarchy; the monks were once again only keepers of History. There would be more to the history of Saint Denis, triggered at first by the French Revolution of 1789, when much would be destroyed and transformed but Basilica Saint Denis, Abbot Suger and the monks remain as icons of the Kingdom of the Franks in the Middle Ages.

Roman Gaul

Gaul at the time of Caesar

Vercingetorix, Caesar and the Roman Conquest of Celtic Gaul

In the autumn of 52 BC, at *Alesia*, the young Gallic warrior Vercingetorix surrendered to Julius Caesar. The Roman general would go on and conquer Gaul before crossing the Rubicon and returning to Rome. The Gaul of Caesar was the future France.

Celtic blood ran through the veins of the tribesmen who battled against the Roman legions at Alesia. In the second half of the fifth century BC, these *Celts* had left the steppes of Russia and the shores of the Baltic Sea, crossed today's Germany and settled further west. There is a romantic view of these migrations of people from the north and east of Europe moving west and south. It holds that these Celts were attracted by milder, friendlier regions and is illustrated by the allegory of the pine tree dreaming of the palm tree used by Heinrich Heine in his poem *Ein Fichtenbaum steht einsam:*

> "Ein Fichtenbaum steht einsam im Norden..."
> (There stands a lonely pine-tree, in the north...)
> "Er traumt von einer Palme die, fern in Morgenland..."
> (He dreameth of a palm-tree, far in the sunrise-land...)

Large groups of Celts settled in what became known as Gaul. One contingent continued further south, crossed the Pyrenees and found a new home in Spain while still another went to a region hence known as *Cisalpine Gaul* in Northern Italy. Around 400 BC, members of a tribe called the Senones left the banks of the upper course of the Seine and moved south. Some stayed along the Adriatic coast between Ancona and Ravenna, others migrated further into the rich land of the Etruscans. These Celts now stood at the door of Rome, a young republic eager to expand into new territories. A confrontation with the men coming from the north became unavoidable. The Senones, full of bravado and relying on the strength of their numbers were undaunted by the Roman warriors entrenched on the banks of the river Allia. In July of 390 BC their savage and primitive hordes overran the defenders of the city and, with their chieftain Brennus at their head, entered Rome. The defeat at Allia remained for a long time a painful memory for the Romans.

Brennus's triumph was short-lived. In February of 389 BC, Camillus, the former consul and dictator, rallied the Romans and inflicted a crushing defeat on the Celts. This was the first of many setbacks for the Cisalpine Gauls who stood in the way of the northward expansion of Rome. Their impetuous and disorganized masses were no match for the disciplined and well-led Roman soldiers.

The Gauls also unsuccessfully faced the Romans in Anatolia. Gallic warriors had invaded Greece during the fifth century BC and then, at the beginning of the third century BC, a large contingent migrated into Asia Minor, and settled in Central Anatolia in a territory thereafter called *Galatia*. There, they sold their services as warriors and lived mostly off plundering.

Attalus I, an ally of Rome, who ruled Pergamon, a Greek city-state in Aeolia near the Aegean Sea, between 241 and 197 BC, decisively defeated the Galatians in Mysia. Numerous sculptures commemorated these events and one in particular *The Dying Gaul* became the representation of the Celtic stereotype, the Celt as barbarian who never prevailed over his enemies.

The Dying Gaul

When the Romans started their own incursions into Asia Minor at the beginning of the second century BC, it was not long before they encountered the Galatians. The Gallo-Greeks, as the Galatians were also known, were so decisively defeated by consul Gnaeus Manlius that his triumph was celebrated extravagantly in Rome.

In the West, after their conquest of Cisalpine Gaul, Rome prepared to expand into Transalpine Gaul, Gaul on the other side of the Alps, and complete its control of the Mediterranean. It seized upon an attack of the Greek city-state of Massilia (Marseilles) in 125 BC by Celtic tribes coming from the southwestern edge of the Alps. The city had forged close ties with Rome and held a strategic position on the Mediterranean coast. The Romans dared to cross the snow-covered Alps, crushed the assailants of Massilia and continued their victorious drive west. Their first settlement was Aquae Sextiae, Aix, and the second, further south on the road to the Pyrenees, Narbo Martius, Narbonne. The new colony was called *Gallia Narbonensis* but the Romans also gave another, more evocative, name to the land conquered in Gallia Transalpina, *Provincia Nostra,* our province, which became Provence, the corner of France whose translucid skies would charm painters and poets in centuries to come.

W hy did the Celts living on both sides of the Southern Alps become known to the people in the Italian Peninsula as *Gauls?* The question is open to debate. Several etymologies have been suggested and a particularly evocative one connects the name to *gallus,* the Latin word for rooster. The rising sun was a dominant theme in the mythology of these Celts and the rooster, associated with the sunrise, became their emblem. Sunrise-rooster-Gallus-Gaul is a credible sequence.

A few years after their conquest of southern Gaul the Romans faced a fearsome foe, Germanic tribes. In 113 BC the Cimbri left Jutland, todays Denmark, migrated into southern Germany and were joined by another Nordic tribe, the Teutons. Cimbri and Teutons drifted into *Provincia Nostra* and defeated the Romans near the town of Orange in 105 BC. This encounter filled the Romans with such terror that its memory would remain vivid for many generations.

It took a great general, Marius, to turn things around. We owe the story of his life to Plutarch, the first-century Greek biographer; his *Life of Marius* offers rare insights into the life of the general. Marius implemented a thorough reorganization of the Roman military, replacing what had been until then a militia with a professional army. He ignored the property qualification for military service and recruited *proletarians,* men whose only contribution to the State were offspring or *proles.* These landless legionnaires would be totally devoted to their leaders. The newly organized legions decisively beat the Teutons near Aix in 102 BC and the Cimbri in Northern Piedmont a year later.

The Marian reform would have profound consequences; the trust placed by landless Roman legionnaires in their leader opened the door for generals to become emperors. Marius would be the last great Roman general who did not use his military victories as a springboard to the throne of Caesar.

The Cimbri, the Teutons and other tribes originally from Scandinavia and the Baltic were constantly on the move, commingling and separating, and in their expansion pushed the Celts further south. These tribesmen would be known as Germans. They had a well-defined physical type: tall, blond, blue-eyed, with elongated heads (dolichocephalic); in modern times they became the symbol of the *pure Aryan* even though there is no Aryan race but only Aryan languages belonging to the Indo-European family of languages. The Germans had displaced the Celts as early as the third century BC; the Helvetii would be among the last Celts to leave Germany.

These people from the north and east of Europe, who kept crossing the Rhine and entering Gaul were *barbarians* in the eyes of the Romans. The philosopher John Armstrong in his book *In Search of Civilization* notes the faintly idiotic origin often assigned to the word barbarian. It would have been coined in ancient Greece as a way of mocking those who did not belong to the Hellenic culture and did not speak one of the Greek dialects, their speech seeming little better than the bleating of a sheep: baa-baa-barbarian. For the Romans the barbarians were those who did not belong to the Empire. However, a barbarian could be a very powerful enemy. This, Armstrong continues, led to the development, in the second half of the nineteenth century, of a different concept: barbarians were not so much people on the outside as those whose spiritual wealth did not match their material prosperity. The mostly nomadic barbarian hordes who would terrorize the Romans during the later years of the Empire possessed great resources, energy and determination but constructed nothing. They lacked an element essential to civilization: they had the external abilities but not the internal spirit.

There is a dearth of documents about the Celts in Gaul and until recent times a lack of interest in their tribal groups. Historians relied mostly on the writings of Julius Caesar and subsequent Latin authors. Only toward the end of the nineteenth century did scholars in France who, up to then, had their focus only on the Greeks and the Romans, turn their attention to the study of the Celts and the Gauls.

These French scholars presented the Gauls as resourceful, generous and honest even though these character traits have been otherwise contested. They were members of various tribes who were very protective of their independence, and the largest ones were often warring with each other. There is little doubt that family ties mattered to them. Religion also provided a strong connective thread with the druids acting as spiritual heads, priests and doctors. Pliny the Elder, the Roman author, immortalized the legend of the druid collecting mistletoe in oak trees.

These were the people that Julius Caesar encountered when he became governor of Cisalpine Gaul in 60 BC and then governor of Gallia Narbonensis. It suited his purposes to be away from Italy and to gain the trust of an army. He had a delicate relationship with the Senate in Rome and, as member of a triumvirate, shared power with Pompey, praised for his recent victories in the Middle East, and Crassus, who had just brought much relief to Rome in defeating Spartacus. Gaul was his to conquer and could mean glory for him and plunder for his troops.

Caesar knew he could count on a meaningful Roman military presence in the south and that he would need to contain the incursions of fierce barbarian tribes coming from the North and crossing the Rhine. He also knew that the ties binding the numerous tribes in Gaul were weak; today's ally could be tomorrow's foe.

In 58 BC the Helvetii decided to leave what is now Switzerland and move westward with the hope of resettling somewhere in southwest Gaul; in all between 200,000 and 300,000 men, women and children were on the move. They avoided the Provincia Nostra and during their migration devastated the land of the Aedui, who were allies of Rome. This was the pretext Caesar needed to give his legionnaires their first serious action in Gaul. The Helvetii were defeated and the survivors forced to return to Switzerland. It marked the beginning of Caesar's eight years of wars in Gaul and the first of many victories for his legions.

Most of what is known about this period comes from the eight books of *De Bello Gallico,* also known as The Gallic Wars, written by Julius Caesar himself. Another account of the feats of the conqueror can be found in Plutarch's *Life of Julius Caesar.*

These opuses and later commentaries described the Gallic warriors as excitable, volatile and less disciplined than the Roman legionnaires. The long-haired Gallic chiefs are presented as eloquent and prone to swear oaths of "win or die." They are pictured adorned with gold bracelets and other ostentatious ornaments, showing great panache when proudly going into battle but too impulsive and lacking the wisdom to attack and withdraw at the right time. This type of behavior seems to foretell the *beau geste* of the French armies many centuries later during the Middle Ages, brave and noble but not pragmatic.

The tribes that Caesar faced were never truly united; too many Gallic chiefs on the field of battle looked out for their own interests. Even when they would entrust Vercingetorix with the destiny of Gaul, they would not give him the degree of allegiance that Caesar received from his legionnaires.

The Gauls rebelled against the Romans soon after Caesar's expedition against the Helvetii, as his legions had all the trappings of conquerors. Resistance flared in several areas of Belgium and Celtic Gaul, and the Gallic warriors gave only temporary reprieves to the Roman legions, harassing them relentlessly even though they were seldom a match for the well-trained Romans. Every summer between 58 and 52 BC Caesar campaigned against the Gauls. There was no military action during the winter, and it was a rare occasion when Caesar did not return to Italy during the cold season.

In 53 BC riots in Rome pushed the Romans in the arms of Pompey, who was named sole consul. Caesar, who was in Italy at the time, thought it wise to postpone his return to Gaul. The Gallic chiefs, informed of their governor's conundrum, saw an opportunity to unleash a general uprising and the Canutes of Cenabum (Orleans) volunteered to instigate the revolt. They were soon followed by the Arveni, their neighbors, who dwelled in today's Auvergne just north of the Roman Provincia. Vercingetorix, a young aristocrat who had previously disapproved of the conciliatory policy towards Rome favored by the leaders of his tribe and had been exiled, was chosen as king of the Arveni. He seemed predestined to be a leader as his name meant *great warrior king.* In a move that was new in a Gaul usually divided, he convinced other Gallic tribes to unite under his leadership. The young warrior, who was barely twenty years old, used the experience he had acquired during a short term of service as a Roman soldier to drill a strict discipline into the troops of the coalition.

Caesar could not wait until spring to return to Gaul. He, at first, reassured the people from Provence and then, in a bold move, despite snow and cold, crossed the Cevennes Mountains in south-central Gaul, and after a forced march reached Sens, where several of his legions were spending the winter. By March he entered Cenabum (Orleans), killed most of the inhabitants and took the survivors as slaves. This was Caesar's retribution for the revolt instigated by the town. He then set his sights on Avaricum (Bourges) and set up camp at the narrow entrance to the fortified settlement or oppidum. Vercingetorix had moved to the other side of the town. Ten Roman legions assisted by allied tribes fought in harsh weather conditions and after twenty-six days entered the town and massacred its inhabitants. The Gallic warriors had been unable to disrupt the supply lines of the Romans, and Vercingetorix had failed to save Avaricum.

Vercingetorix, outmaneuvered by the Romans, then moved to the capital of his tribe, Gergovia, a few miles south of today's Clermont-Ferrand, and implemented his preferred tactic: retreat and trap the enemy. Caesar obliged by moving six legions to the foot of the oppidum (his four other legions had been sent to face rebellions further north). The siege of Gergovia was a defeat for Caesar. He had to retreat, lost a great number of men and faced the defection of his former allies, the Aedui. Vercingetorix had achieved his first major victory.

After Gergovia, Caesar regrouped all of his legions in Sens and recruited German mercenaries to compensate for the defection of his Gallic allies. As for Vercingetorix, he devised a strategy that looked promising. He persuaded his allies in the south to prepare an attack against the Provincia Nostra betting that Caesar would come to its rescue. Long lines of Roman soldiers marching south would give him a favorable position to attack. Caesar obliged and by mid-August 52 BC, as he was about to enter the land of the *Sequani*, the Gauls launched their attack. The combatants on both sides were fearless, but the Germanic cavalrymen enlisted by the Romans had the upper hand. Vercingetorix lost the best part of his cavalry and was forced to retreat to a nearby oppidum, the elevated settlement of Alesia. Caesar followed the Gauls and positioned his legionnaires and German auxiliaries at the foot of the hill.

Vercingetorix was surrounded. He immediately sent messengers to Gallic tribe leaders asking for relief forces. Caesar, who might have been informed of this plan by prisoners or deserters, accelerated the construction of a double line of wooden fortifications around Alesia to isolate Vercingetorix and his men. The first line, called contravallations, faced the oppidum while the second, the circumvallations, oriented towards the outside and surrounded by deadly traps, was destined to slow down the expected Gallic rescue parties. Caesar's strategy would turn out to be brilliant.

The Gallic relief forces were slow in coming, and by the time they set up camp to the south of the oppidum it was early October; food was already in short supply for the men entrenched with Vercingetorix. Gallic cavalrymen made a first attempt to break through the Roman circumvallations while Vercingetorix attacked the contravallations but both attempts were unsuccessful. The relief forces then converged on a weak point of the Roman fortifications, a wooded area along the northern slope. The fighting was fierce and lasted into the night. Once more the German cavalry tipped the balance in favor of Caesar. The Gauls who had come to the rescue were soundly defeated and forced to retreat.

The *pin and pincer strategy* of Vercingetorix, pinning down Caesar's forces and waiting for reinforcement, had failed; he was now isolated in the oppidum of Alesia in a hopeless position. Caesar's leadership had brought the Romans an uncontested victory over the Gauls.

Rome made sure that Vercingetorix paid the price for his rebellion. He was jailed in Rome, then four years later during Caesar's triumph he was paraded through the city before being executed by strangulation. He was twenty five years old.

During the second half of the nineteenth century, it became de rigueur to point to the battle of Alesia as the beginning of the history of France. There was pride in Gallic ancestors and in Vercingetorix, the hero rallying his warriors to fight the invader. He was out-maneuvered by Caesar but defeat did not tarnish his image and legend says that he surrendered nobly, throwing his shield and sword at the feet of his victor. Their defeat at the hands of the Germans in 1870 may have led the French to search for sources of pride in their past. They settled on Vercingetorix and the Gauls, proving once more that what happens in a nation's present influences the recollection of its past.

In the early 1960's, the popular French cartoon series, *Asterix*, written and drawn by the team of Goscinny and Uderzo, told the story of the Gauls resisting the Roman occupation and fighting to regain their independence. In every one of their adventures, the smart, diminutive Asterix, his powerful companion Obelix and the Druid Panoramix, who jealously protects the recipe of the magic potion that gives superhuman strength, outwit the Romans. The French are very fond of this image of themselves: they swallow their pride when they are not the strongest but they always like to be seen as the cleverest.

Alesia, the Battle Site

The precise location of Alesia has long been debated, even in the French Parliament; more than one congressman has wanted this major tourist attraction on his home turf. The case might be closed now in favor of *Alise-Sainte-Reine* in Burgundy near Dijon, only a few hours southeast of Paris by car.

The small village is spread along the western slopes of a compact hill easily accessible from the highway. A steep dirt road leads from the village center to an oppidum.

Since March 2012 a *Centre d'interpretation,* interpretive center, in the new Museo Parc, offers exhibits and interactive displays. Its distinctive design, a concrete drum inside a wood lattice, was conceived by the architect Bernard Tschumi. The Centre is surrounded by a replica of the Roman fortifications, and its shape echoes their circular configuration.

A second structure, an archaeological museum, will be built on the site of the oppidum where Vercingetorix and his troops were trapped. According to the architects, "The round museum will be wrapped in the same local yellow-tinged limestone as used in the stone walls of the Gallic ramparts." Inside it is intended to conjure the state of mind of the thousands of Gallic warriors during the last days of the battle, when they likely lost all hope of breaking through the Roman contravallations.

Vercingetorix by Aime Millet (1865)

A massive statue of a mustachioed, fierce looking, Vercingetorix dominates the site of the battlefield. It was commissioned by Napoleon III at a time when *les Gaulois* ranked as the favorite ancestors of the French and the Emperor was fascinated by Caesar and his Gallic wars.

"Hairy Gaul," a Province of the Roman Empire

The Gallic rebellion did not survive Alesia. Caesar made sure that any pocket of resistance was crushed. The oppression of the Gauls served his political ambitions and he was merciless with anyone resisting the Roman occupation.

Twenty-eight months after Alesia, having nurtured his ambitions and hardened his troops during years of Gallic wars, Caesar took a single legion and crossed the Rubicon, the small river running into the Adriatic where the inflection of the coast signals the beginning of southern Italy. Under Roman law, Caesar could command his army in his Province but not in Italy. In crossing the Rubicon with one legion, he became an outlaw, and the die was cast. Today, *crossing the Rubicon* is one way of saying "passing the point of no return." Caesar was destined to become *Imperator* and to face a cruel death. On March 15, 44 BC he would be stabbed by a throng of Senators. This historical moment will be most often remembered by the last words "Et tu Brute?" spoken by the dying emperor in Shakespeare's *Julius Caesar* when he recognized Brutus among his assassins.

Gaul became a province within the Roman Empire. Caesar had drawn the blueprint of the future France, an isthmus between Northern and Southern lands, at the western end of Europe, bordered by the river Rhine, compact but marked by weak topographical boundaries in the north and the east.

The Roman presence in Gaul would last close to five hundred years and leave behind the key ingredients for the birth of a country: an administrative backbone, a network of roads for the exchange of goods and people, a language for its elite, and a religion for everybody.

In 27 BC, the Senate conferred the name Augustus to Octavian, the adopted son of Julius Caesar; he used this title with great diplomacy, preferring to be known as Princeps, First Citizen. The new emperor spent much of his first years expanding and consolidating the empire.

Concerned with possible unrest in Gaul, he had the newly conquered land report to him. It was divided into three provinces: Aquitanian, Lyonnaise and Belgian. Lugdunum, today's Lyon, was chosen as capital. Caesar had already divided Gaul into three very similar parts and the opening sentence of his *De Bello Gallico* is familiar to Latin students: *Gallia est omnis divisa en partes tres...*

The three Gauls became known as *Gaule chevelue*, hairy Gaul. Why hairy? Most presumably because its people had beards and long hair, possibly also because the Romans pictured the land covered with trees.

In 10 BC, as Augustus was making his third trip to Gaul, he spent time in Lugdunum and gathered the delegates of sixty Gallic civitates (city-states). In their presence, an altar was consecrated to Rome on a spot previously dedicated to *Lug,* the Gallic God of Fire. Up to the third century, representatives of the three Gauls gathered annually in Lugdunum, around the altar, forming what some have viewed as a first pseudo-parliament.

The emperor made an unexpected fourth trip to Gaul in 8 BC and his frequent presence in situ certainly helped keep the *Gaule chevelue* peaceful during his reign. Another Roman emperor, Claudius, born in Lugdunum and hailed emperor by the Praetorian Guard in 41 AD, would be keen to facilitate the integration of Gaul in the empire. He banned the religious activities of the Druids and tried unsuccessfully to give the Gauls access to the senate in Rome.

"Quinctili Vare, Legiones Redde." When the Rhine became a "Lime"

Augustus, who sought peace in Gaul, was also concerned about the risk of barbarian invasions. Over time it became evident that relying on the Rhine and the Danube to be the natural eastern borders of the Empire left hostile Germanic tribes too close to Gaul and Italy. Agrippa, the strategic mind behind Augustus' great military victories, devised an ambitious plan to settle Germania up to the Elbe. Drusus, when he commanded the Roman forces in the German territories, and later Tiberius, successfully occupied land between the Weser and the Elbe but Rome soon received a cruel reminder that Germania had not become a Roman province.

In 9 AD, Governor Publius Quinctilius Varus, who had replaced Tiberius in Germania but was nothing more than a competent administrator, was betrayed by a young Germanic ally on his staff. He was on his way to quell an uprising, or so he thought, when his legions were trapped and massacred in the Teutoburg Forest by barbarians led by the traitor Arminius. This would be remembered by Rome as a terrifying disaster. Legio XVII, XVIII and XIX lost their *aquilae*, their eagle standards, and even though the lost eagles would be recaptured later, the three numbers were never again assigned to a legion, a very symbolic sign that the wound would never heal. For months Augustus sighed "Quinctili Vare, legiones redde," Quinctilius Varus, give me back my legions. The Romans took their revenge a few years later, in 17 AD, under the command of Germanicus but Tiberius, who by then was emperor, made a strategic decision that would have far-reaching consequences: he withdrew his armies from the lands that were far from the Rhine. This decision set the stage for two Germanys: a Germanic in the east sometimes called Germania libera and a Greco-Latin in the west.

The Empire would no longer venture beyond the Rhine and only kept the people living near the right bank under its protection. Trajan, emperor at the turn of the second century AD, relied on a combination of man-made and natural obstacles to protect the land inside the angle formed by the Rhine and the Danube against armed incursions by the barbarians. These so-called limes which stretched from Bonn on the Rhine to Regensburg on the Danube did not form a continuous wall and were intended to warn more than to protect.

The barbarians will overrun the limes starting in the fourth century, the Roman Empire will fall and Gaul and the two Germanias will continue to share a common history.

Besançon, a Gallo-Roman City-State

Besançon is my home town. On my way to the *Lycee*, the high school, I would walk across the Pont Battant and down the Grande Rue. The bridge was the only crossing over the Doubs River in Roman times. Repaired often over the centuries it had been so damaged during the early days of WWII that it could no longer be saved and was destroyed in 1953. The Grande Rue is built on top of the *cardo maximus*, the main north-south road used by the Romans on their way from Italy to the Rhine River.

The Romans called the town Vesontio and it figured prominently on all the maps of the conquest of Gaul. Caesar in *De Bello Gallico* noted its strategic position when he set camp there in 58 BC, during his campaign against Ariovistus, the leader of a Germanic tribe. Roman reinforcements would rest there during their long marches north to the Rhine and the limes. It was the capital of the Sequani, a buffer tribe between the Aedui, the ancestors of the Burgundians, and the Helvetii. Vesontio was on the route of the Helvetii when they began their westward migration.

The Gauls had settled in an oppidum inside the loop formed by the river Doubs, abutting a hill known today as Mont Saint Etienne. This was an exceptional site and they added very little to its natural protections. The Romans extended the oppidum and Vesontio became one of the many city-states founded after the conquest of Gaul, all exhibiting similar layouts with a *cardo*, the main north-south street, and a *decumanus*, an east-west street. Most had one or several public places, a temple, a forum and sometimes an amphitheater. The city that Caesar called Vesontio became known as Bisontium in the fourth century and later Besançon.

In Bisontium, as elsewhere in Gaul, members of the local elite would be granted Roman citizenship, shared in the government of the city and its surroundings, following an administrative blueprint drawn by Rome. These civic leaders were given the nomen (one of the names) of the Roman who had sponsored their citizenship. Most Gallic men of importance thus bore Latin names and this was another means of integrating the Province of Gaul in the Empire. This form of self-government, under the watchful eye of Rome, allowed the imperial political system to be implemented in the colonies with a minimal number of men. More importantly for the future Kingdom of France it gave the Gauls elements of a national identity they were missing before Caesar.

Ruins recall Besançon at the time of Rome. Under Marcus Aurelius, in the second century, a monument known as Porte Noire had been erected at the foot of the hill, at the northern end of the cardo. This triumphal arch, made of soft stone from a local quarry, was richly sculpted and painted in muted colors. It did not age well, the carvings representing mythological and religious scenes darkened and eroded. Fortunately, several successful restorations were undertaken starting in the nineteenth century and most recently in 2011.

Other Roman ruins enrich the oldest sections of Besançon. Eight Corinthian columns excavated by the archeologist Castan in 1870 have been preserved in a small park bearing his name, square Castan and, on the northern bank of the Doubs, the Rue des Arenes is a reminder that an amphitheater once dominated this part of town.

Roman Ruins in Provence.

There are numerous well-preserved Roman ruins in France. The largest concentration of amphitheaters, aqueducts and statuary is found in the old Provincia. A tour of Roman sites along the lower Rhone valley will be most rewarding during the summer months, when the amphitheaters in Orange, Aix and Avignon are the sites of world-renowned music and dance festivals. Aficionados of bullfighting might prefer to time their visit with the September Feria in Nimes, and share in the electrifying atmosphere of a corrida in the Roman arena.

The *Musée Departemental-Arles Antique* has assembled a fine collection of Roman artifacts. The city, founded by Caesar, was an important Roman harbor at the mouth of the Rhone. Most of the imposing buildings which lined the banks of the river were destroyed by the barbarians and, for many years, archeologists and scuba divers have explored the bottom of the river in search of vestiges. In 2007 a team lead by Luc Long struck gold when a diver brought to the surface an imposing marble bust. The archeologists felt they had a major find but waited for the results of elaborate tests before publicizing their discovery. After many anxious months they received the exhilarating confirmation that they had unearthed the only bust of Caesar sculpted during his lifetime. The bust can be seen at the Musée Departemental, where it is now part of a rich collection of sculptured pieces lifted from the silt of the Rhone, statues, elements of temples patiently assembled and rare bronze objects. In 2009 an altar of the Greek goddess Artemis, the Diana of the Romans, was added to the collection.

Buste of Julius Caesar (Arles Museum)

"Christianity, a Successful Sect" (Ernest Renan)

Martyrdom of Blandine (177 A.D.) and the Persecution of Christians

Gods mattered to the emperor as well as to the citizens of Rome. Their pantheon welcomed the Gods worshipped in the conquered lands of an ever-expanding Empire. The Romans gained their favors by making offerings, sacrifices and joining in festivities. All these activities contributed to create a social identity. This is what a *religio* was, a shared element of identity defined by the rites and rituals believed to preserve the goodwill of the Gods.

At the beginning of the first century AD, the *good news* preached by Jesus and the story of His resurrection was spread by Syrian traders, craftsmen from Asia Minor and often by Roman legionnaires. Small communities of believers blossomed along the Rhone valley and then further north. The teachings of Jesus about compassion and respect of others appealed to oppressed minorities, to women and slaves. These believers in the one God, living in a world of polytheists, were constantly at risk, they were persecuted but their communities proved resilient.

In 177 AD, Christians were persecuted in Lugdunum. The believers in the one God were arrested, interrogated, and those who did not renounce their faith were executed or left at the mercy of wild animals in the amphitheater. That year, at least forty met that fate. One in particular, Blandine, a young slave from Asia Minor, is remembered for her steadfast refusal to sacrifice to pagan idols and her ensuing martyrdom. In Christian iconography, she is usually represented tied to a post and surrounded by lions. The tale of Blandine is found in a letter written by an anonymous witness that Eusebius, bishop of Caesarea, incorporated in his *Ecclesiastical History*, the most reliable source of information on the history of the church during the first three centuries. According to this letter, Blandine watched for days the fate of the other Christians and witnessed them proclaiming "I am a Christian" before dying. When her turn came, none of the wild animals did her any harm. She then was left hanging in a net at the mercy of bulls, tossed around and gored to death. She is the patron Saint of the city of Lyon.

The Greek speaking Christian community in Lugdunum was vibrant and was led by Bishop Irenaeus. Born in 140 in Smyrna, a city on the Aegean Sea Coast of Anatolia, he was a man of generous disposition who at a young age listened to Bishop Polycarp recall the teachings of Saint John the Evangelist. Irenaeus would be one of the few bishops who had been two witnesses away from the living Jesus. He was bishop of Lugdunum at the time of Blandine's martyr but could do nothing when the persecutions began.

Romans were exposed to other monotheisms. Mithra, an Indo-Iranian divinity, had a strong following in Rome during the second and third centuries. Roman soldiers had presumably been in contact with Mithraism during military campaigns against the Parthians along the Euphrates. The cult presented its adepts with a mythical history of the world and Mithra as a savior, helping man in his fight between good and evil. The initiated might even have received the promise of an immortal soul.

The sun was venerated in the east of the Empire. The so-called Sol Invictus, the Invincible Sun, was an all-powerful God in Palmyra in Syria. The cult of *Sol Invictus* became widespread in the army and was well suited to the imperial image. It gained such importance that it has been called the sun monotheism. A temple to the sun was built in Rome in 274 by Emperor Aurelian but the cult declined during the fourth century with the rise of Christianity.

The Romans were open-minded on matters of religion but ill at ease with monotheism. They could have included the new religion alongside the Gods they honored and feared but the Christians were adamant, one God and one God only. During the first decades following the death of

Jesus, the few who followed his teachings were treated as superstitious outcasts. Early emperors did not know what to make of them. If these Christians accepted to sacrifice to Roman Gods they could be pardoned but if they refused obstinately how should they be punished? When authorities called for ceremonies to seek the protection of the Gods and they refused to participate shouldn't they be viewed as traitors?

The Romans did not like cults and the first Christians suffered from the stigmatization of minorities and easily became scapegoats. The first persecutions had taken place in 64 when Christians were accused by Nero of burning Rome and put to death for his amusement. The fire had most certainly been set by the emperor himself who was prone to such acts of madness, but he made sure that, when consulted by his priests, the Gods pointed to the Christians. During that same period, around 64-67, the apostles Peter and Paul were put to death in Rome. A hundred years later, in the middle of the second century, Marcus Aurelius, concerned with the growing number of Christians, found it convenient to persecute them and his name remains attached to the first martyrs, Blandine and her companions, in Lugdunum (Lyon). The persecutions started during the annual meeting of the representatives of the three Gauls, a signal by the emperor that there was no room in the empire to stray from strict conformity to the Roman way.

Lyon, Gallo-Roman Ruins

The inhabitants of Lyon had long wondered about the precise location of Blandine's martyrdom when, in 1933, archeologists started major excavations along the slopes of the hill called Fourviere, rising on the right bank of the Saone River. It was known to be where the first Roman colony was founded. They did not uncover the anticipated amphitheater but made another substantial discovery, a Roman theater built presumably at the time of Emperor Augustus. Since 1946 this theater, now known as Theater of Fourvière, has been a renowned outdoors center for Music and the Arts where every summer the *Nuits de Fourvière* offer a choice of music, dance and other performing arts. Overlooking the theater is a modern concrete structure, attached to the hill and camouflaged by earth and vegetation. It houses the museum of Gallo-Roman civilization, consecrated mostly to the history of Lyon. Its superb collection of artifacts and educational displays make it an instructive introduction to the first centuries of the Roman presence in Gaul.

The amphitheater of Blandine's fame was uncovered years later, in 1958, in the Condate section of town, between the Rhone and Saone rivers. The arena and vestiges of the podium where the delegates from the Three Gauls used to gather can be seen along the slope of the hill of the Croix Rousse. The altar dedicated to Rome, though, has long been destroyed, and is known only thanks to its representation on coins (exhibited at the Gallo-Roman museum).

The Great Persecutions and the Tetrarchy

The defiant serenity manifested by the martyrs in Lugdunum and elsewhere in the empire and the public display of their faith encouraged more conversions.

Christian communities led by autocratic bishops became more noticeable, mostly in urban areas, but even though their numbers were growing, they remained outcasts. People in the eastern regions of the empire, particularly the Greeks, mistrusted them; those in the western territories accused them of the worst crimes and vices. Emperor Decius in the middle of the third century took umbrage at their stubborn independence and gave them the choice of sacrificing to the pagan Gods or being put to death; few renounced their monotheism and most remained steadfast even when subjected to the most horrific torture.

Emperor Decius's successor, Valerian, needed a scapegoat when the empire was at its nadir: the Goths had invaded the Balkans, the Franks were threatening Gaul, and Valerian himself was defeated by the Persians and taken prisoner. The persecution of Christians, he thought, would take the mind of his subjects off these disasters. This was also a time when the penetration of Christianity among the Roman elite had become more noticeable and the emperor felt compelled to rid the patrician ranks of its Christian elements.

The worst was yet to come for the Christians in the Roman Empire. It would be the Great Persecutions initiated by Diocletian at the turn of the fourth century (303 to 311) and escalated by his successor Galerius. Anti-Christian edicts were implemented mostly in the eastern territories of the Empire. Several thousand faithful, bishops, soldiers, even children died as martyrs after they refused to renounce their faith in Christ.

Diocletian's fateful policies can be traced back to 286 when he shared the imperial power with Maximian, an experienced general. Diocletian had come to realize that the Empire would be more efficiently managed by a *diarchy*: an emperor of the East, *primus inter pares,* first among equals, and an emperor of the West. This *diarchy* needed an ideological support and Diocletian proclaimed himself descendant of Jupiter and Maximian of Hercules. The new Augusti, leaders of the Empire, had thus promoted themselves to the rank of demi-gods. A few years later, as the Empire was ever more at risk on all its borders, a Caesar, a secondary emperor, was named to assist each Augustus and become his successor-designate. Constantius, surnamed Chlorus because of his pale complexion, was named Caesar of Maximian and settled in Trier on the river Moselle in Germania. He was the father of a young boy born out of wedlock who would become known as Constantine the Great. Constantius and Maximian in the west, and Diocletian and Galerius in the east, formed the *tetrarchy*.

The emperor-Gods could not leave room for dissent and needed to stifle the new religions, Manicheism and Christianity, and give a new impetus to the traditional Gods. Among the four members of the *tetrarchy* Constantius made the least effort to implement the edicts dictating the persecution of Christians, certainly more out of temperament than conviction. This also happened to be a pragmatic policy as it avoided awakening a spirit of independence in the Gauls. Thanks to Constantius Chlorus, the Christians in Gaul were spared the worst of Diocletian's great persecution.

In a surprising move, Diocletian and Maximian abdicated in 305. Constantius and Galerius, as planned, became Augusti but Galerius, who was primus inter pares, imposed Severus, a senior army officer, as Caesar of Constantius. This was a great blow to Constantine's ambitions. The death of his father in July 306 gave a new twist to his fortune. The Roman soldiers who had deeply entrenched dynastic instincts acclaimed him *Augustus*. This was too ambitious a step for the young man, thirty-one at the time, who preferred to be patient; he did not contest Severus's title and stayed far from Rome.

During the following years the orderly succession plans of the tetrarchy collapsed under the weight of egos and ambitions. After years of intrigues and suspicious deaths, the competition for power in the West climaxed when Constantine was pitted against Maxentius, the son of Maximian. In 312, Constantine led his army, spearheaded by cavalrymen from Gaul and Germania, against Maxentius. Even though he was outnumbered, Constantine rode from victory to victory in the Po Valley and inexorably closed in on Rome. On October twenty-eight the two contenders faced each other in the northern outskirts of Rome at the Milvian Bridge. Despite the backing Maxentius received from the elite unit of the Praetorian Guard (later disbanded by Constantine), it was a memorable victory for Constantine. The body of Maxentius was later found on the bank of the Tiber.

Constantine, Pontifex Maximus of the Christian Church

A legend says that while Constantine was marching on Rome, preparing to face Maxentius, he saw a cross in the sky inscribed with the words *in hoc signo vinces*, by this sign you will conquer. The God of the Christians would have foretold his victory. After his success at the Milvian Bridge, he inscribed his labarum, his standard, with the first two letters of the word Christ in Greek, X and P, chi and rho. In the eyes of Constantine, his victory had been willed and assured by the God of the Christians.

Chi and Rho

Rome acclaimed him *Maximus Augustus* and he accepted the title of *Pontifex Maximus*, the greatest pontiff. He did not give thanks to the Roman Gods for his triumph as was customary, neither did he declare himself openly in favor of the new religion. Constantine placed himself under the protection of Apollo, the Sun God and remained in Rome. In 323 he defeated Licinius, the Emperor of the East, and became sole emperor of the Roman Empire. He then moved to his new capital, along the Bosphorus, which became known as Constantinople.

Long before the vision foretelling his victory over Maxentius, Constantine had been introduced to the story of Christ by his father and, throughout his rise to power, had been close to Christian communities and benefited from their support. It is often claimed that he converted and became Christian in October 312 at the time of his victory at the Milvian Bridge. Other texts maintain that it was in 313, after he co-signed with Licinius the historic *Edict of Milan* which granted religious freedom for the first time. The purpose of the Edict had been mostly to preserve civil peace and it did not imply that Constantine was favoring a multi-religious society, but it was a sign of tolerance towards all religious practices and beliefs. Whatever the date of his conversion, Constantine continued to honor the sun and when he reformed the Roman calendar in 321 and introduced the notion of week, the sun was to be celebrated on the day of rest, Sunday. The day of the sun later became the day of the Lord, Die Dominica, which remained as dimanche in French. It was possible in these early days of Christianity to believe in the one God and sacrifice to the sun as Christianity was still loosely defined and rupture with paganism was only beginning. Since Emperor Constantine's attitude towards religion was driven as much by his longing for power as by his faith in the one God, making sacrifices to the sun was a political necessity.

Previous emperors had been called Pontifex Maximus, head of the highest college of priests of the official cult, and Constantine behaved as the true Pontifex Maximus of the Christian Church. He was head of the state and head of the Church; not a God, only the instrument of God on earth.

Eusebius, Bishop of Caesarea, the source of most of what is known about the early years of Christianity, is also the greatest panegyrist of Constantine. He had the opportunity in 336 during the great celebrations of the thirtieth anniversary of Constantine's proclamation as Augustus by his soldiers, to present Constantine's political theology of a Christian empire. The bishop translated Constantine's views as follows: the emperor holds his power from God and the empire can only be a Christian empire; the emperor's kingdom on earth must be like the celestial kingdom, one God for all, one emperor for all.

The belief that a unified empire calls for a unified church was shared by the first Christian Roman emperors and led to the accusation of caesaro-papism. Max Weber, the late nineteenth century sociologist, coined this term to empathize the concept of a Christian Caesar intervening in the affairs of the Church. It is not clear whether Constantine had actually made it his affair to dictate to the church or if he was answering the call of the bishops to settle internal disputes in the Church. What became true though is that the issue of supremacy of the secular over the religious power lingered not only in the eastern orthodox churches but poisoned the relationship between Rome and the French kings in the west. It would be many centuries before the Church extirpated itself from the grip of secular power.

Constantine has been given much credit for the early success of Christianity. He undoubtedly accelerated the process of Christianization of the empire but much had happened since the first conversions to the new creed. Despite constant persecutions, multiple communities of believers had been very active, particularly in the East and around the Mediterranean.

Christianus was the Latin word used by the Romans to designate those belonging to the new sect, which the Jews called Nazarene. At that time, neither term conveyed any connection to a Messiah. The word *Christian* was first used around forty AD. In Acts 11/26 one reads "Saul [Paul] and Barabas met with a large number of people and it was in Antioch that the disciples were first called Christians."

The word *catholic* implying a universal church, not tied to any race or region, appeared in 115 but at that time it was still an empty notion. It would take three powerful catalysts to create a Catholic church: an orthodoxy, a clergy and Rome, the Great Church as it was called by Irenaeus, the Bishop of Lugdunum.

Around the Empire various groups of Christians had given their own interpretation to the message of Christ and by the second century some of them had started assembling the texts that would form a canon. Christians in Smyrna, the present-day Izmir, led the way when they referred to the writings of the Apostles. The greater Christian community was searching for *orthodoxy,* the sharing of the same beliefs. This was in sharp contrast with the *orthopraxy* of the adepts of Greco-Roman cults, the following the same rules and rituals.

The orthodoxy needed to be safeguarded by adequate institutions and a hierarchy. The first in line were the *episcopos,* the bishops. They were assisted by the *presbyteros*, the clergy. The bishops, located in major cities, became guardians of the canon and administrators of their communities.

Rome was the most important city in the Roman empire of the west, at a crossroads of people, ideas and power. It was well placed to become the heart of the Church and its bishop the head of all bishops, the successor to Peter.

The required ingredients for the founding of a Catholic church were ready to coalesce but theological disagreements, dormant during the great Diocletian persecution, still needed to be addressed. One of prime importance for the new church was *the nature of Christ*: what is the relationship between Christ and God? The debate resurfaced at first within the Christian community of Alexandria. Arius, a preacher at one of the many churches of Alexandria, was forceful in teaching that God alone has not been engendered, *agennetos,* and that Christ was not born before all ages. The unity of the church in the diocese of Alexandria was at risk and its bishop, Alexander, could not but expulse Arius. The dissident preacher found disciples at Cesaree and the controversy engulfed the Christian community in the Orient. The moment had come for Constantine, who was working at consolidating his empire, to call for a council.

The bishops gathered at Nicea in 325 debated passionately for two months and at the end of May endorsed the creed of Jesus, man and God, "born of the Father before all ages, God from God, true God from true God, begotten not made…" The Roman Catholics still say these words when they recite the Niceno-Constantinopolitan Creed during their liturgy (the controversy had been conclusively settled at another council, in Constantinople in 381). This did not mark the end of Arianism even though it was now a heresy. It would still be embraced by numerous Germanic tribes and would survive the fall of the Roman Empire of the West in the fifth century.

There was now a Church, with a canon, adequate institutions and its capital was Rome; it was universal and could be called Catholic. The Messiah of the converted Jews had become Christ, the Anointed One, the Son of God. Constantine had endorsed the views of the majority and excluded any right to dissent. The politics of the One, Holy, Catholic and Apostolic Church of Rome would be based over the coming centuries on the fundamental principle that anything that threatens unity goes against the will of God. The same fundamental belief would guide the lay leaders of Christian states and its most ardent adherents would be the kings of France; dissent was to be rooted out.

During the last years of his life Constantine was involved in bitter intrigues. Crispus, his son from his marriage with Minerva, had all the attributes of an Augustus when, in 326, Constantine ordered him tortured and decapitated. Nothing is certain about the events which led to this dramatic death. One possible scenario says that Fausta, his second wife, attempted to seduce the young man, was rejected and in a perverse move convinced Constantine that she had been aggressed by Crispus. There could be some truth to Fausta provoking the filicide as Crispus clearly stood in the way of Fausta's ambitions for her own sons. It would not be long before Constantine saw the light. He started a long mourning and commissioned a gold statue in the effigy of his son. Then, in the early summer of 326, the body of Fausta was found burned to death in a thermal bath. There is little doubt that Constantine had ordered the murder. Later that year, Constantine's mother Helena seeking forgiveness for her son, led the first pilgrimage to the Holy Land in search of the Holy Cross. She found three crosses and brought back the one on which Jesus is believed to have died. This, at the time, was taken as a sign that Constantine's crimes had been forgiven.

Helena is always associated with the rise of Christianity in the Roman Empire but little is known about her. She was a *stabularia*, a servant, working in the stables of an inn when she met Constantius Chlorus and they conceived a son, Constantine, born in 275 in Niš, in today's Serbia. After Constantius married Theodora in 293 Helena left the stage only to reappear when her son was proclaimed Augustus in July 306. Some authors claim that during that period she had been baptized, unafraid of the persecutions that spared few Christians. Her fame and reputation were secured by her trip to Jerusalem and her active role in the building of the Basilica of the Holy Sepulcher.

It was not uncommon at the time to convert very late in life and

Constantine waited to be on his deathbed in 337 before asking to be baptized. Nevertheless, much has been made of his procrastination as it can be seen as a sign of his ambiguous relationship with Christianity.

The Orthodox Church recognized Constantine as a saint. He had been such a great enabler of Christianity that the decapitation of his son Crispus, the killing of several family members and of his wife Fausta were overlooked.

Constantine had stopped all persecutions of Christians after being named emperor. There had been no immediate Christianization of society but Christianity, now an accepted religion, had gained high visibility. It was, quoting the French historian and philosopher Ernest Renan, "a sect that had succeeded." Renan was right, Christianity was a sect, but what made it radical was the divinity of Jesus the man.

Christians would still suffer short bursts of persecution in the Roman Empire. When Julian the Apostate became emperor in 361 he attempted to revive paganism and make it a state religion with him at its head but such anti-Christian policies were too anachronistic and did not survive his reign. His successor, Jovian, ended the revival of paganism and in 380, another emperor, Theodosius I the Great, imposed the Niceno-Constantinopolitan Creed on all his subjects. Henceforth, only Catholic Christians were tolerated.

Constantine's great empire which had been divided among his sons, and then reunited, was split for the last time after the death of Theodosius I. In 395, Arcadius was named emperor of the east and Honorius of the west. The Roman Empire of the East, which became known as *Byzantium*, survived for ten centuries and remained Christian. The Empire of the West survived for less than a century. Christianity became the religion of the kingdoms which emerged after the fall of the empire and this would be the case for the Kingdom of the Franks, the future France.

Barbarians in Gaul

"The Barriers which had separated the Savage and the Civilized Nations were leveled with the Ground" (Edward Gibbon)

On December 31, 406 Alans, Vandals, Burgundians and other barbarian tribes crossed the frozen Rhine River and entered Gaul. They met with little resistance. The Romans had withdrawn troops from the limes to face the threat posed by Alaric, a Visigoth, in Italy and had left their province defenseless. This was not another periodic migration from the east. This was a true invasion and it is said that it marked the beginning of the end of the Roman Empire in the countries beyond the Alps. The English historian Edward Gibbon did much to give this date its historical importance. In *"The History of the Decline and Fall of the Roman Empire"* he stated:

> "And the barriers which had so long separated the savage and the civilized nations of the earth were from that fatal moment leveled with the ground."

Whilst Gaul was *Romanized* and *Christianized*, Germanic tribes dwelling to the east of the territories controlled by Rome, beyond the limes, had continued to be on the move. People from the Nordic regions near the Baltic Sea, from the Great Steppes and beyond the Danube had their sight set on the west and the south. Neither the limes nor the formidable Rhine and Danube would stop their progression into the empire.

As early as the third century, the Alamans had crossed into Northern Italy, the Franks had led a destructive expedition as far as Barcelona and the Goths had entered Greece. These barbarians came to pillage not to conquer and they were not reluctant to occasionally side with the Romans. Warriors would sign up as mercenaries and some became Roman generals helping the Romans fight the next wave of migrating barbarians. Without the contribution of this new blood, Rome would not have survived as long as it did.

Then came the thrust initiated by the Huns. These nomads are remembered as astute and intrepid warriors who knew when to attack and when to retreat and shot arrows with deadly accuracy while mounted on their small horses. They looked ferocious and their actions matched their appearance.

The Huns started to move west from their land near the Aral Sea towards the end of the fourth century, crossing the river Don in 374. Their *Drang nach Westen*, drive toward the west, had a domino effect as they forced Germanic tribes to move further west. The first to be displaced were the Goths who scattered throughout Western Europe. In 401 the most important group of Goths, the Visigoths, led by Alaric, invaded Italy where their progress was halted by Stilicho, the supreme commander of the Roman army.

Stilicho is an intriguing man. His father was a Vandal and his mother a Roman. His adversaries were always quick to point to his barbarian origins but he seems to have followed his mother's culture and religion and have the interest of the Empire at heart. Victim of a conspiracy not unrelated to his barbarian blood, he was decapitated in 408. The order had been given by Honorius, the Roman emperor of the West who was also Stilicho's son in law.

The life of Stilicho's adversary, the barbarian leader Alaric, is a blueprint of the evolution in the relationship between the barbarians and the empire. A true Visigoth, he was an officer of Emperor Theodosius and led federated Visigoth troops into major battles on the side of Rome. He is one of the well-known barbarians who commanded Roman armies. Claiming they did not get a reward they deserved, Alaric and his men broke their alliance with Rome and sought a kingdom of their own. Alaric's invasion of Italy in 401 was stopped by Stilicho but a new campaign several years later was successful and in 410 the Visigoths sacked Rome. This is a perfect case of a barbarian who at first had allied himself with Rome, then struck out to fight on his own and carve a kingdom from the spoils of the Western Empire.

The Romans, unable to push back these hordes, bought time by granting them a special status, *foederati*. This status can be traced back to a time when the Roman republic granted a tribe or nation the right to settle in Roman territory in exchange for providing Rome with military assistance. The first beneficiaries of this strategy in the province of Gaul were the Salian Franks, the Franks from the estuary of the Rhine. Then, in the middle of the fifth century, the Burgundians were allowed to settle as allies and foederati in eastern Gaul, today's Savoy, Franche-Comte and western Switzerland. The Visigoths were granted the same standing in southwest Gaul.

It was just a palliative as the Romans did not intend to partner with the barbarians whose personal character traits and habits they despised. Pluriculturalism was never in the cards but the strategy gained Rome time. It also suited the barbarians initially; they had no grand ambition to replace Rome and were satisfied to stay as parasites. The status quo, though, did not last. The leaders of the barbarians slowly developed a longing for power and as the grip of Rome further weakened, they grabbed control of the territories they already occupied.

The Huns, whose westward move had started a domino effect at the end of the fourth century, reached Gaul in 451. Attila, their leader at the time, would be known as the Scourge of God. After battling the Romans for more than a decade in the east, the ruthless conqueror had turned his sights to the west. He never needed valid reasons to go to war, but a broken marriage promise might have given him a cause. Had Honoria, the daughter of the Roman emperor Valentinian, truly asked Attila to marry her in order to avoid a forced betrothal? Her father saw only a foolish blackmail but the Hun was serious about claiming what he thought was rightfully his. The barbarians scorched their way to Lutetia, the future Paris, and legend says that the town was miraculously saved by Saint Genevieve. Attila bypassed Lutetia and continued his devastation further south on the way to Orleans.

It took one more miracle to save Gaul from the Huns. The Goths and several other Germanic tribes who had settled in Gaul joined forces and, under the command of a Roman general, Aetius, stood ready to face Attila. They pursued the Huns to a spacious plain near Chalons-en-Champagne known as the Catalaunian fields

The battle between these tribal nations whose home grounds spread from the Volga to the Atlantic coast was a carnage, by some accounts as many as three hundred thousand died. Despite the exhortations of their leader, the Huns retreated and left Gaul. They were tracked from afar by Franks, presumably integrated in the army commanded by Aetius; the leader of these Franks was a warrior who some say was the mythical Mérovée. Romans and Germans had joined forces to stop the invading Asiatic tribes and spared Western Europe from further destruction.

This was a very epic moment: the last victory of a Roman general, the end of the devastating migration of Huns into Western Europe and a memorable involvement of the Franks in Gaul. The first French royal dynasty would be the Merovingian named after its founder Mérovée.

Attila would die two years later and discord among his sons will cause his empire to collapse. Aetius will be assassinated in 454 by Emperor Valentinian (had Aetius become too much of a competitor?). A few years later, in 476, Emperor Romulus Augustus will be deposed by Odoacer, the leader of a German tribe, and the territory under his control, mainly Italy, will become another German kingdom.

Romulus Augustus is considered to be the last Western Roman emperor and 476 has been, for convenience sake, retained to date the fall of the Roman Empire of the West. Thus, it also marks the end of Late Antiquity and the dawn of the Middle Ages.

Throughout most of History, the boundaries of these *ages in the middle* were well set: 476, the end of the Roman Empire of the West and 1453, the fall of Constantinople, the capital of the former Roman Empire of the East, at the hands of the Ottoman Turks. These numbers were drilled into the memory of French schoolchildren when dates still mattered. In recent times, medievalists have moved away from this view of the era, arguing convincingly that there had been no discontinuity between historical periods but rather a slow transition. They consider the beginning of the Middle Ages to be a continuation of Late Antiquity. As to its end, everyone has his own opinion. The death of Richard III, the French revolution and other significant historical milestones compete with the fall of Constantinople. Periodization is a difficult exercise, influenced by field of interest, cultural background and other factors. A straightforward approach would fit the Middle Ages between the two bookends of *Antiquity* and the *Renaissance*; Antiquity, the period of the glory of Greece and the grandeur of Rome, born again during the Re-naissance.

Besançon and the Barbarian Migrations

The city was on the path of the great barbarian migrations of the early days of 407. It led, wrote Claude Fohlen in his *Histoire de Besançon*, to a *return to pre-history*. The town was taken over at first by Vandals on their way to Spain then by pagan Alemanni who ferociously massacred the Christians. Luckily for the few survivors, the Alemanni were displaced a few decades later by the more accommodating Burgundians.

The Franks and the Church take the Reins from the Empire

The Gallic elite reached terms of accommodation with its new masters, the barbarians. As Roman influence vanished, the elite cooperated with the new Germanic leaders and learned to live with a lack of Roman oversight. Those belonging to the great Gallo-Roman families continued to honor Roman traditions long after the end of imperial power in the West. Their clans had deep roots in the former major Roman centers, Lugdunum (Lyon), the Roman capital of Gaul, Orange, further south and Arles, Caesar's city. The Gallo-Roman bishops played a most important role in the transition. In their capacity as religious as well as political leaders they headed a Roman-inspired local administration in their dioceses.

The mingling of the barbarians with the Gallo-Romans did not proceed with equal ease across all of Gaul and the speed of the assimilation was heavily influenced by religion.

Christianity had spread rapidly among most barbarian peoples. These were uprooted people, eager to join a new community and the Christians, particularly of the Arian creed, were ready to welcome them in their midst. Many of the Goths in the empire of the East had been converted by an Arian bishop called Wulfila. His Cappadocian parents had been enslaved by the Goths, he had been raised in captivity, had accepted the Arian faith and been ordained by Eusebius of Nicomedia; Wulfila eventually translated the Bible from Greek to the language spoken by the Goths. Other nations along the Danube and the Balkans had been converted to Arianism by Roman soldiers taken prisoner.

The Arian Burgundians would be conciliatory while the Arian Visigoths who settled in Gaul made life difficult for the Gallo-Romans following the Niceo-Constantinopolitan creed. The Alemanni who had remained pagan were also particularly disruptive.

The Franks, who would ultimately dominate Gaul and had also remained pagan, were the most accommodating. A loosely structured coalition of tribes, a new people of sorts, they adapted fairly easily to their new environment. They did not as much conquer the territories they occupied in the north of France as take the reins from the Romans. Clovis, their leader, would be baptized Catholic in 496 and his people followed him in the new religion. The Franks subjected the Visigoths and Burgundians to their rule during the decade that followed but these two peoples stayed true to their Arian beliefs. It would be some time before the Arian churches would fade and the dominant Church in conquered Gaul became the Catholic Christian Church, the church that followed the Niceno-Constantinopolitan creed, the Church of Rome.

The Church gave the barbarians and Gallo-Romans in Gaul a powerful source of identity. It was still modest when Clovis converted and grew rapidly after the fifth century. It replaced the empire as the unifying force in Gaul and became the one body that stood in the way of chaos.

The importance of the Catholic Church in medieval France cannot be overstated. The Kingdom of the Franks will be a catholic kingdom and the religious will be a part of the secular.

Bishops and Monks: Pillars of Church and Society

The Catholic Church in Gaul rested on two pillars, the bishops and the monks. It could count on the support of tightly-knit Christian communities in some cities and of most of the great Gallo-Roman families. Little is known about the religious practices of the people living in the countryside or in small towns. They most probably did observe the rites, mumble the *credo* in a language that they did not understand as only the elite knew some Latin, and were as submissive to the church leaders as they were to their lords. While Catholics in Gaul would profess their faith in the Holy Spirit *qui ex Pater Filioque procedit,* who proceeds from the Father and the Son, their brethren in the Church of the East would always refuse to add *Filioque.*

The bishops were elected by the clergy and the people, *clero et populo*. In the centuries to come, they would also be endorsed by the king and the role played by the temporal powers in the choice of bishops would become a contentious topic. The consecrated bishop acquired the aura of the chosen, the one who speaks in the name of God and is the descendant of the first apostles. His seat, the cathedral, was located in a major town, a metropolis, or at its outskirts. The administration of the Roman Empire had been directed from large urban centers and the Church followed the same pattern.

Most of the bishops came from the Gallo-Roman aristocracy. They had acquired the education and the mastery of Latin which allowed them to preach and gave them the confidence to deal with the caste of warriors. Many were married and had to accept to live with their wife *as brother and sister* when they entered the service of God.

The mission of the bishop was to take care of souls, *cura animarum*, to protect the Catholics of their diocese, to preserve the orthodoxy of the Church and fight heresy. Bishops relied extensively on the cult of saints to propagate the message of the Church. Several of them became saints themselves, the most famous might be Saint Martin, the converted Roman soldier who offered half of his cloak to a poor man, was chosen in 371 by the people of Tours as their bishop. Later, he became the Apostle of Gaul.

Bishops were assisted by other members of the clergy, priests and deacons. The men-only clergy benefited from the same privileges that pagan priests had received; they did not pay taxes, did not have to serve in any civil capacity and were judged only by their peers. The deacons formed a new order which occupied a well-defined place in society. They oversaw social aid, a service rendered by the Christian community which grew in importance during the first three centuries.

The prohibition of marriage by men ordained deacon, priest or bishop was enforced during the fourth century. The need for a canon on celibacy had been much debated since the beginnings of the church. Celibacy did not become a dogma of the Church but remained a discipline asked of the ordained and ordaining only unmarried men became the rule in the eleventh century. There would be exceptions, adaptations and debates but the rules survived in the Church of Rome; the Eastern Christian churches kept their own rules, allowing the ordination of married men as priests (but not access to the episcopate).

The reach of the bishops quickly extended beyond their apostolic mission. As the number of Christians increased and the Roman presence faded, they took charge of critical functions in civil society, and became heads of city governments and administrators. In their dual role as apostles and administrators they were now in a position to influence the political and moral views of the new occupants of Gaul; this would be the message delivered by Bishop Remi when Clovis became the new King of the Franks. The great Gallo-Roman families saw in their bishop the best protector of the Roman way of doing things at a time when barbarians were taking over the administration of the provinces in Gaul. Their strategy was not always altruistic. In Auvergne, for instance, these families encouraged their leading members to seek this consecration when the Visigoths threatened to take over the rewarding and honorific positions they held in society.

The first bishops of Rome considered themselves the descendants of Peter and therefore one step above the bishops of the other major Christian sees; Rome was also the only Christian center in the ex-Western Empire, the other three, Alexandria, Antioch and Constantinople were all in the East. The bishop of Rome became known as the Father of the Catholic Church, the Pope.

Other pillars of the church in the High Middle Ages were the communities of monks. Some of the first Christians had sought a way to God more demanding than a mere conversion. They had opted for an ascesis that would bring them closer to God through a perfect sinless life. They had left "their land, their family and the house of their father," following the instructions that God had given to Abraham, and taken to the road, waiting for a sign from God.

The road had led some to a desert where they walked in the steps of their ideal, Anthony of the Desert, the Egyptian *father of all monks*. The story of his life has been told by Athanase of Alexandria, probably the first hagiographer. Anthony was born in 251, and started leading an ascetic life at the age of eighteen. He detached himself step by step from earthly temptations, and for twenty years lived alone in a desert, reaching apatheia, the conquering of his passions.

This was a most demanding ascesis, and early on the church fathers encouraged a monastic life in a community. The first Christian monastery was founded by Pachome in Upper Egypt in 320. He is one of the fathers of this type of monasticism called *coenobitic.*

Monasticism, both *eremitic* and *coenobitic,* in solitude and in community, found fertile grounds in the Middle East and from there spread to the west, where it blossomed at the end of the fifth century, during the decline of the Roman Empire of the West. Men and women coming overwhelmingly from the educated segment of the population, cherished the challenge to follow their calling. Leaving behind the trappings of secular life, they embraced the *peregrinatio pro Christo.*

Some walked in the footsteps of Christ in the most literal sense and went to the Holy Land. Others waited for their calling in a monastery. Prestigious monasteries, each one following its own rules, became landmarks of the countryside of France and Italy,

The faithful admired the monks who in their eyes were leading a saintly life. They venerated the remains of founders of monasteries and of abbots, giving a new impetus to the cult of relics which would become over time a major source of revenue for the Church.

The Church leaders, on the other hand, were ill at ease with loose communities of free spirits and decided to give the monks a status. A council in 451 decreed that they would report to the bishop and had to stay in monasteries. Their life should be one of contemplation while the clergy would take care of the community of believers. The monks would live a communal life, accept celibacy and could not be ordained.

While closeted in their monasteries, the communities of monks made a major contribution to the Church and society: they safeguarded the wisdom and treasures of Antiquity. The word *cleric* embodies this connection: the cleric is a man of the church and is also the one who writes. Every monastery needed a library and their collections included books on the Holy Scriptures, writings by Church authorities such as Augustine but also a small selection of secular books by Greek philosophers, all handled with care and meticulously catalogued.

The monks had the means, the patience and the need to also make books. Monasteries had *scriptoria,* ateliers in which manuscripts were copied, bound, and the most valued ones illuminated with ornamental designs and lettering in brilliant colors, sometimes encrusted with gold and precious stones. Many of these true works of art survived wars and revolutions and are now dispersed in museums throughout the world.

Bishops and monks held a quasi-monopoly over education. The bishops had been entrusted with education by Emperor Constantine, and his successors had continued this practice. The monks cared for the children of the elite and it was a sign of the times that this was a small body of students. Most people were illiterate, spoke only a vernacular, had memorized a few prayers and had to content themselves with listening to stories of saints and miracles. The education of the members of the elite, though, was a necessary social function as lords and bishops needed a *brain pool*. Monks, considered models of humility and probity, were perfectly suited to teach them reading, writing, arithmetic and singing, all in Latin.

Culture in Antiquity had been represented by the opuses of Greek and Roman authors, the *classics*. The great classical thinkers, Virgil, Seneca and others, faded from the curriculum of western elite when the Church put its imprint on early medieval society. In the minds of theologians they were, after all, pagans. The teaching of the classics would resume after the twelfth century when the Greek classics became available in Latin and the social importance of monasteries started to wane.

Dark Ages

From Bishop Gregoire de Tours' Embellished "Historia Francorum" to Bishop Hincmar's Myth of Clovis' Anointing (498?)

Bishop Gregoire, the Gallo-Roman Bishop of Tours, wrote *Ten Books of Histories* also known as *A History of the Franks,* Historia Francorum. The most quoted source on the beginnings of the Franks and in particular the life of Clovis, the first leader of the Kingdom of the Franks, Bishop Gregoire's writings contained many legends which over time were embellished and enriched.

The name *Francus* was carried by several peoples not necessarily linguistically, culturally or ethnically related. It was a generic name added to the name of a specific ethnic group and appears during the first centuries AD in texts of Roman historians.

The community of Franks was comprised of the *Sicambrian* and *Salian* Franks located in today's southern Netherlands, the *Riparian* Franks on the right bank of the Rhine up to Mainz and several other groups. They all seem to have proudly flaunted their membership in an informal confederation whose members shared some common features. A clue to these is given by the most accepted etymology of Frank which would be derived from *frech*, the Old German word describing proud and brave warriors. The Franks must have seen themselves and be seen as formidable warriors.

This view was presented by the Belgian Godefroid Kurth, an authority on the Frankish people, in *Etudes Franques* published after his death in 1916. Kurth also tracked the various uses of the word *Francia.* It was always applied to the land inhabited by the Franks and over time represented different geographic realities. The Romans called Francia the territories on the right bank of the Rhine north of the Rhine Province. Then the name was given to the land conquered in Gaul by Clovis at the end of the fifth and the beginning of the sixth century. All reference to the Franks living east of the Rhine was not yet lost. When the extensive empire of Charlemagne was partitioned in 843 the territories to the east of the Rhine were called *franci orientalis.* Otto I, the first Saxon emperor of the Holy Roman Empire, crowned in 962, liked to be called *Imperator Romanum et Francorum.* The reference to Francia will be reserved to Gaul only after the tenth century. The land occupied by the Franks living on the east bank of the Rhine is by then referred as Germania. The capital of the country to be called France will be Paris and not Cologne.

The Frankish warriors have been described as tall and powerful but this is the way Latin historians pictured most barbarians. How else would the Romans want to describe the tribesmen who massacred their Legions in the Teutoburg Forest in 9 AD? This claim is supported by archeological research conducted in recent times, i.e. the anthropological study of bodies found in tombs. Then again, there is no easy way to distinguish the remains of Germans from those of Gallo-Romans in these tombs.

The temperament of the Franks is a matter of great subjectivity. Edward Gibbon cites a Greek historian who praised their virtues and urbanity but also quotes Gregoire de Tours who offers a very different picture. The Gallo-Roman bishop is appalled at their savage and corrupt manners.

A history of the Franks, *Liber historiae Francorum,* written at the beginning of the eighth century and then *The Great Chronicles of France,* composed by a very erudite monk of Saint Denis at the end of the thirteenth century, conferred on the Franks glorious and distant origins. These texts speak in great detail of a very popular legend tracing the Franks back to the Trojans and claiming they settled on the banks of the Danube after the Trojan War (1200 BC).

During the first centuries AD so-called Frankish warriors had conducted raids deep into Gaul and beyond while other Franks had served as loyal soldiers in the Roman armies. When the decline of the empire accelerated at the end of the fourth century, the Salian Franks were granted land rights in territories north of the Seine. There, they behaved as settlers and not invaders, farmer-warriors, carving a place for themselves in the Gallo-Roman population which was more Gallo than Roman in this part of Gaul.

By the fifth century the Salian Franks had migrated into Artois and reached the Somme River. Legend has it that one of them, Mérovée, fought against Attila at the side of Romans led by Aetius in 451 and that his son Childeric was allied with the *magister militum Galliarum,* Egidus, when the Romans battled the Visigoths.

Although not much is known about the Salian Franks during the last centuries of the Roman Empire it can be safely assumed that they were around Tournai at the end of the fifth century; Tournai is now in southern Wallonia, close to the border with France. A skeleton surrounded by numerous valuable objects among which a breastplate inscribed *Childirici Regis* was discovered fortuitously in this town in 1653. Experts agree that this was indeed the tomb of Childeric, leader of the Salian Franks and father of Clovis. The contents of the tomb were entrusted to the National Museum of Coins and Antiquities, but the most important items were stolen in 1861. Some of the recovered artifacts including a cloisonné sword hilt can be seen at the *Musée des Monnaies* at the *Bibliothèque Nationale de France* in Paris.

The tomb also contained one artifact of special interest: shreds of a cloak decorated with bees. It has given life to a legend which says that Napoleon chose to have his imperial robe embroidered with stylized bees with wide-open wings, recalling the fleurs de lis, a symbol of French royalty but also the bees on Childeric's cloak. The emperor saw in the baptism of Clovis a marker of the beginning of France and the bees on his imperial robe emphasized the continuity of his reign with that of Clovis's father.

When Childeric died in 481, Roman Gaul was reduced to a sliver of land between the Somme and the Loire Rivers. It was governed by the son of Egidius, Syagrius, called the king of the Romans by Gregoire de Tours and whose headquarters were in Soissons. The greater part of the former Province of Gaul was in the hands of Visigoths and Burgundians.

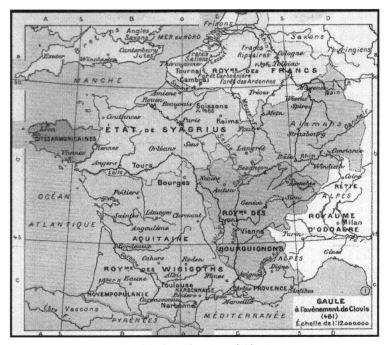

Gaul before the rise of Clovis

Clovis was sixteen years old when he succeeded his father, Childeric. He might have received popular approval and been carried in triumph on his own shield; this tradition was only seldom followed but has made for picturesque illustrations in books on *les Gaulois*. Gregoire de Tours, who could be critical of the Franks, left a favorable portrait of Clovis and would be criticized for his excessive flattery and credulity. The bishop was born 25 years after Clovis's death, never knew the king and had to rely on a plethora of anecdotes and legends. Clovis is portrayed sometimes as intelligent and ambitious, other times as cruel and crafty. In light of his exploits during his mature years, he certainly had all four character traits.

Clovis wore his hair very long, flowing over his shoulders. Long freely hanging hair was clear evidence of his membership in the royal family. Gregoire de Tours wrote about *reges crinite*, long haired kings, and the ceremonial significance attached to long hair is attested by the Merovingian tradition to cut short the hair of deposed kings; as most of them were then secluded in a monastery they would also be tonsured.

Even though Clovis was a pagan, Remi, the Gallo-Roman Bishop of Reims, wrote a letter to the new leader of the Franks encouraging him to stay close to the bishops and follow their advice. It was an invitation for an open cooperation with the Church and a call for a truly Christian government. The advice was eminently pertinent as Clovis and his tribe were no match for the more powerful barbarian groups occupying Gaul and the odds would move in their favor if the Church became their ally.

Clovis and his Franks had settled in *Secundum Belgice*, the second Belgium, that part of today's Belgium closest to the Channel, which was under the command of Siagrius. The legions stationed there represented the remnant of the Roman presence in Gaul. Very little is known about Syagrius and Gregoire de Tours has been the major if not the only source over the years. The Empire of the West by then no longer existed, Syagrius was isolated, without real power and represented a perfect prey. In 486, near Soissons, Clovis overran the Romans and this signaled the beginning of the expansionary drive of the Franks in Gaul.

In 493 Clovis married a Burgundian princess, Clotilde, a catholic Christian. It has often been claimed that she prayed fervently for her husband's conversion.

The *Alemanni*, a Germanic tribe settled on the eastern bank of the Rhine, were the next foe faced by Clovis. They were in constant conflict with the Ripuarian Franks, and threatened the territories controlled by Clovis's Salian Franks. In 496, a fierce battle pitted the two tribes at Tolbiac near Cologne in Germany. Defeat was looming when, according to Gregoire de Tours, Clovis implored the God of his wife, "Give me victory and I will become a faithful believer." He was victorious and the Alemanni recognized his authority. This story belongs to the mythical Clovis. A few months after his victory, in a clever political move, he converted to the religion of his wife and was baptized by Bishop Remi in Reims.

The sequence of events begs the question: which factor carried the greatest weight in Clovis's decision, the passionate prodding by Clotilde or the reversal of fortune on the battlefield at Tolbiac? Whatever the answer, it had a major impact on the history of France and of Christendom in Western Europe. It should not come as a surprise that this episode is reminiscent of the events leading to the conversion of Constantine. Gregoire de Tours, to whom we owe the history of Tolbiac, could not resist making Clovis into a new Constantine.

Bishop Remi would be Clovis's religious mentor. He had understood that the church would benefit from dealing with a strong leader and felt confident that Clovis would allow the Roman and Catholic ways to survive; Clovis, in turn, knew that he needed the support of the bishops as much as they needed his protection.

In becoming Christian, Clovis consolidated his ties to the Gallo-Roman elite. With their help and that of the Church he went on to defeat Alaric II, leader of the Visigoths, at Vouillé near Poitiers, in 507. The Franks had become the dominant Germanic tribe in Gaul.

Soon after defeating the Visigoths, Clovis's warriors searched for the treasure of Alaric. This was a well-established practice. The leaders of barbarian tribes, which Gregoire likes to call kings, were always on the move and traveled with their treasure. Coins and other valuable objects were carried in heavy chests and defeat was consummated when another king seized the treasure. Shortly after his victory at Vouillé, Clovis used some cunning moves to appropriate another treasure, that of the king of the Ripuarian Franks and, Gregoire de Tours wrote, was thus acknowledged as their king.

Clovis was declared *consul* by Anastase, the emperor of the Eastern Roman Empire residing in Constantinople. The bestowed honor and title carried no longer any weight in the Western empire which had become a patchwork of Germanic kingdoms. Clovis's kingdom was the nucleus of a future nation not a province of a defunct empire. The title of *consul* did have a symbolic importance. There was no empire anymore but the shadow of Rome still lingered over the territories in the west now controlled by barbarians.

The Story of the Vase of Soissons

French schoolchildren are still taught about Alaric, Clovis's baptism and Vouille but what they remember best is the story of *Le vase de Soissons.* It was told by Bishop Gregoire de Tours and he claimed the events took place while Clovis was battling Syagrius.

Clovis and his soldiers had pillaged a church, as they were accustomed to do, and had taken an extremely beautiful vase. Plunder had a strategic use as we are reminded by Edward Gibbon when he writes about Clovis:

> "He imitated the example of Caesar who in the same country had acquired wealth by the sword and purchased soldiers with the fruits of conquest."

Bishop Remi sent a messenger to Clovis begging him to return the vase, and the Frankish leader promised he would answer the bishop's request. When the booty was allocated as dictated by custom, Clovis asked to be also given the vessel. Everybody agreed except for one *levis, individus ac facilis,* heedless and impulsive individual, who took his ax, broke the vase and said "You will get only what comes your way." Clovis swallowed his pride and put the incident aside. A year later, the leader of the Franks was reviewing his troops when he recognized the insolent soldier. The legend reaches its climax when Clovis faced the soldier, grabbed his ax, and threw it to the ground saying" Your weapons are not battle ready." As the soldier bent forward to pick up his ax, Clovis wielded his own and split the head of the soldier shouting "This is what you did to the Vase of Soissons."

This story says something about the delicate balance in the early days of the reign of Clovis between abiding by customs and affirming one's authority. Clovis was just "primus inter pares," a far cry from the absolute monarchs who would reign twelve centuries later. It says something about his character and his ability to control his temper and wait for retribution. It also says that, as Clovis had promised to return the vase to the bishop, the cruel punishment he inflicted on the sacrilegious soldier was a public display of his religious zeal.

All his victories on the battlefields and all the legends attached to his name did not in themselves secure Clovis's long lasting myth. It took one more powerful ingredient, the legend attached to his baptism in Reims.

Baptism of Clovis

Almost four centuries after the events, Hincmar, Bishop of Reims, wrote a history of Saint Remi, the bishop who had baptized Clovis. Hincmar borrowed extensively from Gregoire de Tours as was customary and then gave his own interpretation of the baptism of the Frankish king. He began by adding one episode: a dove, in the image of the bird symbolizing the Holy Spirit during the Annunciation, had flown over the baptismal fonts at the beginning of the ceremony, bringing in its beak a vial filled with perfumed oil to anoint Clovis. In the Old Testament the anointed were the chosen, the elected by God and in the New Testament, Christ is the anointed one. Whatever it's biblical origin, anointing carries a message of divine election.

The gentle rubbing of sacred oil on the head is still an essential part of the consecration of bishops and the unction on the forehead is also still at the heart of the ceremony of baptism. The formula for the olive-oil based ointment is found in the Book of Exodus.

Hincmar then subtly introduced one more dimension to Clovis's baptism. He stated that the holy oil brought down from heaven had been used to baptize Clovis *and* anoint him king.

None of the Merovingian kings had ever been anointed and the first French king truly anointed had been the Carolingian Pepin the Short in 751. Hincmar was rewriting history by moving the divine election of the Frankish kings back to the first king, Clovis. As the anointing was done by Remi, he was also giving the church an important institutional role.

Thanks to Hincmar, Clovis and the Frankish kings who succeeded him would be seen as God's choice, benefiting from divine protection and inspiration and the bishop of Reims as the messenger of God's will. The guidebooks at the Cathedral of Reims like to point out that from Charlemagne's son Louis le Pieux in 816 to King Charles X in 1825, all the kings of France have been crowned and anointed in Reims using the sacred oil brought by the dove for the baptism of Clovis.

The French have a tender spot for Vercingetorix and Clovis, the fierce warriors. The first one symbolizes national resistance, and many of those who have reflected on the history of France have been of the mind that the country started with Clovis. The historian Jacques de Bainville is even more affirmative and dates the birth of France to Clovis's conversion to Catholic Christianity. Charles de Gaulle shared this view. He pointed out that Clovis was the leader of the Salian Franks, the Germanic tribe that gave its name to the country, that he became Catholic, and that his capital was the future Paris.

Montagne Sainte Geneviève

Montagne Sainte Geneviève, named after the patron saint of Paris, is rich in *lieux de memoire*.

When Genevieve who had spared the people of *Lutetia*, today's Paris, from the devastations of Attila, died in 512 (some say she died ten years earlier...), her sarcophagus made of granite slabs was placed in a church built at the top of this hill on the left bank of the Seine. The church, dedicated to Saints Peter and Paul, had been commissioned by Clovis to be a resting place for himself, his family and also Genevieve; Clovis and his wife Clotilde much admired the Saint. Genevieve is said to have had a major influence on the conversion of Clovis.

Shortly after Genevieve's death, the word spread that she had performed miracles and possessed supernatural powers, and this reputation would be long-lived. Around 630 Saint Eloi, the goldsmith cum advisor to king Dagobert, created a metal box decorated with precious stones to safekeep her bones. Over the next centuries these remains were honored at times, dishonored at others, and always the cause of much passion.

During the ninth century Clovis's church was enclosed in an abbey, which became highly respected during the High Middle Ages. It was visited by numerous famous preachers and Abelard was one of them.

In 1130 the inhabitants of Paris were afflicted with a deadly epidemic disease, spread by contaminated grain. It was known as *le mal des ardents*. Genevieve's reliquary was carried to Notre Dame and legend says that the sick assembled in the cathedral were all cured. Thereafter, whenever the city was in danger the reliquary was brought in great solemnity to Notre Dame in the hope that Genevieve would perform another miracle. There were still three such processions in the eighteenth century.

By 1220 Clovis's church had become too small to accommodate all the local faithful and a new church was built nearby. It has been remodeled several times since and is known today as Saint Etienne du Mont. The church has preserved the last rood screen in Paris.

In the early days of August 1744 King Louis XV fell suddenly ill and all hope was lost when to everyone's surprise he fully recovered. The king wanted to thank Genevieve for this miracle and ordered the construction of a new church in her honor. The plans called for an imposing basilica in the shape of a Greek cross topped by a majestic dome and the first stone was laid in 1764 not far from Saint Etienne du Mont.

The whirlwind of the Revolution blew over Paris shortly thereafter and, one night, a few fanatics took hold of Genevieve's reliquary, burned her remains and threw the ashes in the Seine. As to the new basilica, it was turned into a *Pantheon* for the great men of France. The use of the building will track the changes in political regimes during the nineteenth century and it will be used alternatively for religious and secular purposes. It has been secular since 1885 and one can read on its pediment "To its great men, a grateful country" More than sixty great men have been buried there since Victor Hugo, the first one, in 1885. The first woman to be so honored was Marie Curie in 1995.

The library of the abbey, famous for its collection of manuscripts dating from the Carolingians, needed to find a new home in 1842 and a facility was built along the Pantheon by the architect Henri Labrouste. The new *Bibliothèque Sainte Geneviève* which today is buzzing with students from the surrounding universities is a stunning piece of architecture. A monumental staircase leads to an elongated reading room inside a metallic structure resting on grooved cast iron columns. It is a pleasure to spend time in this room, filled with light, where the mood created by the green tones of individual lampshades is soft and friendly.

Saint Etienne du Mont is still devoted to Sainte Geneviève. Some of the relics of the Sainte which had been entrusted before the Revolution to several convents were gathered after 1820 and are now safekept in two reliquaries one at Saint Etienne du Mont and the other at Notre Dame de Paris. The magnificent reliquary placed in 2012 in the north transept of the cathedral, in front of a statue of Saint Denis, is the work of the goldsmith Placide Poussielgue-Rusand. The relics at Saint Etienne du Mont have been placed in a chapel on the south side of the church. The stained-glass windows of this chapel illustrate the life of the saint and its entrance is framed by ex-votos, an assemblage of marble tablets expressing gratitude to Genevieve.

The patron saint of Paris has remained dear to many and even Voltaire, the hardened anti-cleric, used to say that he was always moved by the mention of her name and that she was his shepherd.

The hill topped by the Pantheon is a landmark sight in the Latin Quarter in Paris and, as one should expect, is called Montagne Sainte Geneviève.

The Merovingian Dynasty after Clovis: "Fluctuat nec Mergitur"

The *motto* adopted by the City of Paris in the fourteenth century applies well to the Merovingians. The winds tossing the new kingdom originated in the old Frankish tradition of sharing the kingdom of a dead king between his sons. Clovis would be one of those leaders in the High Middle Ages unconcerned by empire building and when he died in 511 his kingdom was shared among his sons. This ancient custom would fade as the nomadic Franks became settlers but as long as it was not effectively replaced by the rule of primogeniture, the survival of proto-France remained precarious. In the meantime, the Church and the concept of unity inherited from the Romans were the threads holding the new kingdom together.

During the hundred or so years following Clovis's death his kingdom was partitioned and reassembled by three generations of descendants as brothers, uncles or cousins, fought for a share of the pie. Four regional entities emerged called *Austrasia, Neustria, Burgundy* and *Aquitaine*. Their borders would remain in constant flux but, broadly, the north and northeast became Austrasia, the west was called Neustria for unknown reasons, the territories that would be conquered from the Burgundians became Burgundy and those taken from the Visigoths, Aquitaine. The large area of Aquitaine did not form ties with the other regional entities while Brittany was never truly integrated in the Merovingian kingdom.

Each of the three generations of Merovingian kings that followed Clovis presided over very somber and cruel times marked by too many crimes, treasons and fratricidal rivalries; the only rays of light came from exceptional women, Radegund and a few others. The kings of this period are at the source of the label *Dark Ages* attached much later by Edward Gibbon on the Middle Ages in general.

The first generation features the three sons that Clovis had with Clotilde plus one, Thierry, with an unknown woman. Thierry was praised by Gregoire de Tours as a very able leader, the sons of Clovis and Clotilde on the other hand were sinister characters. In 532, two of them, Childerbert and Clothar, plotted to share the kingdom of their dead brother Clodomir, and killed their underage nephews. As if in itself their act was not malicious enough, Gregoire de Tours claims that they had presented the children's grand-mother, Clotilde, with their options, strangle the children or cut their hair, the symbol of their royal lineage. "I prefer to see them dead than with their heads shaved" she would have said, in other words, if they cannot be kings I don't want to see them alive.

Left in the hands of such impulsive and savage men the inheritance of Clovis should have crumbled but, to the contrary, Clothar added territories that his father had failed to conquer and between 532 and 534 at last annexed Burgundy to the Kingdom of the Franks. He survived his brothers and from 558 to 561 Clovis's kingdom was united again.

An extraordinary woman, Clothar's wife, Queen Radegund, was a luminous presence in this dark period. She was a Thuringian (Thuringia is a state located more or less at the heart of today's Germany). During the final act of a Thuringian-Frankish war, Clothar and his brothers had killed the Thuringian ruling family, sparing only the six-year old Radegund and her brother and keeping both as spoils of war. When she turned eighteen Radegund was forced to marry Clothar and was powerless when the ruthless Frank, adept at eliminating those who stood in his way, killed her brother. She had the fortitude to flee from her husband's court and, as she had previously converted to Christianity, put herself under the protection of the church. A few years after her escape she founded a convent near Poitiers and remained there for the rest of her life, presiding over a community of nuns abiding by very strict rules.

The land on which the monastery was built had been given by Clothar. This noble gesture embodies the spirit of the time. As Huizinga observed in *The Waning of the Middle Ages*, men were always running to extremes and "life bore the mixed smell of blood and of roses".

Queen Radegund's aura allowed her to acquire a piece of the True Cross from the emperor in Byzantium and this relic became an attraction for pilgrims and a source of profit for her convent. In the ninth century she was canonized and is the patron saint of Jesus College, Cambridge.

The second generation, the children of Clothar and grandchildren of Clovis, presided over a new partitioning of the *Regnum Francorum.*

This generation added to the already long list of murders and cruelties perpetrated by the descendants of Clovis. Chilperic, one of Clothar's sons, had as much blood on his hands as his father but his barbarity paled compared to that of his wife, Fredegonde. She eliminated anyone standing on the path to the throne of her son the future Clothar II. Bishop Gregoire de Tours told the story of her sinister exploits and holds her responsible for the decline of the Merovingian dynasty. She died in 597. The ferocity of mothers protecting the path to the throne of their son is a recurring theme in Late Antiquity and in the early Middle Ages; Fredegonde had illustrious predecessors in the Roman Empire, from Livia, Tiberius's mother to Nero's mother Agrippina.

Clothar II, Clovis's great grandson, became king of a reunified Regnum Francorum. Not only did he add to the list of murdered Merovingians but he also committed his own legendary crime. The victim was Brunehilde, the wife of his uncle, dragged to her death by a wild horse. Brunehilde had been the mortal enemy of Clothar II's mother, Fredegonde.

Then, in 629, came Dagobert, one of the few Merovingians who has a good reputation. He had been eager to be king from a young age and had relentlessly challenged his father Clothar II. After the death of the king he quickly found a role in Aquitaine for his half-brother, Caribert, and took the throne for himself. The great lords accommodated themselves to a united kingdom and never missed a chance to remind Dagobert that he owed them his scepter.

Dagobert was generous to Saint Denis and the Abbey throughout his life. He spent his last hours and died there in 639 after a reign of ten years.

Hincmar, the future bishop of Reims, who resided at the Abbey almost two hundred years later, wrote a *Gesta Dagobert* and was overwhelmingly flattering. He has remained the source of the favorable reputation that Dagobert has kept over the centuries: a diplomat, not a warrior, who reestablished public order in a kingdom that had been shaken by years of civil war, a king who did much for the image of the Frankish royal bloodline.

Most French do not recall much of the lives of Dagobert and Eloi, his trusted advisor but know them well as the two characters of a popular children's song which starts as follows:

> "Le bon roi Dagobert a mis sa culotte a l'envers."
> Good King Dagobert is wearing his culotte backward.

> "Le grand Saint Eloi lui dit, Oh mon roi, votre majesté est mal culottée " Great Saint Eloi said, Oh my king, your majesty is poorly attired.

The song was written during the French Revolution when it was *de rigueur* to ridicule kings and saints; a giveaway is the reference to *culotte*, the short pants which were in use at the time of the Revolution. There are better ways for a king to be remembered but at least Dagobert and Eloi have stayed in France's collective memory.

Eloi, a goldsmith, advised the king wisely on monetary matters, which seems appropriate since gold was the major currency of the time. He was a man of many talents, was named bishop and as is honored as the patron saint of goldsmiths.

The Oldest French Regalia: The Throne of Dagobert

Saint Eloi is said to have sculpted a gilded bronze throne for Dagobert and this artifact can be seen at the Bibliothèque Nationale, Richelieu, in Paris. Some experts doubt that it goes back to the time of the Merovingian king but Suger, in the twelfth century, wrote that the kings sat on this throne when they received the homage of the great lords of the Kingdom of the Franks and Suger is a reliable reference. The tradition of honoring a seated king started after Clovis. Before him, leaders of the Franks were mere successful warlords and it was part of their persona to adopt a martial stance in front of their men. When everyone understood that the authority of the king was conferred by God it befitted his new aura to be seated.

So-called Throne of Dagobert

Dagobert's throne, as it became known, might be the oldest French regalia. It was originally a curule chair, the feet are sculpted panthers and the seat itself must have been made of leather straps. A back and armrests were added at the time of Charles le Chauve, grandson of Charlemagne, in the ninth century. It remained at Saint Denis up to the Revolution and was added to the State Collections of Antiquities in 1791. This throne was used for the last time in 1804 by Emperor Napoleon when he decorated heroic soldiers with the newly created *Legion d'Honneur*.

Mayors of the Palace, Charles Martel and the Battle of Poitiers (732)

The *palace* was the name given to the entourage of the king and during the reign of the grandchildren of Clovis a member of the palace was chosen to assist him, a function with high visibility. The *major domus regiae*, mayor of the palace, handled all matters in the palace in the name of the king. After Dagobert, the kings became mere puppets in the hands of these mayors. They are remembered as the *lazy kings*, a very evocative label said to have first been given to Clovis II, one of Dagobert's sons. The mayors by then decided the fate of the outgoing kings, who should be sent to a monastery or lose his life after they designated the successor. Once in place, the new king merely left the regal affairs in the hands of the major domus regiae.

Power in the three kingdoms of Austrasia, Neustria and Burgundy was wielded by the aristocracy and each kingdom resisted its integration into a unified *Regnum Francorum*, Kingdom of the Franks. Austrasia was particularly reluctant and became ensnared in a bloody rivalry with Neustria. The scale tipped in favor of the Austrasians after the battle of Tertry in 687. Led by their mayor of the palace, Pepin II von Herstal, they routed the Neustrians, captured their king and appropriated his treasury and his palace. From then on the power will be in the hands of the descendants of Pepin, the Pepinides. Pepin II von Herstal will be mayor of the palace during the reign of four kings and will be succeeded by a bastard son surnamed Charles Martel, Charles the Hammer, also known as Charles the Bastard.

Charles the Bastard had the complicated, tortuous life of many bastard sons. His father had chased his legitimate wife Plectrude and her two sons to make room for his mistress Alpaide. Alpaide gave two sons to Pepin II, Charles was one of the two according to *le premier continuateur* of the *Chronique de Fredégaire.* The fate of the mistress was no better than the fate of the wife. She too was humiliated after Pepin's death and so was Charles. None of this mattered after the two legitimate heirs conveniently died and the road was clear for the bastard, who was only twenty-five years of age, to take over the mantle of mayor of the Austrasians.

In his new capacity he held the power to designate the king and he picked a strawman, Clothar IV, who would die shortly after. The official residence of the king was in Metz and Charles stressed his independence by setting his headquarters in Trier. The new *maire de palais* was so convinced that the Kingdom of the Franks should be led by no other than the Austrasians that he set his mind on becoming master of the other two *palais.* He proved to be an intrepid warrior, defeated the Neustrians and the Burgundians and declared himself mayor of the three kingdoms; Eudes, Duke of Aquitaine, who dreamed of an independent kingdom, was no match for Charles' mounted warriors.

Charles was true to his emblem, the Hammer of Thor, the God of Thunder, and to the surname that would be given to him by the pope, Martellus Dei, Hammer of God. This surname, the Hammer, suited him well; he looked like a ram, short legged and barrel chested.

The fame he earned thanks to all his conquests and successful military campaigns would be overshadowed by his victory over raiding Muslims outside of Poitiers in 732. Charles the Hammer became the man of one memorable moment in the history of Western Europe.

Charles Martel at the battle of Poitiers

Edward Gibbon wrote in 1776 that, had the victorious line of march of the Muslims not ended at Poitiers, "the interpretation of the Koran would [now] be taught in the schools of Oxford." Almost a century later the great historian Francois Guizot was convinced that "the civilization of the world depended on it [stopping the Muslims in Poitiers]". The battle of Poitiers has not always been given such importance and during the last century the events have been recast and given different meanings.

The background of *732* starts with the defeat of the Visigoths at the hands of Clovis in 507. The barbarian warriors who had settled in Aquitaine and Languedoc moved across the Pyrenees and Spain became a Visigoth kingdom. North of the Pyrenees they kept control of Languedoc, the Roman Septimania, which remained a frontier province.

A century or so later, on the other side of the Mediterranean Sea, shortly after the death of Muhammad in 632, the Arabs started their formidable expansion out of Arabia. They swiftly overpowered the Roman empire of the east in North Africa. Morocco became part of the Umayyad caliphate of Damascus and then, at the beginning of the eighth century, Tarik and his converted Berbers crossed into Spain. It took them only four years from 711 to 715 to defeat the Visigoths. The Iberian Peninsula became Al-Andalus, a province of the caliphate. This was the beginning of many centuries of Islamic influence in Spain, three in some regions, eight in others.

The Visigoths who had retreated to the north of Spain and into Languedoc tried to gain their independence from al Andalus and sought the assistance of Eudes, Duke of Aquitaine. His duchy was the first line of defense against Arab intrusions north of the Pyrenees and he had already successfully driven back Arab raids. Then, around 731, as infighting among Muslim factions abated, emir Abd ar Rahman turned his attention to the Frankish territories. He crossed the mountains at *Roncevaux*, defeated Eudes, Duke of Aquitaine, sacked Bordeaux and after hearing about the wealth of the Abbey of Saint Martin de Tours continued his raid further north. Meanwhile, a second Muslim army moved across Provence and headed north along the Rhone.

Up until then Charles Martel had shown little concern about the raids and incursions conducted by the Muslims. He was a man of the north and not too displeased that they menaced his enemy, the duke of Aquitaine. He had a change of heart when the Muslims threatened to control all the lands around the *mare nostra* and sprang into action with the full force of his recently formed cavalry. His armies intercepted the Muslims before they reached Poitiers and, according to Latin sources, after a great slaughter, the Muslims abandoned the field of battle and were driven back to the Pyrenees. This was the great Frank victory of 732 which was glorified later by Charles Martel's son, Pepin le Bref, when he seized the crown and was proclaimed king.

Did Charles Martel defeat a mere raiding party as taught in Muslim history books or did he successfully stop the Muslim expansion in Europe? If Abd ar Rahman had been victorious, would the caliphate have been satisfied to consolidate its positions in the south of France or would it have carried its expansion further north into Frank territories? The victors gave their answer and celebrate *732*. The Arabs downplay the event but the Franks did make an impression on them; the Europeans are still called *al-Ifranj* in modern Arabic.

After his successful expedition at Poitiers, Charles Martel drove the Muslims from Provence and, mission accomplished, returned to his northern territories. He died in 741 forever remembered as the Frank who defeated the *Arabs* at Poitiers in 732. Edward Gibbon wrote about stopping the conquering *Muslims*. At the time of Charles Martel, the enemy was called *Saracens* by some, *Moors* by others.

There was no king when Charles died in 741, he had not felt the need to replace Thierry IV, four years earlier. The two mayors of the palace, Carloman and Pepin le Bref, Charles' sons, agreed on the name of the puppet to put on the throne. It would be Childeric III, the last Merovingian king.

Musée des Antiquités Nationales and Château de Saint-Germain-en-Laye

The richest collection of Merovingian archeological artifacts in France is found at the *Musée des Antiquités Nationales* located in the chateau of Saint-Germain-en-Laye, west of Paris. Most items come from tombs of the wealthy as it was the tradition up to the seventh century to dress the body of the dead. The objects uncovered by archeologists are mostly in metal and stone since cloth and wood have not weathered the effect of time. The display of a few swords, numerous belt-buckles, *fibulae* (broaches), and colorful stone jewelry offers a glimpse of western European society during the early Middle Ages, between the fifth and eighth century. The art of this period had been mostly overlooked up to the middle of the nineteenth century when archeologists and medieval historians started collecting artifacts dating from the Merovingian period.

The Morgan Library and Museum in New York also has a fine collection of so-called barbarian jewelry from the *Dark Ages.* It includes brooches, earrings, buckles, belt mounts and jewelry artifacts worn to advertise wealth and status in the new barbarian kingdoms which arose following the fall of the Western Roman Empire.

A trip to Saint-Germain from the Arc de Triomphe takes little more than half an hour on the RER, the high-speed metro. As the escalator reaches street level, the imposing chateau and its park gradually appear and offer a stark contrast to the busy shopping streets of the charming town of Saint-Germain-en-Laye.

The chateau is a compendium of notable French architectural styles and it has welcomed some of France's most illustrious kings. A first *castrum* built in the twelfth century was enlarged by Saint Louis who also commissioned a chapel, consecrated in 1238, which prefigures the Gothic *Sainte Chapelle* in Paris; King Francois I gave the chateau its Renaissance style. At the end of the sixteenth century a *Chateau Neuf* was built next to the old one where Henri IV had stayed with his fourteen children; Louis XIV, the Sun King, was born in the New Chateau and lived in the old one before moving to Versailles. Napoleon III, who was passionate about the conquest of Gaul by Caesar, created a museum for Celtic and Gallo-Roman antiquities in the chateau; this was the precursor to today's Musée des Antiquités Nationales. The purpose of this museum inaugurated in 1867 was to centralize documents and artifacts relating to the history of the people who settled in Gaul from the Paleolithic to the end of the tenth century. This seems overwhelming but the conservators have wisely been selective in the choice of items forming the permanent collections.

The edge of the plateau which overlooks the Seine offers a panoramic view of the river and the western hills of Paris; beyond, is the City of Light. The gardens which decorated the slope and had been the proud contribution of Henri IV are no more. Seven terraces, connected on both ends by symmetrical staircases and brought to life by fountains and grottos represented a rare example of gardens along a slope in France. The Saint-Germain architects had most presumably found their model in the terraced gardens built in Italy after the fifteen century. Marie de Médicis, the Italian wife of Henri IV, must have been influential in their design. Unfortunately, all this was destroyed during the eighteenth century. The property had been poorly maintained for some time and the foundations had collapsed when Louis XVI gave the New Chateau to his brother the count of Artois. The count undertook a much-needed major restoration, the terraces were destroyed and the grottos filled with earth. All that is left to be enjoyed in the twenty-first century is the panoramic view across the Seine.

From Empire to Kingdoms

Pepin's Coup d'Etat (751)

Carloman, who had been mayor of the palace, retired from this world in 747 to find peace in a monastery. His younger brother, Pepin le Bref, now anxious to capitalize on their father's fame, deposed king Childeric III in 751 with the blessing of the pope; Childeric had been the name of the first and would be the name of the last Merovingian king. Pope Zachary had declared that "whoever holds power is the true king". Childeric III was sent to a monastery, and before his exile his long hair was cut depriving him symbolically of the aura of his royal lineage.

The ancestors of Charlemagne replaced the descendants of Clovis 270 years after the Frank had been acclaimed king.

In his seminal work about the Roman Empire published in 1787, Gibbon wrote that the conquest of Gaul by the Franks "was followed by ten centuries of anarchy and ignorance". This is a memorable statement, powerful in its simplicity. Ten centuries is the length of time that can be assigned to the period between the end of Antiquity and the Renaissance, the ages *in the middle.* These were Dark Ages in the eyes of Edward Gibbon and the first 270 years of the Frankish Kingdom most certainly confirm his judgment.

Pepin became king of a country that had seemingly lost much of the civilizing contributions of the Romans. Urban life was in decline and the control of the Mediterranean by the Arabs had reduced the economy to regional trade. The antique culture had been shredded; to wit, Gregoire de Tours wrote the history of Clovis in so-called kitchen Latin. The legal system was dominated by the more primitive laws and traditions of the Germanic tribes. The most useful vestige of the Roman occupation seems to have been the network of roads.

Nevertheless, as the historian Bainville pointed out, Merovingian Gaul had, more than any other part of the Empire, preserved the best that the Romans had brought to the west. The Pepin clan benefited from a home base in the east, the kingdom called Austrasia, the unifying force of Christianity and the Roman concept of state and unity. The pieces of the broken kingdom of Clovis were there, waiting to be reunited one more time.

The new dynasty, the *Carolingian dynasty*, would be named after its illustrious representatives, Pepin's father Charles Martel and his even more illustrious son Charlemagne. Their ancestors, the *Pépinides*, are said to have come from an area close to Liege, near the border between today's Belgium and Germany, not far from Maastricht, known today for the signing of the European treaty in 1992.

The new king was elected by the lords, the *coup d'état* had been a success but it had been a coup nevertheless. Pepin needed a more powerful sign and he looked towards the Church to bless his legitimacy. It was a quasi-dogma that kings were God's representatives on earth but Pepin wanted a public demonstration by the Church that he was the chosen one. The bishops, led by Bishop Boniface, borrowed from the ceremony used for their own consecration and anointed him with the blessed oil used in administering sacraments. Pepin would be elected and anointed but not crowned. It would take a few more years before the rites of the *sacre* crystallized. In 816, Louis le Pieux, Pepin's grandson, was anointed and crowned in the cathedral of Reims and the same rites would be performed for all future French kings. In the years to come, Hincmar, Bishop of Reims, would say that Clovis and not Pepin had been the first anointed king when he had been baptized in Reims.

Pepin wanted also to be assured that the lords would accept one of his two sons as his legitimate successor. In 754, Pope Stephen II came to Saint Denis and anointed Pepin, again, and his two sons, the oldest only six years old.

Centuries later, kings would no longer need a public demonstration that they were the ministers of God. They would still be crowned in a cathedral and it would be a sumptuous affair but it was more a traditional celebration than a blessing by the Church. This change came about when the other lords in the kingdom no longer contested the succession rights of the eldest son of the king.

The anointing of Pepin by the bishop of Rome was one side of a quid pro quo and the king honored his side of the understanding when he led his troops into northern Italy, defeated the Lombards and gave the conquered land to the Pope. This was the so-called *donation of Pepin.*

The Ravenna region of Romagna, along the northern Adriatic coast, became the first of the Papal States.

Pepin would be a good king. He united Gaul, except for the dissident regions of Aquitaine and Brittany. In making sure that his sons were seen as God's choice he had taken the correct first step towards the survival of the dynasty. The choice of a leader was becoming a family affair in the Kingdom of the Franks.

After Pepin's death in 768, true to Frankish custom, his kingdom was shared between his two sons, Charles and Carloman. This made for a difficult transition as the relationship between the two young kings quickly degenerated. Carloman resented the growing stature of his brother after Charles swiftly quelled a rebellion in Aquitaine. Italy, where Carloman sided with the Lombards while Charles strongly supported the pope, became another source of friction. Only Carloman's fortuitous death in 771 avoided a bloody confrontation. His gisant at Saint Denis is on the north side of the transept while the other Carolingians are on the south side. It is doubtful that his body is there since he was presumably buried in Reims. After Carloman's death, his followers presented his crown to Charles and the two Frankish kingdoms were reunited again. In the eyes of Charles, God had chosen him to be the next in line in the Carolingian dynasty.

Charlemagne/ Karl der Grosse

Emperor Charlemagne by Albrecht Durer circa 1512

Charles would be crowned emperor on Christmas day in 800. After his death, his grandson Nithard would call him *Carolus, magnus imperator,* shortened to Charlemagne in French and Karl der Grosse in German. In 1512 Albrecht Durer represented him framed by two escutcheons, one bearing an eagle, the other three fleurs de lys. The celebration in 2014 of the 1200th anniversary of the emperor's death renewed the interest for the Carolingian empire among both German and French medievalists.

Pepin's son would become the most famous man of the High Middle Ages. He owed his reputation to his temperament and his achievements and the laudatory biography, the *Vita Karoli,* Life of Charles, written by Einhard shortly after Charlemagne's death, contributed to this lasting fame. This opus became immensely popular during the Middle Ages and is still re-edited and revised by French as well as German historians. Einhard, a scholar, known as Eginhard by the French, was educated at the court of his master and stayed there for twenty-three years even though he did not hold any specific function. He was a Frank who spoke the same franconian as Charlemagne and wrote in Latin. He composed the *Life of Charles* probably around 829, about fifteen years after the death of the Emperor. Einhard, by that time, was close to Louis le Pieux, Charlemagne's son and this time again did not fill a specific function at the imperial court.

Einhard was the first layman to write the biography of a king in the Middle Ages and he modeled his opus on *The Lives of the Twelve Caesars* by the second century Roman historian Suetonius. In particular, he borrowed the thematic plan used by the Roman: a prologue confirming the legitimacy of the new emperor, his major deeds, a description of the emperor and his personal life, his last moments and his testament. In Einhard's words "the life, the behavior and mostly the noble deeds of my master, he who provided for my sustenance". Vita Karoli is also the work of a man who embodies the *Carolingian Renaissance*, the Renaissance which blossomed during the reign of the emperor.

True to his thematic plan, Einhard starts with a reminder that Charlemagne's father, Pepin le Bref, replaced the last Merovingian who had "the empty title of king" and that Charlemagne became king, with the approval of the Franks, after the (convenient!) death, presumably from natural causes, of his brother. He then proceeds to describe each of the king's military campaigns.

Pepin, Charlemagne's father, had fought the duke of Aquitaine every year from 760 until his death in 768 and Charlemagne brought a victorious end to the campaigns in Aquitaine and Gascony. These two regions that had previously been invaded by the Visigoths had not been truly integrated into the Kingdom of the Franks

He also followed in his father's steps in Italy and was victorious against the Lombards. Father and son had intervened in the peninsula at the urgent plea of the pope and after Didier, leader of the Lombards, surrendered at Pavia, Charlemagne crowned himself "king of the Lombards" to the great surprise of the Pope. This marked the end of the Lombard domination in the peninsula.

Another of Charlemagne's defining campaigns was against the Saxons. It was long and bloody; started in 772 it did not end before 804. Einhard notes that, because the border between the Saxons and the Franks was running through flat countryside, war was unavoidable.

Charlemagne participated only in two battles and one of these took place near the Teutoburg Forest where Quinctilius Varus and his legionnaires had been so dramatically massacred. If conquering land was the ultimate goal of Charlemagne's warriors, serving Christ was no less on their mind. The Saxons converted, rebelled and abjured and by the end of the century were Christians again. By then, the Franks had given up on forced conversions and the Saxon resistance was spent. Warfare ended and the Saxons became trusted allies of the Franks.

Al Andalus, today's Spain, also gave Charlemagne a chance to extend his zone of influence. In 751, the Umayyads had been overthrown by the Abbasids and hunted down as they fled Damascus. Abd al Rahman, the grandson of the emir famous for battling Charles Martel in 732, had escaped the massacre of his family and after months of perilous travel through the Middle East and North Africa had arrived in Spain. Confusion then reigned in Al Andalus as the partisans of the two Caliphates fought for control of the peninsula. Pro-Abbasid rulers in the north enlisted the help of Charlemagne against Abd al Rahman and his Umayyad supporters. The king of the Franks sensing an opportunity to consolidate his southern border against incursions by the Saracens, sent two Frankish armies south of the Pyrenees. One took the eastern route towards Barcelona and will remain engaged in warfare for more than twenty years. The other, led by Charlemagne himself, crossed the western Pyrenees but was forced to return when news arrived of uprisings in Saxony. The Frankish leader had not achieved much, his Muslim allies managed very well without him and were no longer keen to share any power. They compensated him with gold but the Franks did not gain control over any land on the southern slopes of the Pyrenees. This incursion would be worth only a by-line in the life of Charlemagne if it had not been the source of a legendary *fait d'armes* and piece of literature.

The action takes place in August 778 in the Pyrenees. Charles' rearguard led by his nephew Roland is progressing slowly in a single column along a rugged and narrow pass called Roncevaux when it is ambushed by Basques; the Franks are exterminated, and the assailants vanish in the darkness. The coup by the Basques is described at length by Einhard and in one of his manuscripts he specifically mentions Roland, duke of Brittany. Roland became the hero of an extraordinarily popular poem written more than 300 years later, *La Chanson de Roland,* the Song of Roland. It depicts the young knight, victim of his sense of honor, waiting too long to call for reinforcement and overpowered by *Saracens*. It was more in the spirit of a Christian epic to transform a minor battle against Basques into a crusade against Muslims. During the Middle Ages troubadours riding from fortified chateau to fortified chateau would recite the Chanson and Roland became the symbol of the valorous Christian knight fighting the infidels, the perfect knight, loyal to his earthly suzerain and to his other suzerain, God. Roland's folly and temper were the cause of the disaster but warriors in the Middle Ages were admired for their courage, loyalty and prowess more than for their pragmatism. It has been written that Taillefer, William the Conqueror's jester, sang the Chanson before the battle of Hastings in 1066. He knew it would raise the fighting spirit of the Normans.

Charlemagne is at the heart of another legend originating in Spain. It recalls that under the guidance of Saint Jacques he freed the tomb of the Saint in Compostella from the Infidels. In order to dutifully celebrate this event, the French Ministry of Culture has assigned (more or less arbitrarily) the year 813 to this exploit.

A few years after his shortened Spanish expedition, Charlemagne gave the crown of the newly reunited kingdom of Aquitaine to his son Louis and entrusted the Spanish affairs to Guillaume, count of Toulouse. The troubadours in the twelfth century will write and sing about Guillaume's exploits against the Saracen.

Einhard tells of other successful military campaigns, how Charlemagne received the surrender of the Bretons and of Tassilon, duke of Bavaria and mentions that his son Pepin led a long war against the Avars in today's Hungary. At the end of his reign Charlemagne had doubled the size of the kingdom inherited from his father.

Charlemagne participates in almost every one of the campaigns during his reign. He does not hesitate to crisscross Carolingian Europe from the regions bordering Spain and Brittany to Pannonia, from Frisia to the Benevento, all on horseback. He and his men would have covered a wide range of miles par day and his return north after Ronceveaux can serve as a case in point. The *Annals of the Empire* tell us that when he reached Burgundy he was informed of a Saxon rebellion near Cologne and dispatched a *scara*, an elite group, towards the Rhine. There was in the end no encounter with the Saxons which were perhaps only a raiding party. It has been estimated that it might have taken the emperor thirty days to come from the Pyrenees at fifteen miles a day and then only eleven days at thirty miles a day for his mounted elite group to ride to Cologne.

Charlemagne tried to establish diplomatic ties with the Abbasid Caliph of Bagdad. In 797 he sent ambassadors to Harun al-Rachid; four years passed before they returned (Kissinger's shuttle diplomacy would not have worked in the eighth century). They brought back a gift which, legend says, was the one elephant owned by the Caliph. The story became more colorful over time. It was said later that the elephant was white and that it was found dead in 810 at the mouth of the river Lippe next to today's German-Dutch border.

Einhard also echoes the legend that has Harun al-Rachid transferring his authority over Jerusalem to Charlemagne. This happens to be an embellished interpretation of a true story. The Patriarch of Jerusalem had given Charlemagne, a few days before his coronation, the keys to the Saint Sepulcher, thus making him symbolically the protector of the Holy Place. This is only one of the stories referring to ties between the Emperor and the Holy Land. His shadow will loom over the Crusades. When the First Crusaders took their vows in 1096, it was a popular belief that Charlemagne had gone to the Middle East to fight against the Muslims and many Crusaders thought they would walk in the steps of *Carolus Redivivus*, Charles the Born Again, on their way to Jerusalem. Pope Urban II, preaching the First Crusade, cited him to the knights reluctant to take the cross as the model to emulate. In the medieval Germanic world, Karl der Grosse, Charlemagne, was the historic leader of the German crusaders.

Charlemagne is present in one more esoteric legend which finds its source in a letter from Saint Paul to the Thessalonians. This legend says that the last king connected with the Roman Empire will go to Jerusalem, and in the Garden of Gethsemane lay down his crown and his scepter. This will signal the end of the Roman Empire and then, and only then, will the Antichrist appear and fight the Christians. He will be victorious at first but in the end will be defeated by Christ. The prophecy announcing Christ's victory can only be fulfilled after the Christians have returned to the Holy Land. In the minds of the Crusaders, the last king who went to Jerusalem could only have been Charlemagne. Belief in this prophecy was widely spread in the eleventh and twelfth centuries and this says as much about the folklore of legends surrounding the Crusades as about the enduring aura of Charlemagne.

At the end of his long recitation of the commendable deeds of Charlemagne, Einhard mentions the construction of the palace at Aix-la Chapelle, started in 797; in the twenty first century only the chapel is still standing. The emperor wanted to transform Aix into another Constantinople by building a replica of the palace of the Byzantine emperor; Aix was in Austrasia not far from the land of his ancestors. Charlemagne remained a Frank throughout his life, and even after his coronation as Emperor, always saw himself as *King of the Franks and the Lombards.*

The *Life of Charles*, true to the model set by Suetonius, then deals with the private life of the emperor. Charles had been coerced by his mother to marry the daughter of the king of the Lombard, but he divorced after a couple of years and married the noble and virtuous Swabian Hildegarde. They had four sons and five daughters but only three sons and three daughters reached adulthood. He also had two daughters from his third wife Fastrade and several children with concubines. Charlemagne kept his daughters close to him and admired them to a degree that puzzled Einhard; he did not give any away in marriage even though several gave him grandchildren.

Charlemagne was very respectful towards his mother Berthe, called Bertrade. She had played an important political role when he was young, siding with Carloman in favoring the Lombards and forcing Charles to marry Désirée, the daughter of Didier, leader of the Lombards. When Charles realized that it was a political mistake not to honor his commitment to the pope, he repudiated Désirée and kept Berthe at arm's length from the court. He still showed her much affection but she no longer played a political role. Berthe is buried in Saint Denis. In popular culture she is remembered as *Berthe aux grands pieds,* Big Feet Berthe, the heroine of a legend sang by troubadours in the thirteenth century. It is the story of a king, a queen with big feet and a look-alike of the queen; she takes the place of the queen but her small feet give the deception away.

Charlemagne is described as a heavyset, virile, more than six feet tall man with long hair. He dressed in the style of his Frankish ancestors, linen shirt tied around the waist by a silk belt, sandals and a fur overcoat in cold weather. He was a passionate hunter and an accomplished swimmer, was very studious and listened with great attention when he was read Saint Augustine's "The City of God" ("two loves have built two cities: the love of self carried to the exclusion of God and the love of God up to the negation of self" is a well-known citation from Augustine's opus).

Einhard introduces some of Charlemagne's habits and then, seemingly in passing, makes reference to an event which was actually of great importance: Charles crowned *imperator* by the pope.

During the last years of the eighth century the pope had been accused of immorality, simony and other vices and ultimately manhandled by rebel Roman barons. After he was freed, unharmed, Leo III had placed himself under the protection of Charlemagne. The great Christian king had very carefully considered the accusations levied against the pope and in the autumn of 800 had gone to Rome to decide his fate. Leo III appeared in front of a court of prelates and counts and after several weeks of deliberations was exonerated. On December 23, in Saint Peter's Basilica he swore that he was innocent.

Coronation of Charlemagne, workshop of Raphael (1517)

It was two days later, on December 25, at the end of the service at the same Saint Peter's Basilica, that Pope Leo III had crowned Charles emperor following a rite reminiscent of the Roman Empire. He had anointed him with sacred oil and the crowd, gathered in front of the basilica, had acclaimed the new emperor. Historians still debate if

Charlemagne had really wanted to become emperor and be crowned by the pope or if he was surprised when the pope set the crown on his head. There are different accounts of the imperial coronation and Einhard's is clearly meant to express the displeasure of the new emperor. Whatever happened at Saint Peter's Basilica, *imperator* better represented the extent of his power than the title he carried up to then, *king of the Franks and of the Lombards.* By the year 800 he had already achieved all his wide-reaching conquests and reigned over all the Latin Christians except those in the British Isles.

Leo did not ignore that he had no authority to grant this title. The Eastern Roman Empire had survived the collapse of the Western empire and, true to the long-standing Roman concept of universality, the emperor residing in Constantinople considered that his authority extended over the former Western Empire.

In 800 the head of the Roman Empire was Empress Irene. She is remembered as the basileus of the Byzantine Empire but in her days she was seen as the head of the old Imperium Romanum. It was only in the sixteenth century that, for the sake of clarity, the German historian Hieronymus Wolf coined the term Byzantine in reference to the ex-Eastern Roman Empire.

Irene and her entourage did not welcome the rise of a competitor but the pope was not concerned about Irene's displeasure; Byzantium was far away and showed little interest in the territories under its control in the Italian peninsula. The pope also needed protection against the Lombards and he stood a better chance with the leader of the young Frankish kingdom than with Irène. In crowning Charles, the pope had seized an opportunity to distance himself from the east and the Greek Church and throw his lot with the major power of the west.

Even crowned by the pope, Charlemagne's imperial title needed to be acknowledged by the Byzantine emperor. This was done in 812 but the Byzantines stopped short of recognizing him as *Roman* emperor.

This event had far-reaching consequences. It brought a confirmation that Rome was the first of the metropolitan seats of the new empire, the Carolingian empire, and it was the first step towards the forming of a new empire about one hundred and fifty years later, the Holy Roman Empire.

In conferring civil authority to a king, the papacy had reinforced its universal role. Likewise, regal power had been strengthened by a public demonstration of its divine origin. It was of little import that both parties, the *Romanists* and the *Royalists,* could claim victory, during Charlemagne's time, the church was part of the empire. The emperor had been the head of the Church ever since Constantine and, as such, the representative of God on earth and Charlemagne did not see it differently. It would take another four centuries before the Church extirpated itself from the grasp of secular powers. By then, Church and State would still influence and fight one another but two power centers would exist: one for the temporal and the other for the spiritual.

Islam, the other major religion in the Middle Ages, would follow initially a similar path. Muhammad had been acknowledged during the early stages of the development of the Muslim faith as a religious and a secular leader. The successors of the prophet, the *caliphs,* were the representatives of Allah on earth, and were similar to the emperors who were the representative of God; early Islam, during Charlemagne's time, was a single cultural, religious and political force. This unity would be destroyed during medieval times and the Muslim world became the sum of powerful, dispersed, cultural centers. In contrast with the Church of Rome, though, the bond between religious and secular authority was not broken and state and religion stayed one.

The French medievalist Robert Folz gave considerable symbolic importance to the imperial coronation of Charlemagne. He claims that in becoming the head of a Christian empire, the king of the Franks walked in the footsteps of King David and Constantine and made the Franks the chosen people and the ancestors of the French. The legacy of Charlemagne was France itself.

Napoleon, also, was a strong believer that Charlemagne was a founding father of France. It is worth noting that the two emperors represent opposing views on primogeniture. Napoleon would be obsessed by founding a dynasty and having a son inherit his Empire. Charlemagne, on the other hand, only wanted to keep the assets he had inherited and conquered in the hands of his family and did not intend to hand them all to his oldest son; this was detrimental to empire building but was in line with Frankish tradition.

The emperor is not buried at Saint Denis but at Aix-la-Chapelle, not far from the western border of Germany. Karl der Grosse belongs to the German Middle Ages as much as Charlemagne does to the Kingdom of the Franks. The Rhine was at the heart of Charlemagne's empire, an empire which long ago announced twenty-first century Europe, a continental Europe, not a Europe centered on the Mediterranean as it had been at the time of the Romans.

Alcuin of York and the Carolingian Renaissance

Einhard was a disciple of Alcuin, the Anglo-Saxon monk who came to Charlemagne's court in 786 and was labelled the most knowledgeable man of his time. Alcuin became the leader of the ensemble of reforms championed by Charlemagne later called *Carolingian Renaissance*- a convenient label fashioned after the better known *Italian Renaissance*. The foundation of the Carolingian Renaissance, its emblematic document, is a capitulary, ordinance, called *Admonitio Generalis* issued in 789.

Charlemagne's renaissance was driven by a longing for salvation as were similar reforms attempted during that era. He was convinced that he had been called to guide on their way to salvation the people that God had entrusted to him. This meant more than bring them peace, order and prosperity, it also meant facilitate their access to the Bible and the sacred texts. The study of these texts was believed to lead to the understanding of God and therefore language, script and books were enablers of salvation. Charlemagne brought together the best minds of Europe to achieve a much-needed revival of these three domains.

The level of Latin was raised. Charlemagne's mother tongue was a Franconian dialect and the only spoken language he shared with the elite was Latin. The Germanic languages spoken by most of his people bore no relationship to Latin. Latin was also the only written language and had been adulterated over time. It had become necessary to restore the teaching of proper grammar, spelling and reading.

The extensive recourse to capitularies by Charlemagne was an impetus for a purer Latin. These instructions were relayed by his representatives, the counts, scattered around the empire and, in order to fulfill their mission, these representatives needed to be able to read and write Latin. There was one more advantage to having one language clearly understood by the elite, it helped unify the disparate regions forming the empire.

The texts used by the church, also, had long been neglected. At the request of Charlemagne, Alcuin edited the Latin translation of the Bible written by Saint Jerome called *Vulgate*. During the previous four centuries the clerks copying this Bible had accumulated numerous errors which now needed to be corrected.

The reform of script was at the heart of the Carolingian Renaissance. During the Merovingian dynasty the scribes wrote in a cursive style called half-uncial. This script took time to copy, was difficult to read, made arbitrary use of majuscules and used too much space. Charlemagne, around 770, asked the scribes in charge of copying his official documents to create a script that would be easy for all to use. They designed the so-called Carolingian script and made a lasting contribution by standardizing the calligraphy of capital letters, the majuscules, and by introducing the *Carolingian minuscule.* The Caroline quickly replaced the other scripts in the major scriptoria, first at Corbie Abbey, upriver from Amiens, and then shortly after at Saint Martin de Tours where Alcuin had been named Abbott.

The Carolingian minuscule went through various transformations, was superseded during the twelfth century by the Gothic blackletters (commonly known as German script) and was revived by the humanists in the fifteenth century. The so-called Roman alphabet and Carolingian letters are still employed today in most Western countries and their usage has far outgrown the Greek or the Cyrillic of orthodox Christians.

Charlemagne was the first king to assemble his court in one location. His palace at Aix allowed the numerous scholars who belonged to the court to meet and form what Alcuin called the Palatine Academy, a sort of literary salon. The palace also housed a school for artists, painters, calligraphers, architects...which fostered a true cultural and artistic Renaissance. In reviving arts and crafts neglected since the end of Antiquity the emperor was convinced he was allowing a better appreciation of sacred texts.

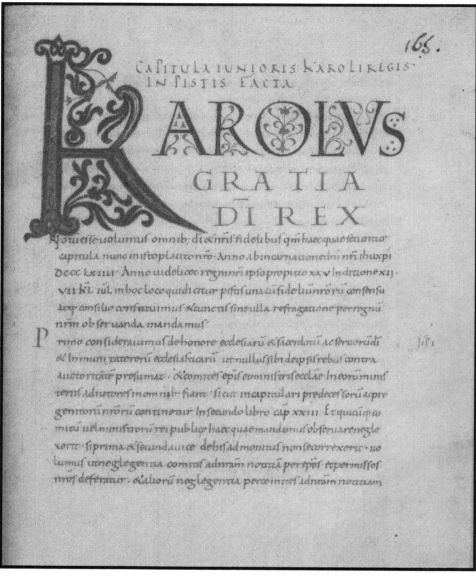

Carolingian minuscule. Ninth century capitulary. Work done at a scriptorium connected with the court of Charles le Chauve

Schools similar to the palace school operated in monasteries and cathedrals. The scriptoriums of the great abbeys at Saint Martin de Tours, Fleury or Corbie handcrafted liturgical books and bibles that were true artistic masterpieces. Some of these are safekept at the Bibliothèque Nationale, rue de Richelieu in Paris and, from time to time, the Museum of the Bibliothèque exhibits illuminated liturgical manuscripts with ivory bindings that once belonged to Charlemagne or his grandson Charles le Chauve, that is, Charles the Bald.

Charles le Chauve would cherish luxury and be a patron of the arts. In the footsteps of his grandfather he would encourage the founding of a Palace School. He was particularly keen to see a flourishing of the art of bookmaking and various uses of precious metals and ivory. Painters, scribes, makers of artifacts and other artists followed the royal court in its peregrinations from Soissons to Saint Denis and often to Compiegne. The Morgan Library in New York has in its collections a masterpiece known as the Lindau Gospels, an illuminated manuscript with a jeweled cover, presumably the work of Charles le Chauve's Palace School at Saint Denis.

This revival called Carolingian Renaissance can be considered as the first blossoming of a European culture. It will end in the ninth century when the Kingdom of the Franks will be ravaged by Vikings, Moors and other invaders.

An anecdote in connection with Admonitio Generalis. One of its articles required the creation in each diocese and monastery of a school for boys seeking to become clerks. A superficial reading of this article is at the origin of the long-lived legend that *Charlemagne invented school*. The very mention of Charlemagne in France recalls the refrain of a 1964 popular song: "good old Charlemagne who had the crazy idea to invent school."

Verdun Treaty: Two Countries in the Making

Charlemagne's successors fought bitterly over his empire. Several partitions would be drawn and the agreement reached in Verdun in 843, almost thirty years after the death of the great emperor, would become the first milestone in the making of France and Germany.

The emperor's sole surviving son, Louis le Pieux, had been crowned in 813 and anointed by the pope in Reims three years later. Louis le Pieux had three sons with his first wife, Ermengarde, and as was customary, had divided his empire soon after his anointment. The succession plan, *Ordinatio Imperii,* stipulated that his sons Louis and Pepin would receive regal authority over kingdoms in the eastern and western parts of the empire. He then introduced a novelty by giving the title of emperor to his oldest son, Lothar, in order to preserve some sense of unity. Louis le Pieux was convinced that the empire could survive in peace, cemented by Christianity. This was unfortunately an anachronism at a time when power trumped Christian principles.

There was another descendant of the emperor, Bernard, an illegitimate grandson. His title of king of Italy was not confirmed by the *Ordinatio* and Bernard, now vassal of his uncle Louis, became tormented by the idea that his kingdom was at risk. He rebelled, was defeated, found guilty of treason and condemned to death; the sentence was ultimately commuted into blinding, but the young man did not survive his mutilation. The revolt and death of Bernard were turning points in the reign of Louis le Pieux, and the heartless treatment of his nephew remains to this day a dark spot on his legacy.

In 819, following the death of Ermengarde, the forty-nine-year-old Louis le Pieux married the fourteen year old Judith. She was a Welf, a Bavarian aristocrat, and the emperor had been seduced by her beauty. Their second child was a son, Charles, born in 823 and Louis could not withstand Judith's aggressive lobbying for her son. He drew a new partition giving Charles a share of the empire. From then on, too many egos and ambitions came into play and dark clouds filled the sky over the empire. Pepin and Louis plotted against their father, his new wife, her son and their older brother Lothar. The old emperor was deposed and imprisoned only to be reinstated a few months later. Pepin died in 838 and Charles claimed the kingdom of Aquitaine. Louis le Pieux died two years later.

Until recently Louis had the image of a weak king, submissive to the bishops (true to his surname *The Pious*) and his name always associated with the partitioning of the empire. He was said to have been a *monkish* sovereign, a pious man not at ease in the everyday world of the Franks. Michelet, the great historian, saw in him a humble Christian, a Saint Louis in the ninth century. Since the middle of the twentieth century several scholars have attempted his rehabilitation. In October 1957 the Belgian medievalist Ganshof wrote an article entitled *Louis le Pieux Reconsidered* in which he claims that, however weak Louis might have been, the Empire was too diverse and unstructured to survive. Only a leader with Charlemagne's charisma had been able to hold its pieces together. How the heir of Charlemagne should be judged was still a topic of great interest among medievalists in 2014 during the celebrations of the 1,200th anniversary of the great emperor's death.

As soon as Lothar, Louis le Pieux's eldest son, was informed of his father's death, he claimed the territories controlled by his brother Louis and his half-brother Charles. Neither of them had any intention of surrendering without a fight and they joined forces, defeating Lothar at Fontenay in a rare Franks against Franks battle. The victorious brothers drew a plan to share the spoils and build upon the territories they already controlled, Bavaria for Louis and Aquitaine for Charles. This was the agreement reached in Verdun in 843 which gave Louis the eastern part of the Empire and Charles the western: East Francia for one, West Francia for the other. Lothar was left with a sliver of land in the middle, extending from north of Aix la Chapelle through northern Italy up to Rome. It would be called *Lotharingia* at times, *Middle Francia* at others. Lothar also received the title of emperor but without suzerain rights over his brothers.

Charles le Chauve, the Bald, was crowned king of West Francia shortly after the Verdun agreement. Some historians have called him *first King of France* and include him in the short list of founding fathers of the country. They argue that Charles was the first king to reign over a territory which would over time be called France. Others deny Charles any primacy among French kings. His Francia was, they claim, just an empty shell and it would be many centuries before it would be filled with the spirit of a French nation.

Middle Francia would not survive the death of Lothar, the anointed emperor, in 855, and Charlemagne's ex-empire would be further partitioned. Italy and the title of emperor went to Lothar's oldest son, Louis, Provence to his son Charles and the third son, Lothar II, received the northern portion which kept the name Lotharingia.

Division of Carolingian Empire, Treaty of Verdun in 843.

Despite this new partition, the Carolingian lords did not doubt that the kingdoms could be brought together again into a great Carolingian empire. Charles le Chauve, for one, dreamed of becoming emperor of a newly reunited Regnum Francorum. His two brothers, Louis and Lothar, had the same ambitions. As early as 858, only fifteen years after the Verdun agreement, Louis the German answered the call of some of Charles le Chauve's vassals and claimed the crown of West Francia. This was a failed attempt. Influenced by Bishop Hincmar, the church stayed faithful to Charles and Louis returned to East Francia claiming that he was abiding by the will of God. Then, after 884, Charles le Gros, a son of Louis, reigned over a reunited Regnum Francorum but for a few years only. During the second half of the ninth and all of the tenth century West and East Francia interfered in each other's affairs but the partition was there to stay, and the suzerainty of the emperors will remain an empty concept. The pieces of Charlemagne's empire would never again be reunited for a sustained period.

The south of Lotharingia, Lorraine, stood in the way of France reaching its *natural* border, the Rhine, the border that Caesar knew should be the eastern limit of his Gaul. The seeds had been planted for recurrent warfare between the states on both sides of the Rhine. This would lead to the very emotionally charged *annexation of Alsace-Lorraine* by the German Reich in 1870 and the return of the territory to France in 1918.

Besançon and the Kingdom of Lothar

After Clothar and his Franks had defeated the Burgundians in 532 the town had become part of the Regnum Francorum. It was the de facto administrative and military center for the western and eastern slopes of the Jura Mountains.

Little is known about Besançon during the *Dark Ages*. It appears on the list of metropolises to which Charlemagne by testament was leaving a donation of gold and other valuables (a metropolis was the seat of an archbishop). It is also mentioned whenever a pope went to Reims to crown a king of the Franks as it was on the pope's route from Rome.

Following the partitioning of Charlemagne's empire, the town was integrated in the kingdom of Lothar.

Oaths of Strasbourg and the Birth of the French Language

East Francia and West Francia already exhibited cultural specificities when these territories were allocated to Charles and Louis. This is evidenced by documents known as the *Oaths of Strasbourg* written a year and a half before the Verdun partition.

After defeating Lothar, Louis and Charles had made mutual pledges of allegiance in front of their soldiers. The event had taken place in Strasbourg, on February 14, 842. Charles had sworn an oath of assistance to Louis in *teudisca lingua*, in front of his brother's army. Louis, in turn, had read a similar oath written in *romana lingua* to the troops from the western territories.

It matters little what these pledges were about, their historical importance lies in the fact that the texts read by the two monarchs were written in vernacular languages. Latin, the language commonly used in the Carolingian empire, had been replaced by languages used in two regions of Louis le Pieux's empire. This in itself pointed to the specificity of western and eastern Francia.

The transcript of the oath in *romana lingua*, Romance, is the birth certificate of the French language. It is usually said that the originals of the Oaths of Strasbourg are archived at the Bibliothèque Nationale in Paris. They actually were lost. The texts have survived thanks to a document by Nithard, a grandson of Charlemagne, *De dissensionibus filiorum Hludovici pii*, on the dissensions of the sons of Louis le Pieux, a chronicle more so than the opus of a historian, composed at the request of Charles le Chauve, probably at the end of the tenth century. During the next centuries *De dissensionibus* followed a very convoluted path. It found its way to an abbey in Paris in the fifteenth century, was sold to Christine, Queen of Sweden, in the seventeenth, donated by the queen to the Vatican library, appropriated by the French in 1797 as part of a larger ensemble of historical texts and never returned to the Vatican.

Oath of Strasbourg in Romance,
the birth certificate of the French language

The two versions of the following text: "For the love of God and for the common salvation of the Christian people and ours" are found in folio 12v to 13v.

> In Romance this text was transcribed as follows: "Pro Deo amur et pro christian poblo et nostro commun salvament," and is legible in the appended image.

> In Tedesco it would read: "In Godes minna ind in thes chritianes folches ind unser bedhero gehaltnissi."

The text in Teudisca lingua bears a stunning resemblance to German while in Romana lingua it is still very close to Latin.

What is the origin of the Romance dialect used in the oath? The answer now favored by eminent philologists is that it was not a dialect spoken in a specific part of Gaul but the language used by the few who knew how to write. This language, called Romance by the clerics, had progressed from spoken to written. How did a language which would become the French language find a niche in the ninth century between the numerous patois which were not written but only spoken and Latin which was written and spoken by the elite and was a tie between the various nations in Europe? The impulse came from the elite and the church was instrumental in the process.

Latin was the language used during religious ceremonies in the first centuries of Christianity in Gaul. Masses and sermons were said in Latin. As early as the sixth century the bishops came to realize that this Latin was less and less *classical* and that there were increasing differences between the spoken and the written languages. Since it mattered that the faithful understand the message of the church, the Council of Tours in 813 recommended that the clerics use their everyday language, *rustica lingua romana.*

The language which, in the Kingdom of the Franks, would become *French* started therefore as a plainer, more rustic form of Latin. The clerics began transcribing words as they were spoken, and the new language took flight. For the masses, nothing much would change for many centuries. They continued to communicate in their local patois or dialect ignoring almost all of this language that was becoming the French language.

The new language owes little to those spoken by the original Celtic populations. The rustic Latin core was sprinkled with Gallic words and then heavily influenced by the languages spoken by the invading Germanic tribes. Political as well as technical factors weighed on these influences. It was socially valorizing to adopt Frankish contributions.

The Germanic lexical, phonetic and syntactic influences would be more pronounced in the north of the country and lead to a *langue d'oil*; they carried less weight in the territories closer to the Mediterranean which would speak the *langue d'oc*; oil and oc are two ways of saying *oui*. At the turn of the fourteenth century, Dante wrote about oc and oil and said he preferred to write poems in *la lingua del si*, Italian.

This genesis of the French language is the one most commonly accepted by the philologists but there are other theories. The most flattering for the French derives the language from classical written Latin and not rustic spoken Latin. Others defend the view that it is a Celtic or Germanic language influenced by Latin.

Similar debates have opposed for centuries those who give more weight to the Gallic, the Frank or the Roman influences in the making of the French temperament. Each theory is usually championed by opposing ends of the political spectrum; the Jacobins during the French Revolution would be on the side of the Gaul while the aristocrats favored the Franks.

A few features of the new language:

- the vocalic system of the spoken Roman languages initially distinguished these languages from classical Latin. The vocalic range of French (front/back, open/closed, rounded or not, nasal/oral) is much richer than the Latin one and is an originality of the French language.

- in the first written texts, the Strasbourg oath for instance, one could read *pro Deo amur*; later the construction *pour l'amour de Dieu* and not *pour Dieu amour* would characterize French.

Side notes: The *lieschbloeme* became the *fleur de lis*, the enduring heraldic symbol of French kings, and the last son of Charlemagne was named *Hlutowigh* before being called Louis. The first leader of the Kingdom of the Franks who no longer spoke a Germanic language was Hugues Capet, crowned in 987. The mother tongue of his predecessor, a descendant of Charlemagne, had been *Franconian*, a Germanic language.

The new *lingua romana* radiated from Paris, the residence chosen by the kings, but it would take the *Ordonnance de Villers-Cotteret* in 1539 during the reign of King Francois I to impose French as the administrative language. English had become an administrative language much earlier. In 1356 the major of London imposed the use of English during council meetings and a few years later the opening of the British parliament was done in English. This break from the use of the French language by the English upper classes must be seen in the context of the political relations between the kingdoms of France and England in the fourteenth century.

The French language, the language of a centralized regal power and of clerics, was imperialistic and led to the extinction of numerous dialects. These disappeared mostly in their written form; spoken dialects and patois were hardy and some of them are still alive in the twenty-first century.

In August 1790, Abbe Henri Grégoire, a deputy to the national convention during the Revolution, initiated a survey of customs. His goal was to find support for his policy to stamp out local dialects and impose the French language. He and other revolutionaries knew that the citizens had to speak French, the language of freedom, in order to fully understand the *ancien regime* and the new world of liberty, equality and fraternity; language and nation were associated for the first time. The report that the Abbe submitted four years later on "the necessity and means of exterminating patois and universalizing the use of the French language" was an eye opener; the new regime had a long way to go. Less than one out of ten people used French as their language around 1790. The country was split between *oil,* north, and *oc,* south, of a line going from Lyon to Bordeaux via Limoges; regional languages dominated mostly in the fringes of the country, from Brittany to the Basque country, Provence to Alsace, shaped by centuries of invasions and fierce spirit of independence. There was, above all, a myriad of patois spoken in every corner of the land. Abbe Grégoire received reports from villages where several idioms were spoken and heard stories of people on one side of a river using different words from those living on the other side.

Almost a century later, in 1880, only one out of every five citizens was comfortable speaking French. It would be only after school attendance was compulsory that the French became familiar with their national language. In 1881-82 the so-called *Lois Jules Ferry* introduced free, secular education for boys and girls from six to thirteen. The implementation of these laws triggered the expansion of the French language outside of Paris and in the countryside. One of the aims of the legislation of the then Republic was to eradicate patois as a first language.

Throughout most of its history the French language has been the affair of the state starting with the Ordonnance of Villers-Cotterets in 1539 and continuing with the *Académie Française* which was established in 1635 and printed its first dictionary in 1694. English dictionaries on the other hand would be collated by dedicated individuals. Samuel Johnson, passionately committed to his endeavor and endlessly in search of patrons, compiled the definition of 40,000 words and published "A Dictionary of the English Language" in 1755.

Viking Age: Rollo Becomes Robert

In 793, three Norwegian ships appeared off the coast of Lindisfarne, a tidal island near the north-east border between England and Scotland. The resident monks expected to welcome traders but in a surprising turn of events were attacked by the Northmen; many were killed and their monastery was sacked. Alcuin, who was at the court of Charlemagne at the time, left a record of the events in several letters written to the king of Northumbria. They reflect his outrage "a place more venerable than all in Britain is given as a prey to pagan peoples." A similar raid would be conducted a few years later on the *Ile de Noirmoutier*, an elongated island south of the mouth of the Loire River. The monastery housing the remains of Saint Philibert was pillaged, a harbinger of more depredations during subsequent years. Lindisfarne had not been the first hostile action by men from the north along the western coasts of Europe but it is commonly taken as the opening act of the Viking Age.

During the early part of the ninth century the raids became more frequent and ever more violent. Men coming from the north sailed up the Loire and Seine rivers, pillaged Nantes, Rouen, and Paris and devastated the countryside. During the first years of Charles le Chauve's reign they returned north for the winter but then increasingly stayed behind, establishing their camps on islands or other protected sites where they would be joined by newcomers from the north.

What had led to the Viking Age which by some accounts would last until the beginning of the eleventh century? Among numerous possible causes two are worth highlighting.

Charlemagne had victoriously led his troops against Danish and Slavic tribes along the Baltic Sea. These expeditions had pitted Christians against pagans and left memories of fear and hostility in northern Europe. The emperor's cruel and long war against the Saxons (thirty-two years) and their forced conversion to Christianity had been even more vexatious. After Charles' great empire had been dismantled and the pieces had fallen in the hands of weak kings, the pagan Norsemen had exploited the fractures within the Christian Carolingian kingdoms. The Norsemen traders whose sailing skills were taking them to faraway lands easily became warriors when they entered defenseless lands.

The Viking Age had also been facilitated by the Norsemen achievements in shipbuilding. In the ninth century, after years of trial and error leading to technical innovations, they possessed the know-how to build highly efficient, long, light boats with large sails; shallow-draft boats steered with side rudders enabled them to sail up rivers. Some of the larger ones with fearful carved dragon shaped bows would be called *Drakkars*, maybe from the Latin *draco* for dragon.

Drakkar in Viking Museum, Oslo

The pagans who sailed south in long ships were known by the common names of Norsemen or Northmen. Those who suffered from their exactions did not care to find out precisely from where they came. Since the nineteenth century they have been called Vikings and there is no consensus on the etymology of the word. They were Scandinavians from Norway, Denmark, Sweden, all were long-distance sea warriors, some by necessity, all for the sake of spoils and glory. These Vikings communicated fairly easily among themselves as the languages they spoke had a common root. They sailed along the Atlantic coast of the Kingdom of the Franks and went up rivers as far south as the Garonne, ravaging and pillaging cities and the countryside.

Their targets of choice were the treasures kept in monasteries and churches. "From the wrath of the Northmen, O Lord, deliver us," the monks needed the apocryphal prayer more than anyone else. The abbeys who had the misfortune of safeguarding *relics* and had benefited from rich offerings of gold, silver and precious stones, were attractive preys. To the monks, the fierce warriors coming from the Nordic regions, who had no fear of the God of the Christians and sacked and burned their abbeys, foretold the Apocalypse.

Money would buy the withdrawal of the raiding Vikings and their leaders often accepted to be baptized as part of the deal but it only gained the Christians a short reprieve.

Charles le Chauve was too preoccupied by his three scourges, imperial ambitions, unruly vassals and rebellious Carolingians, to mount an efficient resistance. He could count on only a handful of vassals in the defense of the kingdom. In the words of a chronicler of the time the king, unable to push his enemies back with his iron (sword), was chasing them away with gold. One bright spot was Robert le Fort who fought courageously and died heroically, killed by Norsemen north of Angers in 866.

In 885-886, Paris was besieged once more by a confederation of northern warriors sailing up the Seine on their way to Burgundy. The city at the time was mostly concentrated in the Ile de la Cite and a large tower protected the west shores of the island. The bishop of Paris and Count Eudes galvanized the defenders of the tower, and time after time stopped the progression of the invaders. They could have ultimately succeeded but for Charles le Gros, a Carolingian from the German branch, who was de facto regent of Western Francia. He had been called to the rescue, had slowly marched his warriors from Metz to the hills north of Paris and then had preferred to negotiate, bribe the Vikings and grant them passage to Burgundy.

Pillaging and claiming tribute had been the first two Viking strategies. The third followed logically: gaining permanent settlements. The name of one king has stayed attached to this phase and to the history of the Vikings in Western Francia: Charles III, surnamed *le Simple* with the meaning of sincere and honest and not as one might assume of simple minded. He was king when, in 911, the Franks benefited, at last, from a reversal of fortune. Led by Robert, Count of Paris, brother of Eudes, they defeated the Vikings near Chartres. Robert convinced the king that it was the opportune time to reach a settlement with the Vikings. The ultimate negotiations took place in *Saint-Clair-sur-Epte* (mid-way between Paris and Rouen). The Vikings were granted control over a territory, presumably between the river Epte and the ocean, which they already occupied and their leader, Rollo, was given the hand of King Charles's daughter Gisla.

As part of the quid pro quo he became the vassal of the king and, shortly thereafter, he and his men converted. Rollo took the name Robert.

Rollo's Vikings belonged to a wave of sea warriors who had already been raiding for many years and they welcomed becoming landlords. Charles III, in turn, saw in them the protectors of the northern coast against further devastations. Indeed, their presence did discourage other Viking raiders. The conquerors became assimilated by the conquered. They married Frankish women and within a few generations lost their language, their laws and their religion. By the turn of the millennium it was more meaningful to call them *Normans* than Vikings.

Rollo's conversion to Christianity had been opportunistic but the Viking leader and his successors understood the importance that the Church would play as they strived to keep control of their newly acquired territory. They followed the example of the Carolingians and associated the hierarchy of the clergy in their secular affairs.

The story of Rollo is known thanks to the *Histoire de la Normandie* written by the monk Dudon of Saint-Quentin. Little is certain about Rollo's origins. He might have displeased the king of Norway and been exiled which would explain his willingness to settle in the Kingdom of the Franks. Rollo's principality became known as Normandy and under his Christian name, Robert, he is traditionally considered the first of a long list of dukes of Normandy. Guillaume le Conquerant, known to the Anglo-Saxons as William the Conqueror, who will appear on the historical stage one hundred and fifty-five years later, is one of his descendants.

Guillaume le Conquerant will not be the only Norman-ex-Viking to be the hero of odysseys during the eleventh century. Others of lower nobility but with the same adventurous spirit went south, earned a reputation as excellent combatants while fighting for the account of the Byzantines, the Lombards, even the pope, and carved kingdoms for themselves in southern Italy.

The sons of Tancrede, Lord of Hauteville, a diocese in lower Normandy, are the best known of these conquerors. Only one of his twelve sons stayed in Normandy, all the others sought fortune in Italy. Robert, surnamed *Guiscard*, the oldest son of a second marriage, arrived in southern Italy around 1045. He fought victoriously against an anti-Norman coalition organized by the pope and then, in a quid pro quo, became vassal of the pope and was named Duke of Puglia and Calabria in 1059. Nearby Sicily was in the hands of several Muslim emirs and the

Normans took advantage of their dissensions. Robert joined forces with his brother Roger and started the conquest of the island in 1061. They reached their goal only in 1091 after thirty years of guerilla-type warfare. Roger became count of Sicily and the Norman kingdom in southern Italy remained in the hands of the direct descendants of the Hauteville for more than one hundred years.

Saxons in the East, Carolingians in the West

The Magdeburger Reiter

The Magdeburger Reiter is one of the best-known equestrian statues north of the Alps. It is part of an ensemble erected in the old market place of Magdeburg, an Eastern German town, most certainly in honor of Emperor Otto I. The emperor, who had been duke of Saxony, had strong ties with Magdeburg. Otto I had been acknowledged as king of Germany by the dukes of East Francia (Franconia, Swabia, and Bavaria) and by Lorraine in 936 and much later, on February second 962, had been crowned emperor by Pope John XII. He was the first of a line later known as the *Holy Roman Emperors* and even later, after the fifteenth century, the *Holy Roman Emperors of the German Nation*.

The Carolingian dynasty in Eastern Francia, unable to protect any longer the kingdom from continuous invasions, had fallen at the beginning of the tenth century. The crown had first gone to a Franconian and then to a Saxon. The end of the Carolingian rulers in Germany had not led to anarchy since tribal ties avoided excessive parceling.

Otto I was a powerful man, the great man of the tenth century, a true Aryan in the eyes of many Germans. As king and then emperor his model had been Charlemagne and his mission had been to foster a Christian empire. He fought hard against the Slavs and his victory against the Magyars near Augsburg in 955 has been given a place of honor in the history of Europe. In the plain of the Lech, the Magyar mounted archers had found their match in the disciplined Ottonian heavy cavalry and had been slaughtered during their retreat from the battlefield. They never returned and this marked the end of their eastern migration into the Latin West. Otto's feat can be compared to Charles Martel's success against the Arabs in 732.

On his western border, the German emperor treated West Francia as a quasi-vassal and his bullying did not meet with much resistance. During the ninth and tenth centuries, the Carolingian dynasty in West Francia was handicapped by the unfortunate early death of several kings. It also had to face the increased competition of the *grands,* the most important lords in the kingdom. Some of these lords had been invigorated by the leading role they played in beating the Vikings. Nevertheless, the dynasty proved to be resilient and remained acknowledged even if constantly challenged.

The fate of these Carolingians was mostly in the hands of the Robertians, the most powerful house in Western Francia at the end of the ninth century. Count Eudes' father, Robert le Fort, can be considered the first Robertian. They had a solid base in the Maine and in Anjou, the support of numerous monasteries and had been at the forefront of the fight against the Vikings. They can be compared to the *Maires de Palais* during Merovingian times but while the Pépinides, the ancestors of Charlemagne, had not waited too long to grab the crown, the Robertians were very patient. They did occupy the throne after Charles le Gros had been deposed and Eudes had been elected king but, after his death, the crown went back to the Carolingians.

In 936, the grandson of Robert le Fort, Hugues le Grand, received the title of duke of the Franks, ranking just below king of the Franks. The title was very honorific but little more. Outside of the Ile de France region, which was at the heart of the land of the Franks, Hugues's authority was only moral. Twice he could have stood for election for king and both times he supported the candidacy of the Carolingian next in line, holding a legitimist discourse and giving primacy to birth rights.

The patience of the Robertians throws an instructive light on the forces at play in the kingdom in the ninth and tenth century. The legitimacy of the anointed king mattered and it was a big step for anyone to usurp the throne. The Robertians could claim they had saved the kingdom from the devastating Viking raids but the *legitimists* did not want to see the equilibrium between the grands unduly broken. Only towards the end of the tenth century, when King Louis V died after a reign of barely a year, and as the legitimate successor was a discredited uncle, did a Robertian cross the Rubicon.

A New Dynasty

Hugues Capet and the Founding of the Capetian Dynasty (987)

Hugues Capet was of good lineage, son of Hugues le Grand and of the sister of Emperor Otto I. The surname Capet was first given to Hughes in the middle of the eleventh century and was widely used only after 1130, long after he had become king. It is commonly said today that it came from the cape which young Martin, a Roman soldier living in the fourth century, had ripped and shared with a poor shivering man. Martin had become a Saint and the Hughes family was the secular head of the collegiate church where Saint Martin was buried. There have been other etymologies; Capet has been associated with the head and with butcher, a reminder of the modest origins of the new king. This latter connection came to prominence at the beginning of the fourteenth century when Hughes Capet became the target of Dante's wit. In the *Divine Comedy,* the Italian poet exhibited his great animosity towards Hughes's descendant, the Capetian king Philippe le Bel, by labelling Hughes a butcher.

The young Hugues was only about twenty years old when he was granted the title *Dux Francorum* and for that and other reasons did not wield as much authority as his predecessors. The imperial ambitions of the Ottons gave him a chance to shine.

The duchy of Lorraine had changed hands several times since the end of the ninth century and had been alternatively controlled by the kings of Western and Eastern Francia. In 978, Lothaire, the Carolingian king of West Francia, decided to recover Lorraine and went on the warpath against the Holy Roman Emperor Otto II. Lothaire rode east at the head of a powerful army, with Hugues Capet at his side, and forced Otto II to leave Aachen so precipitously that meat was still roasting in the fireplace when Lothaire entered the great hall of the palace. The imperial residence was duly pillaged, the bronze eagle majestically crowning the roof and facing west towards Lorraine was turned to face east towards Saxony as it had under the great emperor Charlemagne. Then, as his supplies were running short, the king of West Francia ended his raid and returned west.

Otto II was enraged; he had been taken by surprise and could not wait to have his revenge. The emperor led his own imposing army towards Paris and history has retained that Hugues Capet stopped the Germans before they crossed the Seine in front of Paris. Winter was coming, Otto II ran out of time and was forced to return east, relentlessly pursued across Lorraine by Lothaire and Hugues Capet.

Lothaire did not retain Lorraine but his successes against the Germans would be highly acclaimed. The reaction of the people was seen, centuries later, as an expression of French nationalism and the conflicts as harbingers of Franco-German wars. In the ensuing years Lothaire, Otto II and Hugues Capet, who was proudly wearing an aura newly gained on the battlefield, tried vainly to outmaneuver one another. Their behavior would be symbolic of the feudal times in the tenth century when alliances did not last, passions were violent and grand designs nebulous. Antagonism between the main players was ongoing and expressed itself in guerilla-type warfare more than in wars. Land, cities, dioceses, monasteries were always at risk of changing hands. Despite all the upheaval, feudal society in Francia was surviving.

The archbishop of Reims was one of the powerbrokers in these confrontations and Archbishop Adalberon, in particular, openly showed his allegiance to the Empire and his antagonism toward the kingdom of West Francia. He was from an old *grande famille* of Lotharingia where all the sons destined to prelature where surnamed Adalberon. The family was fiercely pro *Caesar Otto* as they called the emperor of Germany but more fundamentally pro-empire and anti-kingdom of the Franks.

When Lothaire died and the crown was put on the head of his son Louis V, the young king, only nineteen years old, showed his deep dislike of Adalberon. He accused him of having betrayed his father and of favoring the Ottonians. Adalberon of Reims was going to be judged by the *grands* in Compiegne in May 987 when the Carolingians were again struck by fate. Louis V fell from his horse while hunting and died a few days later.

Hughes Capet took charge without delay. The Adalberon affair was swept aside; the bishop was exculpated and the *grands* convened in Senlis to elect a new king. The legitimate successor was Charles, the young king's uncle, but Adalberon's own agenda was to bring an end to the Carolingians in Francia. The first sentence of his well-prepared address to the assembly contains the essence of his demonstration: the throne should not be transmitted by hereditary rights but should be occupied by the lord who surpasses others not only in physical nobility but also in spiritual qualities. He then praised Hughes Capet who would, Adalberon claimed, be a protector of the public weal and of the interests of the grands.

A few days after Adalberon of Reims' grand show, his *partner in crime* Hugues Capet was elected and then crowned king. He was presumably anointed in Noyon on July 3, 987. Election had been allowed to trump legitimacy. In December of the same year, the new king made sure that his son Robert, age fifteen, was also crowned. He did not want him to be subjected to the hazard of an election.

This was the end of the long and eventful downfall of the Carolingians. The Robertians were now kings, kingmakers no more. The new dynasty would be named the Capetian dynasty after Hugues Capet. There was nothing pre-ordained in the fall of one dynasty and the rise of another and it could have taken place long ago. The fall was initially explained by the lack of resources of the last Carolingians but Hugues Capet was not better off than Lothaire. In the nineteenth century, when it became politically correct for the French to favor their Gallic ancestors and disparage the conquering Franks, a new type of justification was presented. It surmised that the people in Francia had no longer trusted the Carolingians, that these Carolingians had close family ties with the German Empire, that they were nostalgic for the time of Charlemagne and not truly faithful to West Francia.

Maybe the Gods had tired of the Carolingians and had given a chance to the Capetians. The results for the country that can now truly be called the Kingdom of the Franks will not be disappointing.

Whatever the underlying causes of the rise of the new dynasty the circumstances of the coup are troubling, particularly since there was only one record of the election of Hughes Capet, written in 995 by the monk Richer from Reims.

Had the crown been usurped? This shadow over the new dynasty was of little import as long as the kings of the new dynasty remained weak. It did matter though towards the end of the twelfth century when the Capetian king was the powerful Philippe Auguste. He had to erase any doubt about the beginnings of his dynasty and Rigord, the historian monk from Saint Denis, provided the necessary arguments. Rigord stressed the election of Hugues Capet and pointed to the continuity between Capetians and Carolingians. The first Capetian kings had married descendants of Charlemagne and Philippe Auguste could be said to have blood from the great emperor flowing through his veins.

Irrespective of the circumstances surrounding the anointing of Hugues Capet, this event is a milestone in the history of France.

It took time, patience and favorable circumstances for the new dynasty to consolidate its hold on the crown. The great lords continued their drive towards autonomy started under Charles le Chauve. Solidly implanted in their domains, some of them far away from Paris, and facing weak suzerains, they could not be prevented from appropriating the political, legislative and juridical power bestowed by control over land. These lords had no longer paid homage to the last Carolingian kings and seldom travelled to the court of the Capetian kings. The descendants of the counts who had sworn allegiance to Charlemagne now considered that their power was *by the grace of God* and did not call themselves *comte du roi* anymore.

This did not imply that the preeminence of the king was questioned. It had been clearly established since Pepin le Bref that the king's power was given by God and this set him above other lords. The king was the linchpin of the seigneurial pyramid, the arbiter; even a weak king was necessary to keep all the *grands* in check. He was the protector of the kingdom against external threats; when Charles le Gros had failed to meet the challenge of the Viking raids, the great lords had been quick to replace him with a Robertian; the deposed Charles le Gros finished his days in the monastery of Reichenau. The king was also the protector of the church; in the middle of the twelfth century, the pope called Louis VII the *very Christian king*.

The first Capetians had the aura of the crown, the support of the church but did not control much land. They had neither the power nor the means to act outside of their territory. Hugues' royal domain stretched from Compiegne, north of Paris, to the Loire valley, a narrow strip of land less than one hundred and twenty-five miles long which he had received from his father.

During his nine year reign, Hugues Capet remained largely unassuming and shared his responsibilities with his son Robert II. There will be three other Capetian kings in the eleventh century and each one will be busy fighting family members, other great lords and the pope. Robert II despite his surname *the Pious* antagonized Rome when he repudiated his first wife. To his credit, he increased the royal domain when he successfully claimed the duchy of Burgundy after the duke, his uncle, had died without heir. The next king, Henri I, will be in conflict with the duke of Normandy during the last years of his reign. The hostile relationship with Normandy will continue under Philippe I. The duke at the time was Guillaume, better known later as William, and he would engage in the fabulous enterprise of the conquest of England in 1066. King Philippe I repudiated his wife despite the pope's strong objections and he, also, was excommunicated.

Abbey of Fleury

The basilica of the Abbey of Fleury in Saint Benoit sur Loire, a small village along the northern banks of the Loire River, southeast of Orleans, is the resting place of Saint Benedict and Philippe I. The king had been a benefactor of the abbey and wanted to rest in close proximity to the Saint. Philippe I is one of the very few kings who chose not to be buried at Saint Denis.

The monastery had been founded circa 630 and a few decades later Mommolus, the second abbot of Fleury, went to Montecassino in southern Italy and brought back the remains of the Saint; Benedict's abbey had been ravaged by the Lombards around 580 and his remains abandoned. The monks of Montecassino still claim that the relics of the great saint are in southern Italy, not along the Loire valley. Fleury was destroyed by the Vikings in the ninth century and Charles le Chauve took from the royal purse to pay for its reconstruction and bring the saintly relics back from Orleans where they had been safely kept. In the tenth century the Abbey of Fleury became one of the beacons of the Benedictine reform calling for a return to Benedict's principles.

A crypt was built in the middle of the eleventh century to accommodate the relics and the construction of a Romanesque basilica began at the same time. It was completed by the end of the twelfth century. The French Revolution caused the community of monks to disperse but monastic life was fully restored in 1944 and was ensured in 2016 by thirty-two brothers.

The abbey is a fine example of early Romanesque architecture. The visitor enters the basilica through its most noted feature, a massif square porch tower; light enters the porch through three openings on two levels. This concept of an add-on to a church, an *augmenta*, goes back to the time of Charlemagne.

The *piece de resistance*, the shrine of the great Saint, is in the crypt, a few feet under the choir and the tomb of King Philippe I. It is a surprisingly large metal reliquary encased in a monumental pillar. Daylight filtering into the crypt creates a mood propitious to meditation, an atmosphere befitting the resting place of the founder of the Benedictine Order.

The Crown's First Glimmer

Abbott Suger, the very Suger intimately associated with Saint Denis, taught Louis VI, Philippe's son, that "it is the duty of kings to repress by their power... the audacity of the nobles...." The king followed this advice and behaved more like a king than a feudal lord. For the first time, more than a hundred years after the beginning of the dynasty, the crown of a Capetian was shining. Suger also did successful public relations for the king and his *Vie de Louis VI* was the panegyric which brought Louis his renown.

Louis VI was tested early in his reign by his nominal vassal Henry, Duke of Normandy, who was also Henry I, King of England, son of William the Conqueror. He conceded quite a few battles to his rival but always kept in mind his ultimate goal, to consolidate and enlarge his base. Luckily for the Capetians, Louis VI, despite his poor health, was never reluctant to ride into battle against his unruly vassals. He also prepared his son well for his succession.

Despite these developments, by the end of the reign of Louis VI, the Kingdom of the Franks was still dominated by great lords, and these lords were at the heart of the so-called *feudal system.*

Feudalism

Vassals and Fiefdoms

One event has been often presented as a landmark in the expansion of the feudal system: the gathering called *plaid* of Charles le Chauve and his counts in *Quierzy-sur-Oise* in Northern France in June 877 and the *capitulary*, ordinance, issued at the end of the plaid.

The plaid had taken place as Charles was on the verge of leading an expedition to Italy to assist the pope threatened by Muslims. The counts, bishops and vassals who had answered the king's call were concerned about their titles and benefits should they die while fighting in faraway lands. Charles reassured them by conceding, among others, that should a count die during the expedition his rights would be transferred to his eldest son. This was a decision dictated by circumstances but after the king died during his return to Francia, the counts treated the measure as permanent. A temporary measure concerning the transfer of titles and benefits had become the rule.

In 1877 a stele was erected in Quierzy-sur-Oise to commemorate the 1,000[th] anniversary of the capitulary and the town was called the birthplace of feudalism. Since then some medievalists have treated with sarcasm the idea that a starting date could be assigned to the feudal age. That age lasted from the ninth to at least the fourteenth century and during that time the evolution of the network of relationships between members of the leading social classes was slow and uneven. In the works on this period Quierzy-sur-Oise has become a footnote and the focus is on *personal homage, allegiance, fief* and one other defining feature of the feudal system, *tradition*.

Homage was a rite, also called *commendatio*, during which a personal bond was sealed between a free man and his lord. The ceremony borrowed much from the Church of Rome. In West Francia similar exchanges of commitments had been familiar to the Merovingians but began to be well-documented during Charlemagne's reign. The free man would put his joined hands between the lord's hands, swear an oath of allegiance and become his *vassal*. Lord and vassal entered into quid pro quo commitments: the vassal committed to render various services to his *seigneur* who in turn promised protection to his man.

Vassalic oath

Another rite, also well-known to the Merovingians, was the *oath of loyalty* during which a subject would swear to respect his master or the king. There were differences in form but the oath of the vassal and the oath of a subject had similar implications and both types were extensively used during the reign of Charlemagne.

The king imposed an oath of loyalty on all his subjects in 789. This mandate might have its source in a bloody conspiracy against him in Germany a few years earlier, in 785. Later, after his coronation, the emperor asked his subjects to renew their oath. This time he broadened the concept of loyalty and asked his subjects to also swear to keep God's commandments and to obey imperial commands.

The oath of loyalty was received in the name of Charlemagne by his counts, a sign of their importance in the empire. The counts and the other grands seigneurs, dukes and marquis in the border territories, were members of the *grandes familles* and of the palatine court. As an institution, the counts predated Charlemagne. About 250 were put in place throughout the empire and were given extensive powers in their counties. They were audited by a much smaller select class of men of higher social status, the *missi dominici*.

As head of a far-reaching empire at a time when information was circulating at the speed of a galloping horse, Charlemagne needed this network of trusted men to implement his instructions and the decisions made during the *conventus generalis*, general plaids. The counts in particular became the true intermediaries between the emperor and his subjects and the executors of his will.

Counts, dukes, marquis, missis, vassals of the emperor, formed the tissue holding the empire together and mattered greatly to its survival. The conquered territories had diverse administrative and legal systems. Franks, Burgundians, Aquitani, each followed their historical laws as did the newer members of the empire. It was neither feasible nor desirable to impose new ways of doing things on people recently conquered. A common administrative super-structure was necessary and this was the role played by the network of counts and dukes.

Charlemagne was always keen to anchor his legitimacy. The oaths of loyalty, the network of counts, a parallel network of bishops, and one more trusted network, the king's vassals, the *vassi dominici* who did not report to the counts, all assured his symbolic presence throughout the empire.

The vassi dominici played an important role in a critical institution, the army. Successful military operations were necessary for the survival of the empire. There was no standing army but every year, in the spring, Charlemagne called on his vassals to join him for a new campaign. The dukes and marquis led this ad-hoc force while the counts commanded the men of their county. The vassi dominici, totally devoted, always on the ready, were the elite soldiers. All the king's vassals had to provide for themselves and their retinue during the yearly campaigns. Over time, this became one facet of a more general issue: how to compensate the agents of the king?

In an economy where money was not widely used, land was the true means of exchange. The compensation of the agents of the king, counts and vassi dominicis in particular, was in the form of *usufruct* of land belonging to the *royal fisc*, the royal domain. This benefit became known as a *feodum* starting in the ninth century. The more the empire expanded, the more the emperor needed to grant usufructs, mostly in the form of usufruct of land. The *fief* became a defining feature of the feudal system.

In the early stages of the feudal system there had been a true quid pro quo and the fiefs had been contingent on services rendered. The land entrusted by Charlemagne to his vassals remained in the royal domain, the fisc; the vassal received the fruit of the land, the usufruct, during his lifetime and at his death the usufruct returned to the fisc. The same process was followed with benefits that were not in the form of land.

As long as Charlemagne remained a charismatic and successful leader, his agents and the men called to be at his side during his military expeditions abided by the terms of this quid pro quo. Three decades after his death this no longer held. The empire had been dismantled, and his grandsons and great-grandsons fought for the empire or a share of the empire. The missi and counts saw in these family feuds a great opportunity to sell their allegiance to one Carolingian or the other. Their price was usually the full ownership of their title and benefit. This process started under Charles le Chauve and the Quierzy agreement had been but one step on the road to feudalization.

Charles le Chauve had already contributed to the extension of the feudal system before the plaid at Quierzy-sur-Oise. While his kingdom was facing the Viking invasions, he had made numerous gifts of land and other estates to his vassals to compensate them for their losses, or to thank them for their military services. Throughout his reign he would grant four times more land fiefs in Western Francia alone than Charlemagne had granted throughout his reign. This inflation had two far reaching consequences. First, the royal domain shrank and regal power weakened considerably, and second, a handful of families gained control over vast amounts of land and became powerful clans.

There was no force strong enough to slow down the ensuing decentralization process as the Kingdom of the Franks was not truly unified. It was not unified politically as the notion of res publica, public order, was limited to personal bonds. Lords agreed on the terms of their relationships with other lords and in doing so were constrained only by feudal customs (which were very empirical) and the teachings of the Church (which were considered immutable). The kingdom was not unified economically as trade remained largely regional and money was not yet used as the main unit of exchange. The gold standard and most sought-after asset was land and its amount was finite. Counts rewarded knights who fought at their side by granting them fiefs in the form of land, knights parted with some of that land when they needed to secure the allegiance of another warrior. The process started with the king and trickled down to the minor knight.

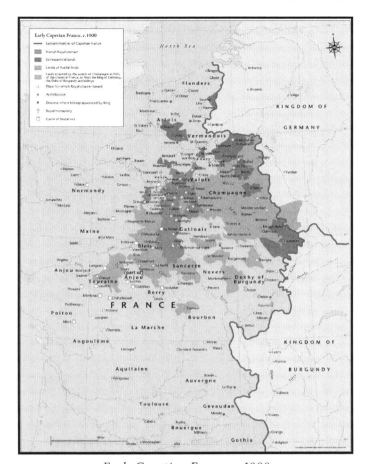

Early Capetian France c. 1000

The resulting partitioning of the territory is reflected in maps of the Kingdom of the Franks at the beginning of the eleventh century, a time when the markers of its eastern border were roughly the Meuse, the Saone and the Rhone.

These maps show an assemblage of duchies and counties, one marquisate and the undersized royal domain. The shape and size of the individual pieces suggest how this picture might change over time. The king, if he is to be more than a passive referee, will need to add to his meager land holdings. His capital, Paris, is within reach of potentially hostile forces coming from the north and the east. The duchy of Aquitaine, formidable in size, and Gascony, are too many riding days away to be controlled from Paris.

The fragmentation of the kingdom had gone too far and, in the words of Norbert Elias in *The Civilizing Process,* centripetal forces had to prevail. These forces had already been put in motion, guardedly, in the middle of the twelfth century by King Louis VI, patiently coached by Suger. Little had the two men known that they were giving the initial impetus to a process that would lead, four centuries later, to the absolute monarchy of another dynasty, the Bourbons.

Elias in his historico-sociological analysis of the feudal system notes that the size of France was well-adapted to a wide-reaching decentralization followed by a powerful centralization. England was too small, only as big as a large principality in France; the opposite was true for Germany, the territories controlled by the German emperor were too extensive to lead to a monopoly by one house and a unified German state will appear only in the nineteenth century. The first Capetians took control of the weak decentralized Kingdom of the Franks during the last years of the tenth century and, by the middle of the seventeenth century, the king of France will have more power than the English king, and even more so than the German emperor.

Besançon, Between Emperor and Archbishop

The kingdom of Burgundy was effectively controlled by counts and bishops and not the king during the early feudal age. The counts were particularly powerful in the diocese of Besançon and this became even more noticeable when the counties in the diocese were in the hands of one count only. The *county of Burgundy*, which will later be called *Franche-Comte,* had all the features of a duchy except for the name and the count of Burgundy kept the king of Burgundy at arm's length.

Rodolph III, king of Burgundy, who was without heir, bequeathed his kingdom to the German emperor Conrad II and when Rodolph died in 1032, the ultimate suzerain of Besançon became the German emperor. A few years later, the archbishop of Besançon, Hugues I de Salins, became the trusted advisor of the then Emperor Henry III and was rewarded with extensive temporal powers in the county. This marked the beginning of the political control of the town by archbishops. At the end of the eleventh century the suzerain of the town was a German emperor and its true master an archbishop.

Fortified Chateaux, the Search for Ostentation

Fortified *chateaux* are archetypes of the feudal age.
Society was mostly rural during the early periods of that age and chateaux scattered in the countryside served multiple functions. They were edifices built for defense, residences for lords and seats of power.

Collective memory has mostly retained their defensive role. Built on elevations and dominating the surrounding countryside, they brought fear to the lord's enemies and comfort to the people living in their shadow. Chateaux, though, were not conceived with wars only in mind. These imposing structures also served as residences of local courts and administrative centers. Whatever their function, civil or military, fortified chateaux expressed ostentation and were physical demonstrations of a lord's power and his search for social recognition.

Castra and other forms of fortifications could already be seen at the time of the Roman Empire. Many were given a second life during the ninth century as they offered an efficient defense against Viking incursions. During the tenth century *motte-and-bailey* castles proliferated across Europe, particularly in Normandy. These were mostly mounds of earth, up to one hundred feet high, surrounded by wooden fences enclosing a courtyard called a *bailey*. The earth would be carted up by villains, serfs who owed labor to their lord. The *Bayeux Tapestry* which tells the story of the conquest of England by William, Duke of Normandy, has several panels depicting mottes and serfs at work. Wooden towers built on top of mottes were called *donjons* from the Latin *dominum,* a reminder that these structures were seats of power.

Starting in the eleventh century, donjons were made increasingly of stones. The construction of these towers became an onerous process as it could not be entrusted to labor owed by villains, and the seigneur needed money to pay masons and carpenters; by then, a tower represented not only power but also wealth.

Normandy paved the way for the construction of these edifices which then spread along the Loire valley; England was dotted with castles and rectangular towers after its conquest by Duke William. The most impressive symbol of William's regal power was the White Tower, still to be seen in the *Tower of London* complex, a fortress which also contained living quarters. The crusaders in the twelfth century brought the concept of such towers to the Middle East where it was further modified by Muslim architects. (T.E.Lawrence, better known as Lawrence of Arabia, wrote, while at Oxford, a thesis entitled: The Influence of the Crusades on European Military Architecture- to the end of the XIIth century).

Towards the very end of the twelfth century, Philippe II, better known as Philippe Auguste, championed the construction of massive round towers which became known as *tours philippiennes.* The first of these towers was the *Grosse Tour du Louvre*, a cylinder resting on a truncated cone. Completed in 1204 it was replicated throughout Europe. (see later chapter entitled "Where the Parisii first dwelled becomes Paris). Round towers allowed for better protection, their smooth round surface efficiently withstood the impact of projectiles flung by siege engines. Their shape though left little room for living quarters as the commonly found thirteen feet thick wall left a diameter of only twenty-six feet of inside space.

Most if not all of the fortifications of towns and chateaux throughout the royal domain were reinforced during the latter part of Philippe II's reign. A round tower at each corner of a rectangular chateau became one of the most visible symbols of regal power.

The great lords in France copied the tours philippiennes and so did their peers in England, Germany and Eastern Europe. The massive towers which dotted the countryside were ostentatious, could be seen from afar and always projected strength.

Great halls in medieval chateaux offered kings and lords another chance to showcase their rank and power. These halls could be modest in size, say one thousand square feet, or as formidable as the fourteen thousand square foot great hall of Westminster palace. They were built mostly on the ground floor in England and on the first floor in the Kingdom of the Franks. By its size, the great hall at the Chateau de Coucy, north-east of Paris, rivaled those of the *chateaux du roi.*

It was in these multi-purpose halls that kings and lords performed their administrative and judiciary duties in front of their peers and subjects. It was there also that they entertained and accommodated their guests.

The communal meals served in the halls were an occasion for the lords to remind the *oratores* and the *laboratores* that the *bellatores*, belonged to the most prestigious class, the warrior class.

Trestle tables were set in these halls (therefore the expression *setting the table*). The flames of wide, high fireplaces where meat was roasted, provided light and heat. Seating was on one side of the table only, arranged according to the rank of the guests. Meals were served *a la française* meaning different dishes of a same course served at the same time. The preferred dish of the bellatores was grilled fowl; beef was not served at their table. Where one was seated, which food he was served and where his lodging was in the chateau all pointed to his rank and status.

Each region in France had its share of medieval chateaux but construction flourished at different times in different parts of the country. Gascony had a construction boom between 1250 and 1350, then came Brittany's turn, while chateaux in Auvergne and the Limousin mushroomed during the second half of the fifteenth century. The Hundred Years Wars (beginning fourteenth to mid fifteenth century) obviously generated a great demand for defensive towers and chateaux in the western half of the country.

Medieval donjons and chateaux belong in France's architectural heritage. In museums and illustrated history books they mostly appear with the heading *military architecture* but these icons of the Middle Ages were mostly social markers and truly belong under the heading *feudal architecture*. Their appearance from afar symbolized the domination of the lords over the surrounding countryside; inside, the lay-out of the space reflected the lord's status and rank.

Medieval chateaux and donjons will generally face one or more of the following destinies: they will be seriously damaged during the Hundred Years War, abandoned when they lost their main purpose at the end of feudal wars, and, in the best case, restored after the second half of the nineteenth century.

Chateau de Coucy

Isometric view of Chateau de Coucy.

The Coucys held one of the four great baronies in France in the thirteenth century and their arrogance was reflected in their motto: "Not king nor prince, duke nor count am I; I am the lord de Coucy."

One of these lords of Coucy, Enguerrand III, whose second wife was a sister of Emperor Otto IV, satisfied his megalomania by starting construction around 1223 of a chateau on a hilltop at Coucy, north-east of Paris, between Soissons and Laon. By its sheer mass it represented as much a threat as a protection to the king of the Franks. The great donjon was 180 feet high and with a diameter of 100 feet was twice as imposing as Philippe Auguste's tower at the Louvre. The great hall and the chapel also outshined those of the king and of other great lords. It was a giant of the giants of feudal architecture.

The German army occupied Coucy during World War I and in a most unforgivable and, as it turned out, needless barbarian act, exploded the tower and the castle before retreating in March 1917. The ruins by themselves are worth a tour but the tourist short of time might learn much about the *Chateau de Coucy* by visiting the *Cite de l'Architecture* in Paris whose permanent collections exhibit models of the towers, the keep and the village, all built for the 1937 Paris Exhibition.

There is in the same section of the Cite a detailed model of another historic medieval castle, the *Crac des Chevaliers,* the imposing structure built by the crusaders and still standing in Syria. It typifies the defensive castles used as barracks favored by the Templars and the Hospitallers in the twelfth century. Long and cavernous halls could accommodate thousands of Christian combatants on campaigns against the Muslims.

The visitor who lingers at the Cite should not miss the sight at sundown of the Eiffel Tower, all lit and sparkling, in full view through a window on the ground floor, framed by the austere moldings of pillars of the Cathedral of Chartres.

Knights and the Ethical Ideal of Chivalry

Knights, the other archetype of feudal society, played a crucial role on the politico-social scene in the early years of feudalism, and then faded away at the end of the fifteenth century. They are the heroes of the romanticized spirit of chivalry and became a rich source of material for action-filled historical novels.

Charles Martel, in the middle of the eighth century, had understood the advantages to be gained on the battlefield by a well-equipped and well-trained cavalry. Europeans had learned the benefits of *stirrups* only long-after they had first been introduced by the Chinese around the fourth century. The foot support gave mounted warriors more stability and allowed for more power in their charges. A new class of warriors had been born which changed the face of battles. The English would call them *knights*, an Anglo-Saxon word for servant. Their name in French,

Italian and Spanish would be derived from horse, *chevalier-cavaliere-caballero* and rider in German, *Ritter*.

By the eleventh century, only nobles could afford to become warriors on horseback. There were notable cases of *sine nobilitate* warriors who found patrons and were knighted but these remained exceptional.

The son of a knight started early in his life to follow a path dictated by tradition and had to submit to a rigorous training. He started as a page, would graduate to squire at the age of fourteen and became the servant of a knight. The select few deemed worthy could be knighted when they turned twenty-one. This was a supreme honor for a young nobleman but the cost of his outfit was a major hurdle on the road to knighthood. The knight-to-be needed a squire, several horses, an armor, helmets, swords and other items, all of which represented a great expense. The oldest son was outfitted by his father; other young men would enlist as mercenaries and those who could not afford the necessary equipment remained squires.

The few who were knighted offered their services for *chevauchées*, going to war on horseback, and hoped for a chance to become a vassal and receive a fief. This was most often decided by acts of bravura and success on the battlefield. These lucky ones could then live off their land, have food for themselves and their retinue, grass for their horses and enough surplus to pay for the maintenance of their equipment and for the squires who would assist them in battle.

By the end of the eleventh century the knights formed a new social class whose control escaped the king, the *chivalry*, a name, as previously mentioned, derived from *cheval*, horse. They had their own code of conduct which they implemented among themselves but which they did not extend to those outside of their class.

Chivalry became imbued with the attributes of an ethical ideal. The knight in his capacity as warrior had to be brave and as vassal his loyalty was expected. The true knight was above all in the service of God and the ceremony of knighthood was a reminder of his vow. A man destined to defend the Holy Church could only be a man of piety and virtue.

Such was the dignified aura of the knight and his chivalric ideals that crystallized during the eleventh century but war was his path to glory and fortune and his life seldom conformed to this romanticized image. It was routinely filled with cruelty, not immune from treason and unfailingly guided by self-interest.

In *The Waning of the Middle Ages,* Johan Huizinga writes that "medieval thought...was permeated by the fiction that chivalry ruled the world" and elsewhere in the same book he notes that in the fifteenth century chivalry would be considered to be "the crown of the whole social system." By then, though, the crown would not be secure anymore; the glorified image of the French chevaliers had been irreparably damaged at the battle of Agincourt in 1415 and a few decades later, as the Hundred Years War approached closure, the knights slowly and inexorably lost the glory of being at the heart of every battle.

Spiritual vs Temporal Powers

Pope Gregory VII and the Reform Bearing his Name

At a time when the emperor had the prerogative to nominate the pontiff and tightly control the investiture of bishops in Germany, the papacy made a daring show of force. During a synod in Rome in 1059, Pope Nicolas II decided that his successors would be elected by the cardinal-bishops and accepted by *clero et populo*. A dramatic confrontation between the two powers became unavoidable and it would be the remembered as the *Canossa Incident.*

These memorable events took place in 1076 when Emperor Henry IV, also King of the Germans, provoked Pope Gregory VII by nominating several bishops in Germany and Italy. Harsh words were exchanged, the emperor stood firm on his claim that he held his power from God while, as he wrote, Hildebrand, the Pope, was a fake monk who had become pope through tricks, money and favors ... A synod gathered in Worms condemned the pope and then the conflict, truly political in nature, climaxed with a surreal sequence of events: the pope excommunicated the emperor—the German bishops sided with the pope—the emperor, dressed as a penitent, walked to the castle of Canossa, north of Tuscany in Italy where the pope had sought refuge, waited for three days at the gates, knelt in front of the pontiff and asked for forgiveness—the pope lifted the ban. This part myth, part reality has been immortalized by the expression *going to Canossa*, synonymous with coerced submission and a strong touch of humiliation. There would be more drama and reversals before an agreement was reached in 1122 in Worms whereby the emperor accepted the free election of the bishops. This marked the end of the imperial church but Church and State will continue to be involved with the same business, the bishops and abbots will still behave like feudal lords and the lords will strongly support their favorite candidates for episcopal positions.

Victor Hugo wrote a play, *Hernani*, featuring Don Carlos about to be elected Charles V, Holy Roman Emperor, at the beginning of the sixteenth century. He calls the two protagonists, the pope and the emperor, "these two halves of God, one the truth, the other the power." History would prove that neither pope nor emperor would be satisfied being only half a God.

The primacy of the emperor had not been seriously contested up until the eighth century. Even though Charlemagne had been crowned by Pope Leo III in 800, the emperor never doubted that he was the leader of the Western Church and consistently reminded the pope of this state of affairs. He kept the right to approve the election of the pope and the bishops acknowledged his authority. Charlemagne followed the footsteps of Constantine who was head of the state and head of the church, i.e the *ecclesia*, the assembly of Christians.

The balance of power had shifted after the death of the emperor as the Church filled the vacuum created by the dereliction of royal authority. The bishops, confronted with weak kings, challenged them openly. During the troubled times of the second part of the ninth century it was the archbishop of Reims, Hincmar, who stood as the arbiter of regal power and successfully championed Charles le Chauve. The Church, led by the archbishops, was now more than a moral force guiding the kings, it was becoming a true political power. The world of God, though, was still guided by the same hands as the world of Caesar and during the eleventh century the Church more forcefully attempted to sever its ties to the emperor.

Wrestling the independence of the Church from the temporal powers was one of the objectives of an ambitious reform of the Church. Depriving the great lords of their prerogatives in the nomination of the pope and of the bishops was a tall order and the Canossa incident had to be expected.

The reform had two other far reaching goals, one to affirm the primacy of the bishop of Rome, the second one to establish moral integrity. The pope was still only an honorary *primus inter pares* and the time had come for the bishops to be truly subordinated to their leader in Rome. As to moral integrity it entailed, among others, condemning the clerical abuse of *simony,* the buying and selling of sacraments and positions in the church

The need for reform had been a preoccupation of the church leaders long before several popes became vigorous advocates of change. Leo IX in 1049 was the first pope of the reform and Gregory VII, pope between 1073 and 1085, gave the greatest impetus to the program which will bear his name, the *Gregorian Reform.*

The investiture controversy carried less weight in the Kingdom of the Franks than in neighboring Germany as the Capetian kings controlled only one third of the diocese, the others having fallen into the hands of the great lords after the death of Charlemagne. The Capetians were not favorable to change as they were addicted to the practice of selling positions in the hierarchy of the Church. The popes used the influence of the monastic orders and the largest abbeys, Cluny in particular, to give momentum to their reform in the Kingdom of the Franks but towards the end of eleventh century Rome, already entangled with Germany, opted for a compromise. A *modus vivendi* was reached and the Frankish King Philip I retained the investiture of bishops for their temporal functions.

It would not be long before the issue of power of church versus power of king would resurface and the separation of Church and State would become a staple of French politics.

In the meantime and during most of the Middle Ages, popes and bishops could rely on fearsome weapons to enforce Church mandates when engaged in disputes with the temporal powers: *excommunication* and *interdict.* They never hesitated to use these as deterrents and the second one, in particular, was dreaded by everyone.

Interdict was a form of territorial excommunication. The *cessatio a divinorum celebratione* meant that nearly all ministrations of the church ceased including last rites and burial in consecrated ground. It was a harsh measure as it touched people indiscriminately. The countryside of France and England became eerie when the church bells, the very bells which set the rhythm of the days, stopped ringing. Innocent III had a particularly aggressive use of this sentence by laying an interdict on France in 1200 when Philippe Auguste obstinately refused to take back his wife Ingeburge of Denmark and part with Agnes de Méranie, and in England in 1208 when King John did not acknowledge the pope's nominee for Archbishop of Canterbury.

Monasteries and the Secular World

Charles Martel had used ecclesiastical assets and positions to reward trusted allies. A lay person named abbot would delegate the spiritual functions, then manage the monastery as a true landlord. These were lucrative rewards, and lay abbots, in turn, could be valuable allies of kings and other seigneurs. This had been a serious fissure in the wall isolating the monks and their abbeys from the secular world.

Another fissure was to be expected from the monks' knowledge of reading and writing which was shared by so few at the time. Under the first Carolingians, monasteries became intellectual centers and a vehicle for cultural exchanges within Western Europe. These would be exciting times for monks; they supplied the brain power for a Church in search of itself and shaped the minds of the elite. These monks were no longer the modest children of God. They were members of a small elite and saw themselves as closer to God, not only than the poor souls living in smoke-filled mud huts in the countryside but also than the other clerics. This sense of superiority was reinforced when several monasteries gained a special status, avoiding the authority of the bishop and reporting directly to the pope.

The *coenobitic monks*, members of an educated elite, had committed to live in a community isolated from the world. Most of these monks accommodated themselves to such a life but some had not renounced their ambition to have a voice in the affairs of the Church and of the kingdom. Among them, several abbots would make their mark as advisors of popes, kings and lords.

Charlemagne's son Louis, King of Aquitaine, was very concerned that the monasteries were too influenced by the secular world. When Louis, surnamed le Pieux, became Emperor, he championed a return to the founding principles of monastic life and a unification of the rules and customs of the monastic world. In 817 the Synod of Aachen decided that these rules should be those of Saint Benedict.

The life of Saint Benedict of Nursia (Nursia, the birthplace of the Saint, is a town in Umbria, in the heart of Italy) is known thanks to

Pope Gregory I, Gregory the Great. According to Gregory I, the Saint founded a monastery at Monte Cassino, south of Rome, in 530, and up to his death in 547 wrote the rules that should be followed by coenobitic monks.

Benedictine monks were asked to live their faith in humility, charity and the love of others. Obedience and silence would guide their daily routine of prayer, study and work. It is unfortunate that Monte Cassino is now better known for the dramatic bombing of the monastery by the Allies in 1944 rather than as the home of the monastery founded by Benedict. The reform met with strong resistance but the idea that a good monk could only be Benedictine was there to stay.

By the time Charles le Chauve, a son of Louis le Pieux, became king of West Francia, the good intentions of Aachen were forgotten. Monasteries were again distributed as rewards to lay people; Charles awarded himself with no less than the abbey of Saint Denis. There was also another source of secular influence: land ownership.

It was commonly believed that prayers shortened the time spent by souls in purgatory, and people made arrangements with monasteries for intercessions, prayers to the Lord for the salvation of the souls of their family members. The covenant might specify a finite number of prayers and the compensation received by the monastery might in that case be modest, but the important requestors usually belonged to the nobility, and in exchange for prayers for the soul of their departed, gifted the most valuable possession of the time, land. The monasteries which benefited from such land donations were carefully selected because, as the historian Barbara Rosenwein wrote, "Property transactions are alliances in the making and part of a network of patronage".

This early monastic model allowed for an inflow of donations but no natural outflow of assets as the monks were celibate. Monasteries did not have to deal with inheritances and family feuds. They eventually controlled strategic positions across the country and became a factor in the battles fought by kings and nobles over the control of territory.

Monasteries had one very unique source of power and wealth: *relics*. These could be precious objects brought back from the Holy Land, bones of prior abbots that had performed miracles, or any other object associated with a saint. Whatever their origin, relics were a source of fame and money. During the eighth and ninth century, when Vikings eagerly searched for treasures in monasteries, monks became adept at hiding their precious relics. A safe place was usually another monastery less easily accessible to the raiders. Some of these relics never found their way back to their initial home.

When their door to the secular world was opened, monasteries were a source of power and prestige. Kings and lords understood that associating the name of their family with a religious community, if possible with a saintly monk, bestowed on them an aura of importance and dignity; being seen as favored by God was a useful asset to anyone seeking political power. They also knew that the monasteries which had benefited from their largesse would remain under their control. A second-born son or a nephew could become abbot or even prior, and this is where they could retreat and weather hard times.

Two Failed Attempts at True Monastic Life: Cluny and Citeaux

In 910, Guillaume le Pieux, Duke of Aquitaine, gave land he owned in Cluny, not far from today's Macon in Burgundy, for the foundation of an abbey. His aspiration was to shield this institution from secular influences and he placed it under the sole protection of the pope.

Blason of Abbey of Cluny
Gules two keys the wards upwards etc...

Cluny's rise to prominence began thanks to a succession of dynamic and powerful Abbots. Odon (927-942), paved the way for monastic reform in the Church and a return to Benedictine rules, Maieul (954-994) and Odilon de Mercoeur (994-1049) spread the Cluniac reform to monasteries throughout France, northern Italy and elsewhere in Europe. In 998, Rome withdrew Cluny from episcopal authority and a few years later the same status was granted to all the institutions of the obedience of Cluny. The Cluniac monastic network then became a church inside of the church, the *ecclesia cluniacensis*, reporting directly to the pope. Cluny reached its pinnacle under Abbot Hugues de Semur (1049-1109). The symbol of its grandeur was the Basilica Cluny III which has been called the entrance to heaven. Its construction was started by Hugues de Semur, it was consecrated in 1130 and would remain the largest basilica until the reconstruction of Saint Peter's in Rome in the sixteenth century.

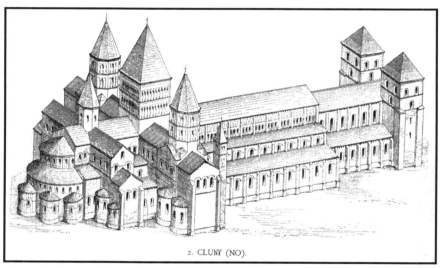

2. CLUNY (NO).

Cluny III

When Cluny III was consecrated by Pope Innocent II, the Cluniac community was an intellectual and spiritual center second only to Rome in Christendom. Cluniac monks had participated actively in the Gregorian reform, several had become bishops and belonged to the curia in Rome; Eudes de Chatillon, who had been at Cluny at the time of Hugues de Semur, had become Pope Urban II, the pope who called for the First Crusade in 1095.

As the eleventh century came to an end, Cluny was still a church inside of the church but had moved away from its initial mission. It had become too affluent and the Cluniac monks too concerned about temporal matters. The monastic community of Cluny was no longer in the spirit of the time, a spirit which favored a life of humility and poverty. Saint Bernard in a famously acerbic diatribe against the Cluniacs pronounced them *humble in words only*.

The inexorable decline of Cluny started as early as the end of the twelfth century. The decline was material as the Order never solved the financial problems created by the huge construction expenditures of Cluny III, and it was moral as discipline in the Abbey became lax and ignored Benedict's precepts.

Centuries later, the Order would be abolished during the French Revolution, the basilica destroyed and used as a quarry. A few ruins were still standing when a young American architect, K.J Conant, received, while walking through the site in the 1920's, "an unforgettable impression of Cluny's greatness." In 1928 he secured financing for excavations and remained a passionate champion of the importance of Cluny III in the history of Romanesque art. Much of the documentation on the basilica still available was gathered by Conant. In the twenty-first century, the visitor discovers the greatness of Cluny mostly thanks to 3D virtual visits.

A century after Cluny had been founded, the return to a stricter observance of the rules of Saint Benedict, once again, inspired the founders of a new order, the Cistercians. In 1098, Robert, Alberic, Stephen and eighteen other monks settled in a marshy forest about fifteen miles south of today's Dijon. They had broken away from the Abbey of Molesme aspiring to an authentic monastic life; Molesme had been founded by Robert a few decades earlier and had slowly lost its rigor. The archbishop of Lyon blessed the *Novum Monasterium*, new monastery, and local lords were generous in giving land for the abbey. The new order settled in Citeaux, a word derived from *cistel,* the reed found in the marshes of Burgundy, and became known as the order of the Cistercians. Its first church was dedicated to Mary as would all future Cistercian churches and the monks wore white robes as a symbol of purity.

The saintly life led by the first Cistercian monks attracted new recruits. In 1113 a party, about thirty strong, asked for permission to join the community at Citeaux. A young man, the son of the Lord of

Fontaines, had convinced family members and friends, all belonging to the local nobility, to join him in a new life of reflection and prayer. His name was Bernard. By 1115 he became abbot of Clairvaux, one of the *daughter* abbeys of Citeaux, and there he devoted much time to building a network of affiliated abbeys. He became a passionate advocate of the Cistercian commitment to work and contemplation and publically chastised the Clunisians for their laxity. Following his example, the white monks became the model of monastic reformation. In 1250 they were present in six hundred and fifty abbeys in France and were scattered across Europe but by then the decline of the order had already started. Success had taken the Cistercians ever further from their initial principles and the fate of Cluny would also be theirs.

The Cistercian community, known as the white monks, is still alive in France in the twenty-first century. More than forty Cistercian monasteries are scattered around France even if few, such as Senanque in Provence or Citeaux in Burgundy, still serve their original purpose of work and worship. The best preserved abbeys, Fontfroide in Languedoc, Royaumont near Paris or Fontenay in Burgundy, have found a second life housing seminars, exhibitions, music festivals and other cultural activities.

Bernard de Clairvaux

Young Bernard who knocked at the door of the Novum Monasterium in the forest of Citeaux stood in sharp contrast to his five brothers. They were the product of the physically demanding preparation for knighthood while the frail young man had the intense look of one who has spent his childhood at a school of secular canons. In the seclusion of the *collégiale* at Chatillon-sur-Seine he had been an avid reader of the Bible, theology and Latin authors and his extreme sensitivity and intelligence had allowed him to blossom in this spiritual environment. Throughout his life he would use his sharp intelligence and analytical mind to brilliantly address sacred and profane issues of the Church and the Kingdom of the Franks.

Neither knight nor monk, he took the path that he believed God had destined for him. Three years after joining the Novum Monasterium he was sent to found the abbey of Clairvaux and his name will remain foremost and forever attached to the Cistercian community. Throughout his life he would be a prolific writer and his texts, sermons and dissertations on monastic life left an indelible imprint on the order.

Bernard was a traditionalist and, today, would be labeled a fundamentalist, intransigent with his faith but also relentless with those who did not share his views. His controversy with Abelard, the Abelard unfortunately most often remembered for his heart-breaking and tragic love of Heloise than his teachings, belongs in the anthology of theological debates. Abelard argued that "in doubting we are enticed to search and in searching we reach truth." This was the antithesis of the monastic ethic preached so passionately by Bernard, an ethic based on obedience and the surrendering of self. He condemned the scholastic and dialectic approach which he feared was infecting the universities in Paris. By 1137, when the political winds at the court of the Frankish Kingdom and in Rome shifted in his favor, Bernard, in the words of Henry Adams, "made short work of all that tried to resist him." In 1140 a council in Sens, with no other than Bernard as prosecuting attorney, silenced Abelard.

Bernard-the-Mystic was also a man with great personal charm. He built a network of relationships which led him to become involved not only in the affairs of the Church but also in the critical issues of the secular world. He counseled Alienor of Aquitaine, scolded her husband King Louis VII, passionately preached the Second Crusade and relentlessly defended not only the independence of the Church but also its ascendancy over the affairs of lords and kings.

Very saintly at times, very human at others, he left no one indifferent and induced much passion.

Twenty-one years after his death he was canonized and became Saint Bernard.

Abbey of Fontenay.

The lilacs were in bloom when our party set out for Fontenay in northern Burgundy on a warm sunny day in May. The road wound lazily through fields of pale green wheat and bright yellow corn. Nature was generous in rewarding men's labor.

Fontenay, the Abbey and its manicured French gardens, at the bottom of a green valley, suddenly come into full view after one more turn of the road. It is the oldest Cistercian complex still standing. It was founded in 1118, a daughter of Bernard's Clairvaux (one might also call it a grand-daughter of Citeaux). In 1134 an assembly of Cistercian abbots set the norms for churches and other gathering places in their monasteries. They decreed that statues should not be painted and glass windows should remain unstained. Cistercian churches did not need to display passages from the Old and New Testaments; monks knew how to read the Bible and were not to be distracted during their meditation. The buildings erected in 1139 in the marsh of Fontenay embodied this Cistercian ethic and became the template for other abbeys of this order.

While Fontenay was coming to life, Abbot Suger was launching the rebuilding of Saint Denis and the contrast is still striking between the spare church born from Saint Bernard's vision and the glorious Abbey willed by Suger, between a spire pointing to the sky and an edifice solidly implanted in the soil of Burgundy, between a work of art in Paris built to welcome kings and a building which shuns the seduction of art and decoration.

The day was still young when we entered the empty Romanesque church. Neither the columns nor the ceilings were decorated, and the bareness of the edifice was only broken by a few gisants, these sepulchral sculptures, next to a modest altar at the end of the nave. The apse was bathed by the morning sun, the glass windows revealing the green of the trees and the blue of the sky. The mood in the church is conducive to contemplation and undisturbed meditation, even the casual visitor feels inner peace and is inclined to stay and pray. The wishes and vision of Saint Bernard are respected at Fontenay.

Abbey of Fontenay

In the back of the church, to the right of the entrance, is a barely noticeable door. It was used by the *converts*, men from the countryside, illiterates living in the Abbey, possibly to be closer to God and certainly to secure food and lodging. They used that door to enter the Church and this is where they stayed during service. They were the factotums of the monastery and without them there would not have been trout breeding, or iron work or any of the activities which were commercial successes for the Abbey. At its peak Fontenay housed 200 converts and only 120 monks.

The monks, who most commonly were knights or sons of knights, believed that everyone has an assigned place in society and a specific role to play; the knight fights, the monk prays and the convert works. When a knight becomes a monk he makes a vow of humility, charity and fraternal love but he does not renounce his place in a social order where all men are not equal. The converts belong in the back of the church, the monks near the altar. The modest door in the back of the church is a reminder that at the time of Saint Bernard the monasteries were built for lords and knights, the well-off who also might be the ones who knew how to read; the masses remained on the fringes, and knew this community was not theirs.

The Abbey of Fontenay became public property at the time of the Revolution. By then it had been neglected and seriously damaged by wars and housed only a few monks. Later, it was sold to private hands. Since 1906 the family of the current owners, the Aynard, has undertaken a large and meticulous restoration. Fontenay remains the template of Cistercian Abbeys even if some buildings no longer exist, the sleeping quarters of the converts among others, and some have been built after the twelfth century.

The countryside around the abbey has a sprinkling of medieval villages; nature is restful, food delightful and people friendly. During the Middle Ages, Burgundy was the source of a political and religious energy that the king of France could not ignore. Today it is a peaceful rural province, so pleasant to visit when the lilacs are in bloom.

The highways converging on Paris from Burgundy in the east and Normandy and Anjou in the west are furrows parting endless wheat fields. The rich plain encircling Paris between the Loire and the Somme belongs to a larger geological region called the *Bassin Parisien,* a limestone plateau well-irrigated and topped with silt, the same fertile soil which has been cultivated in the low plains of Europe since prehistoric times. Historians claim that, as early as the fourth century BC, farming people from Central Europe brought their techniques and life style to the core of the Bassin Parisien. It has been called the granary of France.

In the eyes of Michelet this fertile region was the engine that drove the unification of France. Paris, the capital of the Franks and the heart of the domain of the Capetians, is in the center of the Bassin. In the twelfth century the city was primed to become one of the major metropolises in Europe. The Seine, the Marne and the Oise River brought cereal, wine and meat to feed its growing population. The city had an open access to the Atlantic Ocean but it would remain continental and France a continental country. The die was cast when the capital of the country grew on and around the Ile de la Cite and not in Rouen. Later, mostly after the end of the sixteenth century, the need to vigilantly protect its eastern borders stood in the way of France becoming a maritime force. The geopolitical consequences of this continental option were for all to see when England grew into an uncontested major colonial power.

Wine and the Kingdom of the Franks

From the "Savoir Vivre" of Romans to the "Savoir Faire" of Monks

Histories of wine always postulate that the planting of vineyards in Gaul was advanced by the symbolic importance of wine for Christians and its use during the rite of communion. This is a fair assumption but one must recall that wine was present there several centuries before the country was Christianized and that the Gauls were drinking wine long before making their own.

The Greeks had invented the art of *domesticating* a wild grapevine and grew grapes yielding a liquid pleasant to drink. The Gauls had first encountered this beverage in the Greek colony founded around *Massalia*, today's Marseilles, along the Mediterranean, at the beginning of the six century BC. Later, the Roman occupation of Provence in the first century BC encouraged the consumption of imports from Italy. During the same time period grapevines planted by Roman citizens could be seen growing further west, in Gallia Narbonensis.

The Romans, who had learned the art of wine making from the Greeks, enjoyed drinking their wine in various fashions, hot or cold, usually cut with water. When amphoras were replaced by wooden barrels, spices were added to hide the taste of the tar that lined the insides. Wine went well with olive oil in the diet of the Romans. They were proud of these attributes of their culture that distinguished them from barbaric Gauls who drank beer and cooked their food in animal fat and lard. The Gauls drank their wine pure, uncut with water, further inflaming their hot tempers. It was, in the eyes of the Romans, another sign of their uncivilized manners.

The emperors considered that introducing the Gauls to the Roman gustatory traditions was a feature of their civilizing mission. In the wake of their conquest, olive trees and grapevines made a slow and modest appearance in the south of Gaul. For a long time, only the well-off could afford the expensive imports from Italy, and it has been written that some avid consumers did not hesitate to trade their slaves for wine-filled amphoras.

The consumption of wine after the first century AD followed the major trading routes. Barges fighting the currents of the Rhone delivered amphoras, and later wood barrels, to Lugdunum, today's Lyon, and from there were transported further north on the Saone, the Moselle and the Rhine. In the western part of Gaul, Italian wines reached the Atlantic by way of the *isthmus of Gaul* as the Greek geographer Strabo called the narrow passage from the Mediterranean to the Atlantic which starts near Narbonne and follows the Garonne up to Bordeaux. There, they would be loaded on ships bound for the British Isles.

Bringing the enjoyment of the products of vineyards and olive groves to their colonies, wherever the climate allowed, was a noble goal, but wine was more than a proud element of the Roman culture; it was also a source of wealth and a political tool. The Romans became conflicted about whether to develop local production or to protect a profitable trade for the Italian merchants. Emperor Domitian at the end of the first century forbade the planting of vineyards in the colonies in order to protect the Italian producers; about two hundred years later, however, in 276, Emperor Probus allowed all Gauls, *gallis omnibus*, to have vineyards; he needed their support in his wars against the barbarians. In the interim, imports remained the principal source of wine in Gaul.

Two regions in Gaul benefited from Probus' edict: the valleys of the Rhone in the east and of the Garonne in the west. Numerous fragments of amphoras are still dug out from the silt of the two rivers and attest to the importance of the commerce of wine along these major trade routes. A map of Gaul shows clearly that they were the natural paths for delivering further north and west the products unloaded in the harbors along the Mediterranean. The planting of grapevines would naturally progress along the same axis. The soil and climatic conditions along the Rhone valley were favorable up to Vienne, south of Lyon; the same held true for the isthmus up to Gaillac, between Toulouse and Albi. Experience and patience were needed to obtain a reliable harvest north of Vienne and west of Gaillac, but it was only a matter of time before grapevines would be planted on the western slopes of the Saone valley and in the Bordeaux area.

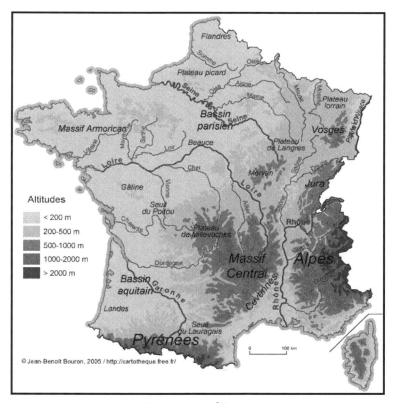

Main rivers of France

A handful of questionable sources attest to the beginnings of wine in Burgundy during the third century. The Romans had granted a few cities in Burgundy the privilege to produce their own wine even before Probus' edict. The *Musée du Vin de Bourgogne* in the town of Beaune has preserved written documents relating to wine making in Burgundy during the fourth century. The modest museum also has well-preserved amphoras that had brought wine from Italy and Greece, and next to the amphoras, wooden barrels said to have been used by the Gauls as early as the first century to store their beer, *cervoise*. The musée contains folkloric reminders that the Gauls venerated a so-called *Dieu au Tonneau* (Barrel God).

The time frame for the initial production of wine in the southwest of Gaul was similar to Burgundy's. During the first century AD, grapes originally from Greece made their way to the Bordeaux area; called biturica they evolved into today's carmenets that is, the cabernet sauvignon, merlot and related varieties. It seems that the grapes had acclimated to northern Spain at the time of Emperor Augustus and then were found suitable for southwestern Gaul. The physical conditions for wine growing were not optimal around Burdaglia, as Bordeaux was then called, but it was a major *emporium*, market, that had been supplied with wine by Gaillac for a long time and was favorably located for shipments to the Nordic countries. Bordeaux was destined to become a major wine production and trade center.

As the barbarians overran Gaul and the wine-making skills acquired during the previous centuries were at risk of being forgotten, bishops and monks made sure that the vineyards were not left untended. Wine was needed for Christian rites, but its production was preserved mostly because it was a symbol of social status and a means of honoring guests. The bishops had become the most respected personalities in the civitates (towns where the bishop resided) and in their new capacity as leading citizens they entertained distinguished visitors and wanted to be proud of their wine.

White wine, also called French wine, was in abundant supply throughout the Middle Ages, as white grapes were more resistant than red grapes to extreme weather conditions. Demand, however, made red the dominant type of wine after the end of the thirteenth century.

Up to the eighteenth century, only red wine was used to celebrate mass. This made sense to Christians who believe that the wine they drink during the sacrament of the Eucharist had been transubstantiated into the blood of Christ. In recent times, white wine has been used more often. The reason is down-to-earth, the spots made by white wine on the white cloths of the altar are easier to wash away. Even though quantities remain negligible, mass wine has a niche of its own in the wine trade. Priests have their preferences, and in rural areas where the Church of Rome has long been present there are mass wine fairs and traditions of offering the wine for Sunday mass.

Wine production continued during the Carolingian dynasty, but its successful progress in the south of France came to a halt during the terrible ninth and tenth centuries when trade became difficult and unsafe. The Vikings controlled the Atlantic coast, the Seine, and the other major rivers and the Saracens, pushed back into Spain by Charles Martel in the eighth century, were again conducting destructive raids in the south of France; the commerce of Bordeaux and Burgundy wines with potential markets in the northern regions became more hazardous. Quality vines survived around cathedrals, monasteries and chateaux, and local consumption was satisfied by less noble wines. The economic loss for the south became a temporary gain for the northern regions as wine production gained ground along the Seine and the Rhine, where climatic conditions had never been favorable and reliable.

In the twelfth century, the expansion of the network of Cistercian abbeys gave a new impulse to the production of wine. The Cistercian monks devoted much of their time to manual labor, a distinctive feature of their way of life. They relied on *cruce et aratro*, cross and plow, to save their souls and feed their bodies. The monks who handled precious books in *scriptoria* and taught the children of the elite, showed the same patience in caring for vineyards.

Over the years, the monks became so industrious and efficient that the fruit of their labor exceeded their consumption and surplus was available for sale or barter. They learned to steer between their vows of poverty and simplicity and the pragmatism of the world of commerce. Monks could afford to be patient in their search for the best products. This was a most useful asset in creating quality wines. The monastic communities took meticulous care of their vineyards and wines, slowly and consistently improving the grapes they planted around their abbeys and the oenological techniques they closely guarded. Grape vines could be seen carefully tied to wood posts next to monasteries even in regions where soil and climate were unfriendly.

The abbeys scattered around the kingdom acted as *auberges* and attracted a clientele of lords and knights during their long travels on horseback. Abbots and bishops considered it their duty to welcome all visitors *as Christ.* They offered wine to honor guests and in turn, the travelers who had enjoyed the hospitality of the abbeys contributed to the reputation of the best vintages.

Clos de Vougeot

Pious donors gave land near Vougeot south of Dijon to the monks who had abandoned Cluny and had settled in Citeaux. There, they planted vineyards and by the twelfth century produced what is known today as *Clos de Vougeot*. The land was not favorable for growing grapes, and the Cistercian monks had to work patiently and diligently, to test and select the best techniques for planting and pruning. By the end of the century, they were serving a pinot that delighted their guests. Most of the wines made from the grapes coming from the *Clos de Vougeot* are still *grands crus* (grands crus and premiers crus are wines from top ranking-vineyards).

Vougeot has its own *climat*. This does not refer to meteorological conditions but is the local word for terroir, for the elements "forming together within a vineyard characters that constitute a personality, unique to one terroir and one cru" as defined in the successful candidature of Burgundy for *Unesco World Heritage Listing* in July 2015.

The first time my wife and I visited the Cote de Nuits in Burgundy our timing was unusual. Any well-prepared visitor aims at touring that part of France in October or maybe in the spring; unfortunately our itinerary took us between Dijon and Beaune in the middle of winter. We stayed at the *Chateau Hotel de Gilly* and could not have hoped for a better fit with our search. In the fourteenth century, the Citeaux monks had bought a priory in Gilly, which was subsequently fortified and transformed into a chateau. More recently, it joined the collection of *Relais et Chateaux* hotels; one of its unique features is its ancient ribbed vaulted wine cellar transformed into a dining room. Citeaux, the first Cistercian Abbey, is ten or so miles away and the Chateau du Clos de Vougeot is within two miles.

The only taxi driver in the village of Gilly was away hunting when we needed his services and so we walked to the Clos. It was cold but it was exhilarating to be on the narrow paths which take little space away from the precious land on which vines grow. We saw the vineyards as few visitors see them: bare, the grey gnarled roots of the vines, larger than one expects, aligned in perfect geometric rows along the gently sloping hillside. Acres and acres of vineyards tended knowledgeably by human hands; rows of roots tied to wires, each one the noticeable object of loving care.

The road runs along a low wall which symbolically encloses the grapes yielding the premium wines. Along a gentle hill is the *clos*, the enclosed vineyard, and, halfway up the hill a stone arch signals the path leading to the Chateau. It was bought in 1944 by the *Confrérie du Tastevin* and every year the Confrérie organizes sixteen celebrations of food, good spirits and, of course, wine; two well-attended tastings also take place during the year. The tourist crowd was sparse in the chateau; we had to satisfy ourselves with an unguided and unheated tour.

The clos has preserved testimonies of the wine-making techniques of the monks. Wood vessels and presses are on display in a *cuverie*. The grapes were trampled in the vessels and then crushed in the presses; two of the four presses date back to the middle of the twelfth century, their levers made of six oak beams, held together by metal hooks. These are not technical marvels but merely formidable wooden structures.

The monks stored wine in a cellar above ground. This cellar has thick walls, a ceiling lined with densely packed wood beams and is said to have the perfect natural temperature for keeping wine; this is where the soirees of the Confréries are held.

There would be no wine tasting for us at the Clos but the sommelier at the Hotel de Gilly made sure we had the fullness of the experience in the vaulted dining room of the hotel.

Beaune

An early morning local train took us from le Clos de Vougeot to *Beaune*, crossing a countryside draped in white frost. The Musée du Vin de Bourgogne could not afford to heat more than one room and the winter weather did not make the Hotel-Dieu more hospitable.

The Hotel-Dieu better known as *les Hospices de Beaune* was built in 1443. The Hundred Years war was coming to a close and gangs of disbanded soldiers were spreading misery and famine throughout Burgundy. God-fearing nobles, looking to save their souls, decided to come to the help of the needy. The chancellor of Duke Philippe le Bon and his wife founded a hospital for the poor, an institution that still welcomes old and indigent patients. The chancellor and later other noblemen donated works of art, tapestries etc. and, most importantly, vineyards, scattered along several of the best known *cotes*, particularly

Cotes de Beaune and Cotes de Nuits. Today, the Hospices de Beaune recall two images: the Gothic former hospital in the center of town and a yearly wine auction.

The trademark of the building is its polychrome slate roof, a symphony of geometric figures where each shape is colored in flamboyant black, orange or yellow. The builders might have found their inspiration in central Europe and the style became typical of Burgundy. Inside of the Hospices the *Grande salle des Pôvres,* grand room for the poor, is a superbly restored medieval hospital room under a carved wooden ceiling in the shape of a boat hull. The Hospices also house a Flemish masterpiece, a fifteenth century polyptych representing the last Judgment.

Every year, on the third Sunday of November, the wines of the Hospices are auctioned in Beaune. This very traditional ceremony goes back in its current form to the middle of the nineteenth century, and is always the occasion for much wining and dining.

The attraction of Burgundy goes beyond good wine and good food. It is also a heaven for people in search of peace. Many on a pilgrimage to Compostella find comfort in the basilica of Vézelay; further south, very near Cluny, young Christians will gather at the ecumenical community at *Taizé.* A Taizé prayer service is a quiet, meditative experience known to Catholics and Protestants around the world. The historical connection between the region and worship is still alive.

The Good Fortune of Bordeaux Wines

At the beginning of the twelfth century, as trade routes became safer, the economics of wine, previously led by supply from the south, became driven by demand from the north. At the same time, demand was impacted by changes in the political landscape which exposed landed gentry and aristocrats in England to quality Bordeaux wines and made them knowledgeable consumers.

The context which favored the wines of the Bordeaux region was the marriage, in 1152, of Alienor of Aquitaine with the future king of England, Henry II. Alienor became queen of the vast so-called Plantagenet Empire but, throughout her long life, (she was 82 when she died and she outlived Henry by 15 years) she remained deeply attached to Aquitaine. It is during her reign and that of her sons King Richard I and King John that England learned to appreciate *claret wines*. It would be a long-lasting legacy. Claret, here, must be understood in the twenty first century sense of the word; in the Middle Ages, claret designated a spiced wine.

At the very end of the century, Queen Alienor, who was also Duchess of Aquitaine, answered the pressing requests of the burghers of Bordeaux and cancelled certain feudal customs which handicapped the local wine producers. Alienor's steady interest in the prosperity of Bordeaux was not surprising. She was born nearby, had spent her youth in the *Palais de l'Ombrière* which dominated the medieval town and her marriage to Louis VII had been celebrated in the Cathedral. Her son Richard would be governor of Aquitaine and learn to enjoy the local wine during his sojourns in the town. Alienor's ruling was a good sign for the winemakers of Bordeaux and they gained trust in royal protection. This mattered greatly as their ambition was to make their wine a regular feature on the table of the king of England. The competition was stiff. The Plantagenet had roots in Anjou, and the wines from Poitou and Anjou were well introduced in England. At the beginning of the thirteenth century, Poitou and the neighboring city of La Rochelle were still exporting more wine to the northern countries than Gascony.

In their competition against La Rochelle the burghers of Bordeaux played their cards very well and their trump card, loyalty, won the day. In 1206 when the king of Castille marched into Aquitaine, the town sided with King John. Later, in 1224, when Louis VIII was successfully conquering Poitou and progressing towards Guyenne and as La Rochelle opened its doors to the French when they set siege to the town, Bordeaux made sure it was seen as a city of the English. The town was rewarded for its faithfulness while La Rochelle saw its ships locked out of the harbors controlled by the English. This won the economic battle for Bordeaux, and its wines took over the share of the rival town. From then on, Aquitaine supplied more than three quarters of the wine consumed in the royal castles in England. The Bordeaux wine became a *must* at any celebration of the English aristocracy.

The Good Fortune of Burgundy Wines

More than a century later the Burgundy wines had their turn at good fortune. In 1369, Philippe le Hardi, Duke of Burgundy, married Margaret, Countess of Flanders, and the duke became an ambassador of the Burgundy wines in his northern provinces. The duke was particularly keen to encourage the export of Beaune wine. These were times when kings and nobles took a strong interest in wine, reminiscent of the close attention paid by the Roman emperors. Their goals were financial but heavily tainted with cultural pride. In 1395 the duke forbade the cultivation of the *Gamay* grape which he considered as inferior, the "very bad and unfaithful Gamay...whose wine is much harmful to humans... full of great and terrible bitterness" as he described it in a memorable edict. He praised the black grapes thereafter called *Pinot* which gave a much-appreciated vermillion wine. The successors of le Hardi continued to favor the pinot and it would stay at the top of the hierarchy of wine up to the eighteenth century.

When the popes were domiciled in *Avignon* during the fourteenth century, the duke of Burgundy made sure that each new pope was greeted with generous quantities of grands crus of Beaune. Thus, in 1395, Philippe le Hardi had 4,000 liters of his best wine delivered to two cardinals in the entourage of Benedict XIII, the very controversial antipope *Papa de Luna*. Popes and cardinals lauded the products from Beaune. The popes, who were gracious ambassadors for the Burgundy products, also owned vineyards and made their own wines. The still famous Chateauneuf du Pape was one of them. Burgundy wines became highly appreciated not only in Avignon but in the north of Europe and in Paris. This wine was expensive to transport to Paris as the Burgundy region lacked a network of rivers giving access to the Seine, but the handicap was more than compensated by its quality and reputation.

Guillaume Becomes William

Guillaume, Duc de Normandie

Guillaume had a remarkable father, Robert, sixth duke of Normandy. He would be surnamed *The Magnificient* but should more appropriately be remembered as *The Enigmatic*. His adventurous life is known to us thanks to Guillaume de Jumièges *Gesta Normannorum Ducum*. Robert had rebelled when his brother had become Duke Richard III. A year later Richard had died, possibly poisoned. Did Robert have a hand in the death of his brother? In any case, he then successfully fought for the title of Duke Robert I of Normandy

During his undisciplined years, the future duke had met Herleva, Arlette, whose life offers enough material for several legends. She was the daughter of a tanner and obviously of a much lower social rank. Guillaume was born out of wedlock in 1027(?). A generation earlier his mother would have been acknowledged as a legitimate wife. This was the "more danico," the Danish way to do things, but the Church had been fighting these pagan traditions and Guillaume would remain a bastard. For reasons mostly unknown, Duke Robert I of Normandy went on a pilgrimage in 1035 and died during his return from Jerusalem. Before his departure the great lords of Normandy had accepted Guillaume as his successor and he became duke at the age of eight.

The young man seemed an easy prey for the lords of Normandy and the duchy suffered a long period of anarchy. In 1047, Guillaume, with the reluctant help of the king of the Franks, quelled a rebellion led mostly by members of his extended family. The duke had called on King Henri I, his feudal lord, and the king could not but stand by his vassal. Feeling more secure in his position as duke, Guillaume could now think of his dynasty. Without the pressure of a father or a mother, he was one of the rare great lords who was in a position to choose his future wife and he elected Mathilde of Flanders. The wedding took place around 1050 despite the objections of the pope for the usual cause of co-sanguinity. It would be a very successful marriage, and it would seem that Guillaume truly loved and remained faithful to Mathilde.

A few years later Guillaume was perceived by King Henri as a threat and hostile action became unavoidable. During two military campaigns, in 1054 and 1057, the forces of the duke defeated the men of the king. Guillaume was revealed as a keen tactician and an astute strategist. Henri died in 1060, his successor, eight years old Philippe I, was no match for Guillaume. The duke could now look beyond Normandy, towards England and the succession of its weakening King Edward.

The Great Viking Invasions of England

Lindisfarne had been followed by other incursions west of the Channel. Norwegian and Danish sea warriors had burned abbeys, loaded their boats with slaves and extorted *danegeld*. Then, towards the middle of the ninth century, they had landed in greater numbers and stayed longer. In 865-66 they conquered Northumbria and then defeated the Saxons in East Anglia and Mercia. Only Wessex stood on the way of the Vikings becoming masters of all of England. King Alfred of Wessex led the resistance for many years, galvanized the Saxons and forced the Vikings to settle for the control of only north-eastern England. This is when Alfred began to be called King of the Anglo-Saxons and earned the title of *Alfred the Great* given to him by the Tudors centuries later.

Alfred had several successful successors and one in particular, Athelstan, would be the first to unite the territories held by the Anglo-Saxons and the so-called Danelaw regions. Then came Aethelred, surnamed the Unready with the meaning of *no counsel*, possibly the most maligned English king. On Saint Brice's Day 1002, Aethelred-the-Unready became Aetherel-the-Unwise when he ordered the execution of the Danes who had stayed behind after the fall of the Danelaw kingdoms. Sveyn Forkbeard, King of Denmark, swore revenge and launched yearly raids on England. The Vikings had returned to spread terror. Aethelred negotiated truces and paid Danegeld but as Rudyard Kipling wrote later," ...once you paid him the Dane-geld, you never get rid of the Dane." Then, in 1013, the Danish king led a massive invasion and the Danes had again control over much of England.

Sveyn died shortly after his successful conquest and it was a few years before the crown was secure on the head of his son Cnut. At long last, at the death of the Anglo-Saxon king Edmund, a son of Aethelred, the English nobility pledged loyalty to Cnut (Note: the old English term *atheling* designates a noble of royal descent, the equivalent of *nobiles* in Latin; *aethel* is the prefix of the name of several of the first English kings). The new king left the Saxon institutions in place, agreed to follow English laws and ruled as a true Christian king. Cnut sought the advice of natives and relied heavily on a South-Saxon, Godwine, a shrewd man who would be rewarded with large estates in Wessex and become earl. The English want to remember Cnut as a Viking who became king of England but he was much more. At the time of his death in 1035 he was a Christian monarch ruling over a north European empire extending over Denmark, Norway, and England, and had jurisdiction over the king of Sweden. He ended his life culturally neither Scandinavian nor English but something in between, truly a great European monarch.

A Weak Saxon, a Strong Scandinavian or a Foreign Norman?

Throughout these early years of Anglo-Saxon kingdoms, the relationship between Normandy and England had been continuous if often conflicting. In 1002, in a spirit of goodwill, Duke Richard II's sister, Emma, had wedded Aethelred. After his defeat at the hand of the Danes, the Anglo-Saxon king and his family had found refuge in Normandy. There, his two sons, Alfred and Edward, were brought up with the children of the duke of Normandy.

When news spread of the death of Cnut the two boys saw an opportunity to regain the power once held by their family. They sailed to England but had tragically misread the situation. Alfred was savagely massacred and his brother wisely returned to Normandy. Edward's chance came again when Cnut's direct line ended a few years later. Godwine was very persuasive in convincing the elders to ignore the Scandinavian candidates and crown the Saxon; for Godwine, a weak Saxon was better than a strong Scandinavian.

Edward had to contend with the power of the Godwines. He attempted to shake free from the earl and was successful during a few years after 1050 but then, as he did not receive the support of the earls from the north who resented his choice of Norman advisors, Godwine was quickly back as powerful as ever. This turning point in the king's struggle for power became a turning point in his life. During the last fifteen years of his reign he concentrated on the spiritual and earned his surname *Edward the Confessor*. He will be canonized in 1161 and become the favorite patron saint of the Plantagenets.

The elder Godwine did not benefit long from his power, he died in 1053, but his clan survived. The next in line, his son Harold, succeeded him as earl of Wessex. He was, in the words of Simon Schama "tall, charismatically good looking …. with the gangsterish rough surface buffed up into aristocratic polish." Shortly after, another son, Tostig, gained control of Northumbria. The Godwines were powerful indeed.

In 1064, King Edward sent Harold on a mission to the court of Guillaume in Normandy. The voyage is told by Guillaume de Poitiers in his *"Gesta Guillelmi ducis Normannorum et regis Anglorum."* The king was without heir, and it is probable that the mission had to do with his succession. Edward might have known Guillaume, who we will now call by his English name of William, when the young Anglo-Saxon was in exile in Normandy but it is more certain that they met later when one was king of England and the other duke of Normandy. Was King Edward's intention to confide to William that he intended to make him his successor? Would William or the Godwines clan rule England? What happens next is told in picturesque details in a tapestry which has been in Bayeux ever since these events took place.

Bayeux Tapestry: The Illustrated Story of the Conquest of England

A tour of historical Normandy can be an instructive and moving experience for anyone visiting France and *Bayeux* is a good starting point.

The tapestry is preserved in a former seminary within walking distance of the train station, and billboards along the way encourage visitors to tour the landing beaches, Arromanches, Omaha and Utah less than ten miles away.

The inscription on the nearby Second World War British Memorial recalls in simple and poignant terms the two momentous events which link Normandy and England:

> "We who have been conquered have liberated the land of the conqueror"

Bayeux miraculously escaped destruction in June 1944, and the cathedral consecrated by William's half-brother Odo in 1077 still towers over the town. It points the way to the Musée where the tapestry is kept.

Where and when the tapestry was embroidered is still debated. It might have been commissioned by William's wife Mathilde or by Odo; it might have been crafted by Norman hands or in Anglo-Saxon workshops. A plausible story gives credit to Odo and says that the work done in 1077 was meant to be exposed in the Bayeux Cathedral. At a time when few entering a church were literate, paintings, engravings, embroideries and stained-glass windows were educational.

The tapestry illustrates events that took place in Normandy and England between 1064 and 1066. It is a succession of 57 panels each 50 centimeters high and adding to a length of 68 meters.

The embroidery makes use of wool threads of ten different colors. The rendering of perspective and movement is rudimentary, the emotions of the main protagonists are crudely but clearly rendered; the hand reaching down from heaven when Edward is buried is one of the few reflective touches in a composition otherwise filled with great vitality. There is no doubt that the work was intended to be a message for posterity but what message? The background of the tapestry is so nebulous that its reliability as a historical document will always be contested. Deciphering this testimony remains a tantalizing exercise.

The first series of panels recalls the adventurous journey of Harold to Normandy in 1064 and his sojourn with William. Then comes panel number 23 perhaps the most important of the entire composition. It depicts Harold, in the presence of a regal looking William, swearing an oath with each hand on holy relics. The next scene shows Harold returning to England and sheepishly relating his trip to Edward. Why did Harold come to Normandy and what happened between him and William during his stay remain a source of disagreement between France and England.

The Normans claim that Harold paid feudal homage to William and took a vow to defend his rights to the throne of England. The English call this a dubious interpretation by treacherous Frenchmen; the tapestry is after all a piece of propaganda in their eyes. The oath was given under duress, they claim, while Harold had come to inform William of his own intention to secure the throne of England. This might have been the first of many cases of mistrust between France and England.

The next series of panels, a visual rendering of the events after Harold returns to England, do not record the feud with his brother Tostig. These events, perhaps purposely left untold, weigh so heavily on the outcome of the upcoming battle between Harold and William that they need to be woven into the story told by the tapestry.

The feud had started when nobles from Northumbria rebelled against Tostig. Harold had sided with the rebels and agreed to the removal of his brother from the earldom. A furious Tostig then went into exile in Flanders bent on seeking revenge.

On January 6, 1066, King Edward dies. He has no direct heir and the witan, the council of Anglo-Saxon elders, presents the crown to Harold. Halley's Comet which crosses the sky a few months later is an ominous sign for the new king. The danger for his throne comes from the Nordic countries as well as from the other side of the channel as William is vexed by the decision of the elders. Can he claim perjury against Harold? He convinces the pope to side with him against the Godwine gang, enlists the Norman lords with promises of rich rewards and prepares to invade England.

It will be a stunning logistical achievement. Twenty-five thousand men coming from Flanders in the north to Brittany in the south, thousands of horses, tons of food and equipment, all had to be transported across the Channel. Even though the duke's vassals provided close to eight hundred vessels, more were needed. During nine months all the harbors of the duchy succumbed to a fever of shipbuilding. On September 10, the invasion fleet gathered on the River Dives, northwest of Caen, set sail, at last, only to be blown to Saint-Valery, at the mouth of the Somme. There, the armada waited again for favorable winds.

The wait turns out to benefit the duke as, during that time, Tostig returned from exile and, followed by a formidable army of Norwegians, landed in Northumbria. He had made an alliance with the Norwegian king Harald Hardrada who had a legitimate claim to the throne of England. The confrontation between the Northumbrians and Norwegians on one side and the Anglo-Saxons on the other took place on the 25th at *Stamford Bridge*, a few miles east of York. Against all odds, Harold routed his foes; Tostig and Harald Hardrada were killed and their death ended the threat of an Anglo-Scandinavian state. Before returning to Norway, Hardrada's son swore he would never attack England again and so ended three centuries of Viking invasions and attempts to rule England.

Harold had no time to savor his victory. The winds had shifted in William's favor a few days after Stamford Bridge and the Normans had landed near Pevensey on the south coast of England. One of the panels of the tapestry shows clearly the colorful drakkars crossing the Channel. Harold's forces, badly bruised by their battle against the Nordics, regrouped in London and set out without delay to face the Normans.

The last section of the tapestry is a vivid representation of the dramatic confrontation that took place on October 14 between the Anglo-Saxons and the Normans.

The battle at Hastings

The battle that history books say took place at Hastings, saw the Norman horsemen butting endlessly against a wall of shields and a swarm of spears. Several panels are magnificent tableaux of the Norman cavalry and the elite *housecarls* protecting Harold.

The Gods of War took a long time before siding with William. Harold was struck by an arrow in the eye and his death marked the end of the Godwine saga.

Despite the controversy surrounding its very historical accuracy, the Bayeux Tapestry, is one of France's most enduring *lieu de memoire.*

Guillaume le Conquerant, that is, William the Conqueror, King of England (1066)

William now the *Conqueror* was crowned in Westminster Abbey on Christmas Day 1066, the first of a line of rulers who, in Simon Schama's words, "for better or for worse redefined sovereignty in England." His victory over Harold was the first step in a long and bloody conquest, the conquest of the north in particular would be protracted and very destructive. The new English king might have sought reconciliation at first but by 1070, in reaction to rebellions, he became tyrannical

The duke cum king made good on his promise to deliver the spoils of war to those Norman vassals who had fought at his side. The conquerors replaced the Saxon ruling class and introduced feudalism to England. This would be the most far-reaching socio-political change that England would ever see. Land owned by over 4,000 lords went to the new royal family, to the Church and baronies, altogether less than 250 people.

In 1085, William commissioned a thorough inventory of English wealth. The meticulously collected data was recorded in what became known as the *Domesday Book,* a most extraordinary compilation that had many potential uses beyond the initial one of assessing the resources that could be taxed. In recent times it was used to measure the economic impact of the Norman invasion but despite this wealth of data no reliable conclusion has been drawn. It was most certainly a catastrophe at first but it can be claimed that, in the longer term, the conquest helped the English economy, thanks in particular to a burgeoning external commerce.

One of the most often quoted sources about the period is Orderic

Vitalis. A monk born in England of an English mother and Norman father, Orderic (1075-1142?) spent most of his life in Normandy and wrote a monumental opus *The Ecclesiastical History of England and Normandy.* The nineteenth century French historian and politician Francois Guizot noted in his preface to the translation published by the Historical Society of France "no book contains so much and such valuable information on the history of the eleventh and twelfth century in the West of Europe." Of particular interest is Vitalis's account of the reign of William the Conqueror. He did not shy from a critical appreciation of the violence during this period and wrote in Book IV of the Ecclesiastical History:

> "Possessed of enormous wealth, gathered by others, the Normans gave the reins to their pride and fury and put to death without compunction the native inhabitants, who for their sins were subjected by divine Providence to the scourge."

William's conquest did not bode well for the future relationship between France and England. The Anglo-Saxons saw the Normans as perfidious in their manipulation of Edward's succession and as brutal colonizers.

On the other side of the channel, the possessions of the duke of Normandy cum king of England rivaled in importance those of his suzerain, the king of the Franks, and this made for an unsettling state of affairs. At a time when power was tied to control over land, today's vassal could quickly become tomorrow's suzerain.

The first two antagonists were William and Philippe I, King of the Franks. Their relationship had long been tense and confrontational and remained so after the conquest. King William jealously protected the borders of his Norman duchy and became embroiled in numerous territorial wars. In 1087 he led a punitive expedition in the *Vexin*, a county under the suzerainty of the king of the Franks, and burned the town of Mantes to the ground. While riding through smoldering ashes, his horse bucked, threw him against the pommel of his saddle, and his spleen was fatally punctured. His second surviving son was crowned William II, King of England, as his oldest son, Robert Curthose, had already been granted the dukedom of Normandy.

The third surviving son, Henry, received money and when William II died in a hunting accident in 1100 (was it an accident?) he was the first to reach Winchester and was crowned Henry I. During these early years of Anglo-Norman monarchy there was no established succession process and the first to reach the royal treasury at Winchester had the best chances of being crowned. A few years later, at the end of a fratricidal battle Henry I, gained control of Normandy.

Plantagenets vs Capetians

Matilda and Geoffrey: The First Plantagenets

Anjou in western France was known for its mild climate, lush vegetation and game-rich forests. Some of the most magnificent Renaissance chateaux would be built along the banks of the Loire which crosses the region to the south. Normandy is to the north, and at the end of the Middle Ages both duchies became important building blocks of the Kingdom of France. In the twelfth century, long before the Kingdom coalesced, hostilities were recurring between the two neighboring regions and this weighed in the decision of Henry I when, in 1128, he married his daughter Matilda to Geoffrey of Anjou; Geoffrey's father was Fulk, the Count of Anjou, and his mother had been Countess of Maine.

A few years after securing the hand of Matilda for his son, Fulk, now a widower, married the daughter of Baudouin II, the King of Jerusalem, at the instigation of King Louis VI. Fulk would succeed his father-in-law in 1131, unfortunately, his reign was cut short by a hunting accident in Acre in 1143. He had been a wise and successful ruler. Geoffrey was of very good stock.

Matilda was the only surviving child of Henry I. The legitimate successor to Henry I, William, named after his grandfather, had died in the tragic accident of *La Blanche Nef*, the *White Ship*, in November 1120. The boat had sailed for England carrying the flower of Norman nobility and sank at night, off the coast of Barfleur. More than 140 knights and noble young men and women and an equal number of crew members perished in the freezing waters of the Channel. Only Bérold, the butcher, held on up to morning and survived to tell the story.

When Henry I died in 1135 Matilda, his only direct heir, became the designated successor but the crown was hotly contested by her cousin Stephen of Blois, the son of Adela, the redoubtable daughter of the Conqueror. Stephen was the first to reach Winchester and grab the royal treasury but Matilda was not one to shy away from a fight. It took a long civil war, appropriately remembered as the *Anarchy,* for Stephen to secure the crown of England in 1141. On the Continent, Geoffrey fought for what he saw as the rightful inheritance of his wife, and by 1144 he had conquered all of Normandy. This large territory facing the Channel and stretching along the Seine west of Paris was strategically located. Geoffrey, Count of Anjou and Maine since his father's departure for Jerusalem, now also Duke of Normandy, was a powerful lord.

The son of Geoffrey and Matilda, Henry II, would become the first Norman-Angevin king of England and his descendants would shape the country during the Middle Ages. Geoffrey's surname was *Plantagenet*, a name borrowed from the *Planta Genesta,* yellow broom, that he would wear on his hat. It was adopted by the partisans of Richard of York at the onset of the first War of the Roses in the fifteenth century and has remained the name of the dynasty founded by Geoffrey's descendants.

Louis VII and Henry II, Rival Kings

In the spring of 1137 Guillaume X, Duke of Aquitaine, weakened by dysentery, died on the road to Compostella. He had no male heir and had known for some time that he should not leave his vast duchy in the hands of a daughter, at the mercy of rapacious neighbor lords. In his last wishes the duke had offered the guardianship of Alienor, his oldest daughter, to his suzerain, the king of the Franks.

The emissaries of the dying Guillaume reached the French court in early June. They met with Suger and King Louis VI who, without further ado, promised to give the hand of his private and reserved sixteen year old son Louis to vivacious Alienor. Louis VI was moribund and there was some urgency in concluding this affair. The wedding in Bordeaux was a sumptuous affair but, due to Louis' poor health, was cut short. Not surprisingly, during their return to Paris, the couple received news that the king had died. Young Louis was now Louis VII, *Rex Francorum*, King of the Franks and *Dux Aquitanorum,* Duke of Aquitaine. It was fortunate that Suger had taught him the art of being a king.

Fifteen years later, the archbishop who had celebrated their wedding in Bordeaux dissolved the marriage of Louis and Alienor. The divorce procedures had been started by the French king under the pretext of consanguinity, the very pretext given in those days when an official reason was needed, and had convinced an assembly of bishops to declare the nullity of his marriage.

Why had Louis initiated a separation so costly for the crown? Two reasons have been given. Louis VII, the very Christian King, would have reacted to the undignified behavior that rumor said his wife had while they were on a Crusade. Alienor would have been further at fault in his eyes because she had given him only daughters (The French King would be proven wrong when Alienor had six sons with her second husband).

Raison d'état dictated that the king remarry without delay. The beautiful new queen, Constance of Castille, died while giving birth to their second daughter and it was not before August 1165 that Louis's third wife, Adele, gave him his only son, the future Philippe Auguste, appropriately surnamed Dieudonné, God-given.

After her divorce, Alienor cherished her newly reacquired freedom but quickly realized that it was too risky for a woman to try and manage state affairs on her own. Besides, she had been quite smitten for a while with Henry, Geoffrey Plantagenet's eldest son. She wasted no time making her feelings known and on May 18, 1152, Henry and Alienor were married in Poitiers.

There were political considerations behind this union but it was not the traditional marriage of convenience between people of noble birth. They had sought each other and in an even more modern gesture, she, the woman, had made the advance. Alienor, at the age of thirty, was a beautiful woman, headstrong and passionate. Her charm and temperament would have made her an attractive party in any circumstance and the titles she held to the large territory called Aquitaine which at the time comprised the provinces of *Guyenne, Gascony, Limousin* and *Poitou* made her even more appealing,

Ten years Alienor's junior, Henry was sturdy and muscular, excelled at physical exercises and was proud of his knowledge of the classics. A true Angevin, he was prone to fits of anger which curdled the blood of his entourage and earned him the label *mad king*, but he truly was a gifted statesman who used fits of anger as a management tool.

A few months before his son's marriage, Geoffrey Plantagenet had a sudden bout of fever and died. Henry succeeded him in Maine and Anjou. He did not inherit the kingdom of England from his mother, Matilda, but the crown became his through his own valor. In early 1153 Henry Plantagenet now twenty and newly married embarked in *Barfleur* with an army of 3,000 men of arms and 140 knights and crossed the Channel to claim his mother's rights to the English crown. Stephen was not keen to fight Henry's formidable army and, after the death of his oldest son, Eustace, accepted the offer to keep the throne up to his death and name the Plantagenet his successor. Henry was crowned in Westminster Abbey in December 1154 shortly after Stephen's death.

Duke of Normandy, head of the House of Anjou since his father's death and suzerain of Aquitaine through his marriage to Alienor, young Henry was now also Henry II King of England. These territories became the building blocks of the Plantagenet Empire, also called the *Norman Empire* and, in the late nineteenth century, the Angevin Empire. The Angevin still point out that if Henry was a descendant of William the Conqueror through his mother, his father was from Anjou.

Royal domain and English possessions

It was not in Henry's temperament to ask for the approval of his suzerain, King Louis VII, when he married Alienor. This had led Louis, still reeling from his separation with Alienor, to challenge Henry and unfortunately to be at the losing end of a short war with the Plantagenet. This first act in a rivalry between two men, Henry and Louis, grew into a conflict between their two houses. From 1152 (marriage of Alienor and Henry) to 1259 (Paris Peace Treaty) four generations of Capetians and three generations of Plantagenets will clash on the battlefields. During the second half of the twelfth century, the domain of the king of the Franks will be ever more dwarfed by the fiefdoms of the king of England on the continent. The two kings and their descendants will vie for these fiefs during the *First Hundred Years War* and a constant state of war will be only interrupted by short periods of peace. The fate of the kingdom of the Capetians will often be at stake and its star fade dangerously before shining brightly.

The conflict was truly between rulers, not between sovereign states. The regions which would ultimately form France and England had not yet coalesced. Subjects knew little about faraway kings; they were immersed in vernacular cultures and felt close only to local lords. The enmity was between kings and lords, between ruling families sharing blood lines, speaking the same language and faithful to the same religion. The knights and foot soldiers who stood at the side of the kings on the fields of battle fought for personal reward or were honor-bound to render military service to their suzerain; most of them were protective of the honor of their *tribe* but did not feel French or English and were yet to be driven by any form of nationalism.

In his conflict with Henry, Louis gained a moral advantage when his nemesis became entangled in the Thomas Becket Controversy. Thomas Becket, who had been the English king's Chancellor and made Archbishop of Canterbury in 1161, challenged Henry's claim that the Church in his realm was subject to the king's jurisdiction. The Archbishop stood firm on the principle that the temporal rulers were the servants of the church and any matter concerning the Church was *saving the honor of God.* By the end of 1164 his obstinate opposition to the will of his erstwhile friend the king had put him at risk of being charged with treason, and he fled England. Becket ultimately sought refuge in the Cistercian Abbey of Pontigny, south of Paris, an environment conducive to the hardening of his resolve. His choice of an abbey in France was also a symbolic gesture and Louis VII was more than happy to offer asylum to this eminent man of the cloth involved in a dispute with the king of England.

The denouement of this episode would come many years later. Several attempts had been made at reconciliation but the stand-off persisted up to the end of 1170. After one more dramatic face to face with the king, Becket accepted to return to England "whether to peace or punishment he could not surely say." Henry himself left their last confrontation storming about the arrogance of the prelate, and at that point is said to have all but encouraged his entourage to *make the problem go away.* Among those who heeded him, four knights were anxious to show their devotion to the king by taking his muttering literally. They tracked down Becket, followed him inside Canterbury Cathedral and on December 29, 1170 after one more proud and stubborn stand by the priest of God, the knights did what they had come to do. Out came the swords, one sliced through the top of the archbishop's head before another one decapitated him.

Pope Alexander III placed the king and his territories on the continent under interdict, a harsh punishment for Christians in the

Middle Ages. Only after lengthy negotiations was Henry II reconciled with the Church.

In a world with only a few guiding forces, civil and religious authorities could not ignore each other with impunity.

While this dramatic confrontation was unfolding Henry II, whose health was declining, decided to share his kingdom among his four sons. The oldest known as Henry the Young was to reign over England, Normandy and Anjou; Richard would receive Aquitaine, Geoffrey gain control of Brittany and little was left for John, who thereafter would be surnamed Lackland. Before any of this had become a reality Henry II recovered, changed his mind and reclaimed all his powers to the great frustration of his offspring and their mother. Henry the Young had been crowned king in 1170 but had never received any realm to rule and been left short of money.

Alienor had her own source of frustration. Fourteen years and eight children into their marriage, Henry made no mystery of his affair with *fair Rosamond*. The relationship between Henry and Alienor became stormy and she left England to return to Poitiers where she felt at ease in the court life that had been hers during her youth. She sided with her sons, particularly with her favorite, Richard, when they turned against their father during the Great Revolt of 1173-74.

The French King, Louis VII, saw a chance to score points against his old enemy by joining the Great Revolt. Unfortunately for the members of the coalition, Henry II remained a powerful warrior. He defeated his sons and Louis VII, then arrested Alienor. She would be kept secluded in various castles in England up to Henry's death; the king had remained adamant that she would not go free as long as he lived. Alienor would survive him by fifteen years and during that time became again a *maitresse femme*, reasserting herself as a formidable female force, at first next to her son King Richard and then protecting young King John.

It was during the Great Revolt, in July 1174, that Henry II, upon arriving in England, rode to Canterbury to make public penance at the tomb of Thomas Becket. He walked barefoot for three miles, knelt before the tomb, was flagellated by a long cortege of men of the robe, and then stayed prone up to morning. It was a well-staged demonstration of contrition destined to impress the Church. According to the *Chronicle of Roger of Hoveden* it paid immediate dividends as "the Lord granted into him the victory over his enemies." De facto, the next day King William of Scotland, an ally of Henry the Young, was taken prisoner, and within three weeks all the fortified places in England were delivered into the king's hands.

Louis VII never was a match for Henry II on the battlefield. He was not meant to be a warrior. He had become heir to the throne following the death of his brother Philippe in a riding accident. Philippe had been a proud and arrogant troublemaker while his younger brother Louis had cherished the quiet and contemplative mood of the Abbey of Saint Denis. Alienor is said to have made the acerbic comment that she had married a monk and not a king.

Louis VII was left paralyzed by a stroke during the summer of 1179. He was too weak to make the trip to Reims in November when his son was anointed Philippe II. The new king who would be known as Philippe Auguste did not wait too long to grab the royal seal from the hands of his incapacitated father and was already immersed in royal family affairs when Louis died on September 18, 1180.

Philippe Auguste: Two Inglorious Moves and One Lucky Strike

The new French king would prove to be a strong believer in realpolitik, and exhibited traits of a modern statesman. He was pious but his piety will be too often tainted by political expediency. In 1180 he expulsed the Jews from the royal domain only to let them come back years later against payment of a tax (he would unfortunately not be the only French king using such expedients) and his policies towards the Cathars and other heretics would not be more commendable.

The state of war between the French and English royal houses became protracted. Philippe II's strategy was to take every advantage of the feuds in the English royal family. After Henry the Young, Henry's designated successor, died in 1183, and Richard, the next in line, quarreled with Geoffrey, Philippe II gave a warm welcome to Geoffrey in Paris. When the young English prince died three years later, killed during a jousting tournament, Philippe II became close to Richard. King Henry felt threatened by their open friendship and alliances between the three protagonists, Henry, Richard and Philippe formed and broke. The last act of this drama was played in 1189. Early in the year, Philippe II and Richard conspired to force the king to acknowledge Richard as his successor. The old king rejected the *diktat* and warfare flared again. In June, Philippe II and Richard closed in on the aging Henry near Le Mans. The town was set on fire, Henry escaped, and, surprisingly, rode towards Chinon and not the safety of Normandy. He knew that his end was near and must have wanted to die in the peaceful surroundings of the Loire valley. The two kings met at the *commanderie* of the local Templars where Henry surrendered and named Richard his heir. Defeated and sick, he was carried in a litter to his chateau in Chinon.

King Henry's final moments were near. Philippe II had given him the list of all those who had betrayed him and now, lying weakened in Chinon, he listened to the names of the traitors read aloud and was devastated by the revelation that his favorite son, John Lackland, had sided with his enemies. The will to live left him, he turned away from the lords at his bedside and died three days later. It was July 6, 1189, and he had reigned for thirty four years. His trusted companion, the man who had been at his side during his last years, William the Marchal, made the arrangements for the funeral at Fontevraud.

Richard was the new king and he was the first English king to use the *three lions passant guardant* (facing the viewer while striding left) which still appear on the Royal Arms of England. Two lions/leopards came from the arms of Normandy and had already been used by William the Conqueror and the third came from the arms of Aquitaine.

Royal Arms of England (1198-1340)

Early in 1188, Philippe had vowed to go on a crusade, following the lead of Richard who had made the same commitment a few months earlier. It took the two lords some time to raise the huge sums necessary to finance their expeditions and to prepare their kingdoms for their absence. Philippe II dictated a *testament*, a meaningful document for historians as it reflected a concept of public good which was a novelty for the times. At last, in July 1190, Philippe and Richard were on their way to the Holy Land. The Third Crusade had started. It would be remembered as the Kings' Crusade but would be foremost Richard's Crusade.

Philippe II would re-embark for France as early as July 1191 leaving Richard alone to face Saladin, the fiercest adversary of the Kingdom of Jerusalem. As they parted, the two kings renewed the non-aggression pact they had signed before leaving for Jerusalem. It soon would become clear that Philippe II had no intention of honoring his signature; already on his way through Rome he tried unsuccessfully to get the pope to release him from his commitment.

Why had Philippe deserted Richard in the Holy Land and returned to Europe? The two men had been quarreling ever since they had landed in Sicily as old unresolved issues kept resurfacing, particularly Richard's marriage to Philippe's sister Aelis; the engagement had been concluded twenty years earlier but Richard kept postponing the wedding. There was also jealousy; Richard was immensely popular and Philippe II paled next to the extravert English king. The official reason given by Philippe for his departure was his poor health but truth is that he wanted to take care of business in his kingdom while Richard was away. This was a first inglorious move.

Richard had an adventurous return in autumn 1192. His ship capsized, he was captured by Duke Leopold of Austria and detained by the German Emperor. Richard's mother, Alienor, did raise the huge ransom to secure his freedom and he finally reached England in March 1194. During Richard's detention Philippe schemed to avoid the release of the English king, formed an alliance with John Lackland, Richard's younger brother, and invaded Normandy.

Sometime after his return to France, in August 1193, Philippe II married Ingeborg, the sister of the King of Denmark. This surprising choice ended in a tragi-comedy which kept the Church busy for another twenty years. Two days after the wedding and one day after her coronation, Philippe II sequestered the new queen in a convent and started divorce procedures. He twisted enough arms to have his marriage annulled and in June 1196 married Agnes de Mélanie, a German princess. When Innocent III became pope two years later he revisited the previous decision and ordered Philippe to part with Agnes and return Ingeborg to her rightful place. As the French king did no such thing he was excommunicated and shortly thereafter the Church imposed an interdict on his kingdom. This was a terrible state of affairs for the people and Philippe II had to make enough promises for the Church to end the punishment. The interdict was lifted but the king still kept Ingeborg in sequestration. Méranie died in 1201; she had given Philippe two children which, the church said, were legitimate. Ingeborg was freed only in 1213; she had been kept in seclusion for nineteen years and subjected to all manners of humiliations and privations. This was a second inglorious move.

There has been much speculation about Philippe's motivations. He claimed to have been bewitched which might be a way of saying that he was impotent in her presence. He might also have lost interest in consolidating an alliance with Denmark in his fight against England.

Breaking his commitment to Richard during the Third Crusade and later, scheming to avoid his release, were true to the temperament of a man who was cunning, quick at taking advantage of the weaknesses of his opponents and unabashed at discarding a friend when it could benefit his Kingdom of France. Philippe's strategic moves helped turn France into a powerful state in Europe but he needed luck along the way, even more than luck, nothing short of a miracle.

After Richard's return from the Holy Land, Philippe's fortune took a turn for the worse. During five long years the two kings battled for control of the all-important duchy of Normandy and Philippe would be on the losing side. Many of the French king's great vassals felt close to the Plantagenets and he had to fall back on the support of the bourgeois and the clerics, in other words, the city people. His unlucky streak started with a debacle at Fréteval in July 1194, then, three years later, the counts of Hainaut and Flanders switched their allegiance to the English. In 1198, another disastrous year for Philippe II, an impressive list of French knights were captured at Vernon and Gisors. The pope attempted a mediation but Richard stubbornly resisted, still ruminating the treachery of Philippe during the crusade. There would be no peace agreement, just a five years truce.

Early in 1199 Richard went on a punitive expedition in the Limousin against some of his vassals who had sided with the French king. On March 26, he was at the foot of the chateau at *Chalus*, south of Limoges, preparing for an assault, when an arrow deeply entered his left shoulder. The wound, poorly treated, became infected and Richard understood his end was near. Alienor rushed from Fontevraud only to have her son die in her arms. This is the popular version of the death of Richard which has been romanticized in many ways. Whatever the true circumstances, the French and their King who had been under much pressure from Richard were thankful for the *miracle of Chalus.*

The deadly arrow had been fired by Pierre Basile, the feudal lord. Basile was not given a chance to be a living hero. After his surrender he was swiftly punished for his successful marksmanship. Richard had pardoned him a few days before dying but Mercadier, the feared leader of Richard's mercenaries, had little respect for last wills and Basile-the-hero died a horrible death, skinned alive.

There were two candidates for the succession to the English throne: John Lackland, the sole surviving son of Henry II, and Arthur of Brittany, a boy of 12, son of Geoffrey, Lackland's elder brother.

The Angevins and King Philippe II favored young Arthur but the English nobility picked John Lackland. The old Queen Alienor also favored her thirty-two year old son who, she thought, would give a better fight to the Capetians. John rushed to London and was crowned at Westminster in April 1199. Unfortunately for the English dynasty, the young king suffered from a pathetic sense of insecurity and would be no match for his barons and the king of the Franks.

Alienor, always on the alert and versed in feudal law, went to Tours to meet Philippe II and paid homage for all her fiefs; shortly thereafter she transferred her land rights to John. This was an excellent one-two punch which made it difficult for the Capetian to move aggressively against the Plantagenet, now a vassal for the land he controlled in the southwest. John, though, was always his worst enemy and gave the advantage back to Philippe in one impetuous move.

In the spring of 1200, King John, in the process of obtaining the annulment of his marriage to Isabelle of Gloucester, was a guest at the engagement festivities of Isabelle of Angouleme with Hughes IX of Lusignan, a baron from Poitou. For whatever reasons, probably strategic, possibly sentimental, John eloped with the very charming, very young Isabelle of Angouleme.

The Lusignans had a strong case to ask for reparation after King John abducted Isabelle but were treated with contempt. Hughes asked for the judgment of King Philippe II, suzerain of both parties. The French king was more than happy to turn the simmering feud to his advantage. John was summoned to present his case to the court of the king in April 1202, and when he did nothing of the sort, he was stripped of all his rights as landowner and feudal lord in Normandy, Maine, Anjou and Touraine.

The court had given Philippe what he hoped for, a just cause to pursue militarily his rights. He moved troops into Normandy and sent Arthur to campaign in Anjou. There, the young lord would face his tragic destiny. He was taken prisoner at Mirebeau and it is said that, shortly after, he was strangled and his body thrown in the Seine, all under the eyes of his uncle John.

Philippe II's progress into Normandy was only slowed by Chateau Gaillard. The formidable castle had been built by Richard between 1196 and 1198 at a time when the French controlled the Seine upstream and the English needed to protect the eastern access to their Norman territories. When it first had come in Richard's sight, at the top of a steep hill, the English king had found the castle *gaillard,* valiant, and it has been called *Chateau Gaillard* ever since.

Chateau Gaillard was reputed to be impregnable, protected by solid fortifications to the south, ditches to the east and precipices to the west and north. It stood in the way of Philippe's conquest of Normandy and in September 1203 the French king ordered a siege and, a few months later, an assault. The French knew that the Anglo-Normans had stocked great amounts of food and weapons and decided to avoid what could become a long standoff. Every chateau has its Achilles' heel and this one was no exception. A small group of French soldiers made their way inside the lower court of the chateau through a castle toilet. Why the English builders had left this opening unprotected a few feet above ground level on the eastern wall of the fortification remains a mystery. This story reads like a legend but the truth is that the garrison surrendered on March 6, 1204 and by the middle of the year the king of France was in control of all the Plantagenet territories north of the Loire valley. Anjou, Maine and Normandy became part of the royal domain.

The men of the king sent to administer the newly conquered territories showed flexibility, integrating Normandy in the Kingdom of the Franks while preserving local customs. The administration in Normandy which had been put in place by the first duke, and influenced by the English, in turn served as a blueprint for a reform of the administrative system in the French royal domain. This reform, which gave the men of the king more power over local leaders and introduced more rigor, had in fact been on the drawing board before the conquest but the lessons learned in Normandy certainly accelerated its implementation.

Chateau Gaillard

About seventy miles west of Paris, shortly before entering Normandy, the little town of Les Andelys spreads out along the Seine. The river, on its way to Rouen and the Atlantic, meanders lazily and captures several islands in its loops. Looming over the town and the river are the ruins of the imposing Chateau Gaillard.

Richard's chateau had several moments of fame after its capture by Philippe, one in particular at the beginning of the fourteenth century when Marguerite and Blanche, the adulterous daughters-in-law of King Philippe le Bel, were imprisoned in the chateau. Marguerite died there in 1315, possibly at the hand of an assassin sent by her husband; Blanche was kept in seclusion for eight years and after her release joined the Abbey of Maubuisson where she died in 1326. Catholics found refuge in Chateau Gaillard during the Religious Wars at the end of the sixteenth century and, shortly thereafter, Richelieu ordered the demolition of the keep.

Chateau Gaillard has been on the list of French Historical Landmarks since 1862 and welcomes numerous visitors in spring and summer. They come for the historical site and have the bonus of a sweeping panoramic view of the Seine and the Normandy countryside.

Where the Parisii First Dwelled Becomes Paris

Before leaving for the Crusade in 1190 and going to the *Orient* as the lands along the southern coast of the Mediterranean were called at the time, Philippe II thought it wise to fortify Paris. His enemy, the Plantagenets, would come from the north and the first line of defense needed to be in *le Marais,* marshes, the flatlands north of the Seine. He surrounded the Marais with an imposing defensive wall, a solid mass of stones held together by mortar, six to eight meters high, punctuated every seventy meters by round watchtowers. The western corner along the Seine was a particularly weak spot and Philippe II commissioned the building of the Louvre, a chateau flanked with defensive towers and a keep, the Grosse Tour, at its center.

The nascent Latin Quarter on the south bank, better known today as the Left Bank, would be enclosed a few years later with a similar wall. Construction on the right bank was completed by 1200 and paid for by the local bourgeoisie while funds for the enceinte, the enclosure, on the left bank came from the King's treasury.

Philippe II would later be surnamed Philippe Auguste and the wall surrounding Paris is remembered as *l'enceinte de Philippe Auguste.* In *Paris in the Middle Ages,* the historian Simone Roux notes "The history of Paris as an urban space begins with Philippe Auguste's order for the construction of the enceinte." When it ran through cultivated marshland in the Marais and vineyards on the left bank the enclosure delimited land *ad domos faciendas,* reserved for homes, a true urban space. It gave a concrete reality to the city. Paris had its place on the map.

So-called Braun Map published in 1572, clearly showing Philippe Auguste's walls within the enceinte built by Charles V in the fourteenth century.

Numerous remains of Philippe Auguste's wall are scattered throughout the Marais and the Latin Quarter. A well-preserved example stands behind the Church of Saint Paul-Saint Louis in the Marais, at the corner of rue Charlemagne and rue des Jardins. The playground built along the medieval wall leaves it in full view. The area is pleasant, and numerous shops nearby have found a home in a web of connecting courtyards. The area called *village Saint Paul* is a destination for many guided tours of the Marais.

The foundations of the original fortress of the Louvre were unearthed during archaeological excavations in the mid-1980's. The upper sections of the massive *Grosse tour* had been destroyed when the medieval chateau was replaced by a Renaissance palace at the beginning of the sixteenth century but the bottom section of the Tower and elements of the stone walls can now be seen in the lower level of the *Suffren* wing of the *Musée du Louvre*.

The Louvre lost its defensive role and its strategic importance in the middle of the fourteenth century when Charles V built a new rampart about half a mile beyond Philippe Auguste's walls. Access to the city was through fortified gates which are still in place in the twenty-first century (Porte Saint Martin, Porte Saint Denis…).

Bouvines, Communal Infantry and Magna Carta (1215)

The surname Auguste given to Philippe will be sealed by one exceptional event during his reign: his victory at the battle of *Bouvines.*

King John's defeats in Normandy called for revenge and the hostilities between the Plantagenet and the Capetian knew no reprieve. The English king kept his war chest well-filled thanks to constant levies of new taxes in England and could be generous with his allies on the continent. He knew that the vassals of the French king put their interests ahead of those of their suzerain and their loyalty could be bought. Alliances and friendships were easily broken. By 1214, two great vassals of the Capetian had declared for the Plantagenet: Ferrand, Count of Flanders who was also the son of the king of Portugal, and Renaud de Dammartin, Count of Boulogne. It was to be expected that Ferrand would side with John; he loathed Philippe. The *treason* of Renaud angered the French king to a much greater degree. They had been friends during their youth and partners in crime when Philippe had encouraged Renaud to abduct Ida of Boulogne in 1190.

This abduction is a very memorable episode. Ida had become Countess of Boulogne when her father passed away while she was only thirteen years old. She had two marriages of convenience, lost both husbands and at the age of thirty fell passionately in love with Arnould II de Guines. Arnould was not insensitive to her attention. She was a catch and this had not escaped the attention of another knight, Renaud de Dammartin. Renaud abducted the countess and for good measure captured Arnould who had rushed to the rescue of his Dulcinea. The countess married her abductor and Philippe II was more than happy to see the county of Boulogne in the hands of Renaud.

Philippe II did not benefit long from Renaud's coup. The abduction of Ida had left a trail of resentment. The de Dreux, cousins of the king, and other prominent lords turned against Renaud. Feeling trapped, the Count of Boulogne threw his lot with the enemy of the Capetian, the English.

The remarkable adventures of Ida and Renaud were not uncommon in the Middle Ages. Lords and knights were conscious of the importance of marital ties. Next to exploits on the battlefield they offered the best chances to climb the social ladder. Marriages also highly mattered for a family and a clan; they could consolidate alliances, seal peace agreements or pacify an enemy. Sons and daughters were assets not to be wasted in unproductive marriages and feelings came second behind strategic needs. It was not rare for men to part with a partner that had served her purpose, to elope with a woman engaged to someone else or to marry a child. The popes were kept busy deciding on annulment requests, annulment being the politically correct way of describing a divorce and the most common *diriment impediment* was consanguinity.

King John secured one more powerful member for his anti-Philippe Auguste coalition, Otto IV of Brunswick, Holy Roman Emperor and King of Germany. Shortly after being crowned emperor in October 1209, Otto had betrayed the interests of the pope and become entangled in Italian politics. At the instigation of Philippe Auguste, the pope had campaigned for the election of another German king, Frederick. Otto saw in the French king his strongest obstacle in his wild ambition to become the successor of Charlemagne. He also knew that John would be very generous if he turned against the French king.

The English king decided on a two-pronged attack. He would take the fight to Poitou and the south while Otto, Ferrand, Renaud and other circumstantial allies closed in on the French from the north. In February 1214, King John landed in La Rochelle. Philippe didn't take the bait. He knew the real danger would come from the north and sent his son, the future Louis VIII, to fight the English while he set out for Flanders. Lords coming mostly from the heart of the Frankish kingdom joined the *ost du roi*, the king's army; none of his vassals south of the Loire felt concerned by the confrontation.

Philippe II could count on close to 3,000 knights, as many sergeants on horseback and up to 6,000 men on foot, a group the English called the *communal infantry* which would play a prominent role in the mythology of the upcoming battle. The French king had granted numerous tax exemptions to villages and cities in the north of France, and they, in turn, owed him military assistance; these *laboratores* from more than thirty-nine such communes had converged on the battlefield to form a great mass of foot soldiers. The enemy coalition was at least of equal strength. All in all, it would be a formidable concentration of military power.

The *ost* of the French king pillaged and ravaged as it rode through enemy territory in Flanders and reached Tournai on July 26. On the morning of that very day the king was informed that Otto and the other members of the enemy coalition were only a short distance to the south, along the border with the Empire. The French were in inhospitable terrain, deep into Flanders and at first Philippe II made the safe move and took his forces west towards the bridge at Bouvines, halfway between Lille and Tournai. Then, he faced a tactical choice: retreat and pull the enemy further away from the border with Germany or stand his ground. Fate took the call from his hands. The next day, July 27, was a Sunday, the Lord's Day, a day when the swords should stay in their scabbards but no force could hold the warriors apart any longer. The *oriflamme* brought from Saint Denis had yet to be raised on the front line of Philippe II's troops when fighting started. Otto fled the field while the battle was still raging and by sunset the coalition was in retreat. It had been a heroic confrontation, a true battle, a rare event at a time when ambushes, raids and sieges were the ordinary course of wars.

The encounters had been true to chivalric codes: few knights had been killed, many were taken prisoner and would be set free against payment of a *ransom*. This is how knights made a living; a dead enemy knight was a waste of a good reward. This is also how a rich but unlucky knight could become a poor knight. The payment of his ransom was a personal commitment — he followed a banner into battle but was on his own once taken prisoner. The defeated knight surrendered to his victor on the battlefield and the two sides settled their affairs later, sometimes much later, after the money for the ransom had been raised. It was a strong moral obligation that true knights did not dare break.

The king was the grand prize. Philippe II was pulled down from his horse by hooks swirled by foot soldiers and about to be captured when a handful of devoted knights came to the rescue.

The battle was chronicled by Guillaume le Breton, Philippe's chaplain, a cantor close to the king, who had been at his side during the battle. Guillaume started on the minutes as soon as victory had been declared. Over time, Bouvines was given a symbolic aura, the legends taking precedence over the facts. A favorite tale says that before riding into battle, Philippe II placed his scepter and his crown on an altar, and loudly proclaimed that if someone was worthier than he to defend the crown he was ready to move aside. The soldiers, moved by his words, cried out *long live the king*. The illustrated version of this episode would commonly be given a place of honor in history books during the early twentieth century.

Philippe Auguste before the battle of Bouvines

Philippe Auguste's victory on the field of battle had far-reaching consequences. He had shown his might to the vassals who had betrayed their oath of loyalty and they would be severely punished; Renaud, who had sworn to kill the king, was imprisoned for life at Peronne. Philippe Auguste had triumphed over a coalition masterminded by John. The English king, who had also been defeated by Philippe's son, would sign a peace agreement a few months later. The vassals of the French king who stood on the sidelines waiting for the outcome lost their leverage; playing John against Philippe was no longer an option.

The stature of Bouvines grew during the nineteenth century. It became a *lieu de memoire*, a building block of the patrimony of France. Over time it was given appropriate symbolic interpretations. The French Revolution and the subsequent Republics handed the decisive role in the battle to the communal infantry; Bouvines became the victory of the people of France against a coalition of foreign lords. After France had been cruelly defeated by Bismarck in 1870, the memory of Bouvines was glorified as a triumph primarily over the German Emperor, Otto.

Bouvines was Philippe Auguste's swan song. In the autumn of 1222 his health deteriorated and by July of 1223 he was dead. He had decided, despite his weakness, to travel to Paris to supervise the preparation of another Crusade and did not survive the trip. His body was taken to Saint Denis and his tomb placed next to Dagobert's.

The surname Auguste given to Philippe came from the pen of Rigord, the monk at Saint Denis who chronicled the life of the king in his *Gesta Philippi Augusti*. Rigord was acknowledging a successful reign marked, among other achievements, by a sizeable territorial expansion of the kingdom. After the death of Rigord around 1207, the *Gesta* was continued by Guillaume le Breton and others.

The battle at Bouvines had also been a turning point for England. King John's wars were costly. His defeats and those of his allies on the continent encouraged the English barons to rebel against the heavy tax burden that he imposed, and against his abuse of power. John, pressured to negotiate with the barons, signed the agreement later known as the *Magna Carta* in June 1215, a catalogue of things he could no longer do. The Charter was a reminder to the king that he was not the alpha and omega of his kingdom; there was a higher order of justice by which he had to abide. Chapter thirty-nine of the original asserts that "no free man shall be seized or imprisoned... except by lawful judgment of his equals or by the law of the land." Over time the Magna Carta seemed to belong more to the Americans than to the English. The rebellious colonists referred to the Charter and echoes of the quoted chapter are audible in the American Bill of Rights.

The Magna Carta did not bring peace between King John and the Barons. Their antagonism was still heated when the king died suddenly in October 1216. As to the widowed queen of England there will be more extravagant stories in her life. Isabelle married Hughes X of Lusignan, the son of Hughes IX, the Lusignan to whom she had been engaged when she was abducted by John. She had taken her daughter to be wedded with Hughes X but the young seigneur de Lusignan preferred the mother to the daughter.

Renaissance of the Twelfth Century

A Renaissance!

The Renaissance of the Twelfth Century, is the iconoclastic title of a book written in 1927 by Charles Homer Haskins, the great American medieval historian.

How daring of a man writing in the early twentieth century to apply a label commonly attached to the *bright* Italian Renaissance of the fifteenth century to a period of the *dark* Middle Ages. Haskins did note in the preface that his title appears to contain a flagrant contradiction. It is resolved, he writes, when one realizes that the Middle Ages were less dark and static and the Italian Renaissance less bright than once supposed.

It was only in the middle of the nineteenth century that *Renaissance,* in the context of Haskins' title, became the qualifier for a defined period in the history of art and literature. Without the label, the *Quattrocento* had previously been acknowledged as a period of renewal and one of its most passionate extollers had been Petrarch. The poet had gone to Rome in 1341 and had an epiphany at the sight of Roman ruins. In his eyes, how splendid the city must have been during the *historiae antiquae!* By contrast, the centuries since the fall of the Western Roman Empire, the *historiae novae*, became the Dark Ages. Christianity had expanded during these more recent times and the celebrated poet became an acerbic critic of the Church. His ire was directed particularly at the popes in Avignon. Petrarch had lived in Avignon during his youth and benefited from the largesse of the pope but this did not stop him from being a harsh critic of the Church which, in his days, was not the Church *in* Rome but the Church *in* Avignon.

In awe of Greek and Roman antiquity and critical of Christianity, Petrarch was receptive to an artistic revival which he saw budding at the court of King Robert in Naples. The poet much admired this Angevin dynasty that did so much for the arts and in particular its champion, Giotto, who had completed the decoration of the Scrovegni Chapel in Padua in 1305. Petrarch, Boccaccio and other humanists *introduced the notion* of revival later called Renaissance and, by contrast, the darkness of the bygone Middle Ages.

It would become an unfortunate practice, in the footsteps of the humanists, to lump the centuries after the fall of Rome into one dark age and thus overlook beautiful periods of *light.* There had been, within the Middle Ages, intellectual revivals which, for convenience sake, were called Renaissance. The first one, at the time of Charlemagne, the Carolingian Renaissance, was primarily concerned with language (Latin), script and bookmaking. This first revival was modest in scope, and mostly the product of the court for the benefit of the elite of the monarchy and the church. The next Renaissance was Haskins' in the twelfth century.

This Renaissance saw the revival of architecture, law, philosophy and learning. It was actually, in Haskins's words, more an intensification of intellectual life rather than new creations, and it was so truly widespread that in his opus the American historian confined himself to one topic, the revival of learning in the broadest sense.

The terrain was favorable. The economy had grown at a healthy rate, and in those days this meant, above all, an increase in agricultural output. Famine had receded due to better farming techniques and more favorable climatic conditions; it had been abnormally warm in the North Atlantic between 1000 and 1300, a climatic period known as the Little Optimum (which would be followed by the Little Ice Age). Population growth was noticeable; during these three centuries the number of inhabitants in the Kingdom of the Franks doubled to about 17 million (this is more an approximation than a reliable absolute number; demographic data relating to the Middle Ages are usually very soft.) The trend would be reversed when the *Black Death,* the plague in the middle of the fourteenth century, and the Hundred Years' War, caused a serious decline of the population in the kingdom.

The development of urban centers created an environment favorable for a more intense intellectual life. Urban schools took the baton from monastic schools. They were mostly so-called cathedral and canonical schools and operated under the authority of the bishops. These bishops had been the beneficiaries of the Gregorian Reform and now played an important role in the life of the church. They had urban residences and the centers of gravity of the Church moved to the cities.

The curriculum in the urban schools no longer focused on Latin and the exegesis of the Bible and now incorporated subjects neglected since Antiquity. It still started with the *trivium* of grammar, rhetoric and dialectic and the *quadrivium* of arithmetic, geometry, astronomy and music and then added new areas of learning in science and philosophy.

Most of the added body of knowledge came from the Greeks and the Arabs. The great works of the Greeks had remained untranslated in classical antiquity. The Greek tradition had stayed alive in the eastern empire but the ancient classics had not been available in the Latin West. Then, in the ninth century, works which had been left to gather dust by the Byzantines, were brought to life by the Arabs. Scholars from the so-called House of Wisdom in Bagdad had translated these texts from Greek to Arabic. A House of Wisdom might never have actually existed but a translation movement destined to make ancient Greek texts available to Arabs had become particularly active. The philosophical works of Plato and Aristotle and, as importantly, the medical books of Galen and Hippocrates were translated. These opuses which had been taken east by heretic Christians, Monophysites and Nestorians, made their way west. It is often said that the clerics who followed the knights during the Crusades and were in close contact with the Byzantine Empire, gained access to these and other documents. Most probably, the books written in Greek and transcribed in Arabic followed numerous routes to reach the Latin West. Haskins notes that North Africa was the great highway between the East and Spain and most of the new learning reached Western Europe through the Spanish peninsula. There, starting in the twelfth century, the opuses were translated into Latin; Toledo was one of the best known translation centers. The direct route through Sicily and the Italian peninsula was another major axis and along the route, Pisa was a vibrant translation center.

The cathedral schools where the expanded curriculum would be taught, were not tangible brick and mortar facilities, there was no fixed term of studies. A school was an itinerant body of students sharing a devotion to certain teachers. They met here and there, in a room or a hallway near the cathedral. Teachers lectured there for a while and then continued their wandering. Abelard, one of the most admired masters of the time, famous for his debates with Bernard de Clairvaux, pitting dialectic against faith, always drew great crowds of students. He taught at the Cathedral School of Notre Dame de Paris and the Collegiate Church of Sainte-Geneviève and his students followed him for extended periods of time to Corbeil or Melun.

At one point, the cathedral school morphed into a new institution called *university.* The first official acknowledgment of a University of Paris goes back to 1200 when King Philippe Auguste granted his protection and the privilege to be judged by ecclesiastical tribunals to the *Universitatis magistorum et scolarium parisiensium,* in other words, the community of teachers and students in Paris. This marks the origin of the name of the institution and the first acknowledgement of a body of scholars. The by-laws would be written a few years later and approved by the pope.

The king's decision was prompted by a bloody battle between students and the men of the marshal of Paris. Marshal Thomas had been heavy-handed in breaking up a fight in a tavern, resulting in the death of five students. During the following days, the teachers had threatened to leave Paris if the men of the marshal were not severely punished. The king knew how important it was to pacify students and teachers who increasingly contributed to the fame of Paris. The marshal paid the price; he spent the rest of his life in jail. The students, on the other hand, received the benefit of a *privilegium regale*, regal privilege.

Thanks to this brawl the name of Philippe Auguste has remained attached to the early history of the University of Paris. This is hardly a deserved legacy as the king would otherwise not show much interest in intellectual matters during his reign. Paris would become the template for other universities in the kingdom. During the last centuries of the Middle Ages, the University of Paris would break its ties with the Church and become one of the great intellectual and cultural centers in Western Europe. It would earn great repute for the quality of its philosophy and theology departments, becoming the reference for religious doctrine and known as the *shield of faith.* Students came from all over Europe;

language was not an issue as Latin was the lingua franca of the day. Latin gave its name to the section of town with the highest concentration of schools, the *Quartier Latin,* the Latin Quarter.

An open urban environment was more conducive to the propagation of ideas than isolated, rural monasteries, and this is where the new mendicant orders thrived.

The mendicants preached in vernacular, not in Latin, and did so mostly in cities. They belonged to new religious orders offering an alternative to coenobitic monasticism and introducing a spirit of renewal in the Church. The monks had been immune to the changes affecting society, and the spirituality of the followers of the rule of Saint Benedict no longer corresponded to the aspirations of society in the kingdom. All the while, a recruitment limited to members of the aristocracy had slowly eroded the discipline in their communities. The impact of these unfavorable trends had been considerable. The number of new monasteries had floundered between 1200 and 1300 and very few had been created thereafter.

The most influential mendicants would be the Dominicans, disciples of the Spaniard Saint Dominic, born in 1170, and the Franciscans, followers of Saint Francis of Assisi, born in Italy in 1181. While the Benedictine monks had been searching for God through an ascetic life, isolated from the world, the Dominicans, known as Blackfriars in England, and the Franciscans, wanted to spread the Good News among lay people. They vowed to embrace poverty and live at the mercy of charity. The tone had been set in a spectacular manner by Saint Francis, the son of a rich cloth merchant, who, unmoved by the pleas of his father to renounce his vow of poverty, publicly stripped off all his fine clothing and left his town to live like a beggar.

There was another noteworthy institution known as *college* intended for poor students. In 1253, Robert de Sorbon founded the college which bears his name, the Sorbonne. A few years earlier the Cistercians, encouraged by the pope, had established the College Saint Bernard in Paris, better known today as *College des Bernardins.* For four centuries it was a center of excellence for Catholic teaching and research, but it did not survive the Revolution in 1789. The medieval building was being used as a fire station when it was bought by the City of Paris in 2001; the archbishop of Paris then decided to use it again as a center for learning and reflections. Now, fully restored and opened to the public, the beauty of its peaceful architecture and the quality of its symposia and conferences make it one of the jewels of Paris.

The Time of the Cathedrals

The conditions favoring a revival of social and artistic life also enabled the rise of a new architectural style. It started in France, spread to neighboring countries, England at the end of the twelfth century, Germany sometime later and then both countries gave it their own interpretation. This new style was disparagingly called Gothic as early as the sixteen century and this label has been commonly used since the nineteenth century. Saint Denis, consecrated in 1144, is recognized as the first Gothic religious building and Chartres, built between 1184 and 1220 as the queen of all Gothic cathedrals.

While Romanesque architecture had found a home mostly in rural areas of southern France, this was an urban art. The style of the massive cathedrals rising amidst cobwebs of narrow streets became contemptuously named after the barbaric Goths by men in awe of the Renaissance. Those who praised the re-birth of art, the Italian Renaissance, could not bring themselves to give credit to the architectural masterpieces of the twelfth century. They would say that the builders had found their inspiration in the impenetrable forests of Germania, that the pointed arch reminded them of overlapping treetops. They could not foresee that these cathedrals so disparagingly called Gothic would become one of the glories of French architecture.

Broken arches and ribs seemingly floating in space, awe-inspiring rose windows at both ends of transepts, are clues of a Gothic style inside of religious edifices; outside, flying buttresses, these strong shoulders of stones that enclose the vessel and seem to carry its weight, are one more defining feature. Pointed arches, rib vaulting and flying buttresses allow elevation and light and are the hallmarks of Gothic edifices.

Churches and abbeys built in the Romanesque style of rounded arches and heavy walls offered an environment propitious for prayer and meditation. By contrast, the Gothic cathedrals are all verticality and luminosity. The rays of the sun piercing through the rose windows are ladders to the sky; there is room for imagination while the previous architectural style had inspired restraint. The Romanesque walls enclosed the penitent and protected his solitary reflection; the Gothic rose windows would invite him to find a way to God.

Despite what appears today as striking differences, there was no abrupt break between Romanesque and Gothic styles. In many structures, barrel and pointed vaults coexist and in France and elsewhere, the new style evolved during and after the twelfth century. Nevertheless, a new style did come into its own, was called Gothic and gained respectability in the nineteenth century.

What is known about the process of building a Gothic cathedral in the north of France during the second half of the twelfth century? Nothing much actually. There are no archives of maps and drawings; the names of the architects/ builders are best-guesses and so are the sources of the financing of these colossal projects which lasted for decades. Who made the decisions before and during construction? The bishop and the chapter of the canons head the list, next in line are the architects/master builders and then, possibly, a patron interested in attaching his name to the venture, a successful urban bourgeois trying to rival the castles of rural lords.

What drove bishops, canons, master builders and patrons to seek taller, brighter, unobstructed places to worship and show piety? There is no easy answer. The search for light and elevation might have been driven by the Neo-Platonist concept that light is a measure of beauty and the belief that the rays of the sun filtering into the cathedrals would help the faithful find the way to God. Suger sought *lux continua* and is given much credit for the transformation of the Basilica of Saint Denis (2018) in the twelfth century.

A prosaic view would be that more light might have been permitted by technical innovations; flying buttresses have supported the choir at Notre Dame in Paris as early as 1170 and better glass making and high quality staining was achieved during the same period. Which was the driving force, the theology or the technology? The answer might best be found in the merging of several trends, a spiritual, a social and a technological—as Philip Ball writes in *Universe of Stone*, these cathedrals are the embodiment of a period.

Over time these giants of stone have suffered multiple scars, being mutilated by nature and man. Fires and floods, bombs and desecrations have not spared them. It seems to be in the nature of Gothic cathedrals to be damaged, even destroyed. The wooden frame and elevation, the central location in urban areas and the high visibility make them particularly vulnerable. But they are such symbols of man's esthetic achievements that after each wound that could be fatal the community finds the will and the means to reconstruct, restore and preserve. This was the case again in April 2019 after a fire devastated the wood structure, the forest as it was called, and the roof of Notre Dame in Paris. Notre Dame and other emblematic Gothic cathedrals speak to the secular as much as to the religious and belong to the patrimony of mankind.

Saint Denis: Visiting the Basilica

The first ever Gothic religious building bears the name of the legendary historical figure of Saint Denis, and its relevance in any *Tour of French History* is uncontested.

Basilica of Saint Denis (2018)

The front and back of the Gothic Basilica of Saint Denis were built between 1135 and 1144. The vaults in the narthex are ribbed and pointed and, in the easternmost part of the basilica, the stained glass windows behind the double ambulatory capture every ray of morning sunlight. The basilica bears the mark of Suger but he did not see it in its full glory; he died at least a hundred years before the middle section of the Romanesque building was transformed during the High Gothic period. This middle section is characterized by a triforium with glass windows, one more feature allowing ever more light to enter the basilica.

The royal necropolis at Saint Denis went through troubled times at the end of the eighteenth century. In early August 1793 the elected assembly called *Convention* decided to destroy the *fastueux mausolees,* sumptuous mausoleums. The extremists who pushed for total destruction of everything having to do with kings did come to a compromise with the moderates who saw a French monument that deserved to be preserved: the remains found in the tombs would be thrown in a common grave and most of the empty gisants would be preserved for posterity.

Restoration of the inside and the outside of the basilica was ongoing in the nineteenth century and was led during the first half of that century by the architect Francois Debret. His name remains attached to the controversy surrounding the north tower and spire. Violent storms in 1842 and 43 and a hurricane in 1845 seriously damaged the north tower and Debret decided to take down the spire. For that and other reasons he was the victim of a cabal and resigned in 1846. As soon as Viollet-le-Duc, his successor, who had been no stranger to this affair, was in place, he removed the north tower and made plans to restore the façade and rebuild the north tower and spire. This project remained dormant as Viollet-le-Duc's attention was diverted to other priorities.

Since 1987, the reconstruction of the tower and the flèche, spire, have been again under consideration. Then, in 2012, this venture received renewed interest when the façade was restored and in 2017 its chances of success further increased when it was endorsed by the State, landlord of the Basilica. The latest project calls for the construction of a true replica of the original at the time of Viollet-le-Duc, based on plans and drawings archived since 1847; stones kept during all these years in the gardens will be reused. As expected, not everyone in the world of architecture praises this choice. This is par for the course whenever a major renovation or construction is planned on a building as iconic as the Basilica.

The construction site will make good use of a novel concept—the craftsmen will use medieval techniques and tools and it will be opened to the public. Visitors will see stonemasons, glassmakers, blacksmiths and other craftsmen at work. Then, thanks to a one hundred and thirty feet high metal structure to be built along its northern face, they will have a unique and close-up overview of the Basilica and the site.

As of the middle of 2019, the green light for this project, which should take more than ten years to complete, was pending resolution of some technical issues. Entry fees to the site will be the major source of funding and the commune of Saint Denis expects that word about this project will benefit its image.

The basilica is best visited with a guide. The nave, off-limits for tourists, is bathed in light and radiates a feeling of warmth but the building itself usually remains cold. The guided tour starts in the south side of the transept. On both sides of the nave are fourteen of the sixteen gisants commissioned by Saint Louis. The Merovingians are represented by Clovis II, Dagobert's son and the first Carolingians by Charles Martel and Pepin le Bref near the south entrance. The early Capetians, Robert the Pious and Henri I, son and grandson of Hugues Capet, are on the other side of the nave. The symbolic placement of Philippe Auguste in the middle of the nave to represent the critical link between the dynasties has not survived wars and revolutions.

When Saint Louis ordered the repositioning of the gisants, Dagobert was left in his original place, looking at Saint Denis, and a monumental tomb was built in his honor. The Merovingian king is lying on his left side, at the base of an imposing tympanum divided into three sections, each one rich in sculpted characters. They act out a fable that became popular in the thirteenth century. The soul of the king, represented as a naked child and surrounded by other sinners, bound for hell, is pulled by Saint Denis from the grasp of the devils and taken to paradise. The message is clear: kings, whatever your sins, if you are buried in the basilica, Saint Denis will take you through the doors of heaven.

Tomb of Henri II (1519-1559)

The imposing Renaissance tombs of Francois I and Henri II in the south and north wings of the transept, inspired by Italian sculptors, are in marked contrast to the medieval gisants. After generations of leaders who, at the time of their deaths, showed humility and acknowledged divine power, the kings of the Renaissance sought glorification. The double-decker tombs combine the recumbent king and queen naked, elderly and very dead with, on top of the monument, the royal couple, resurrected to its glorious appearance, kneeling and praying.

The tour ends in the crypt where the vestiges of the original church and ancient Merovingian sarcophagi have been preserved. The crypt is also the sepulture of members of the last dynasty, the Bourbons, six austere black tombstones near the ossuary. The nostalgic of the *ancien régime* gather there to pay their respect to Louis XVI and Marie Antoinette, the tragic victims of the revolution of 1789. They come mostly every January 21 to commemorate the anniversary of the beheading of the king.

It is always cold in the basilica in January but this does not deter large crowds from making the pilgrimage to honor the king's memory; navy blue winter coats with the regal touch of long white scarves are *de rigueur*. For most it was an adventure of sorts to come to this part of

Paris even more so when they rub elbows with the locals during their subway ride. The mood during a long mass in Latin and a sermon fondly recalling the king's life is solemn, as befits the circumstances. The most emotional moment comes after the *Ite missa est*, when the testament of the king is read. It is the confession of a man who knew he was not going to be assisted by a priest at the time of death. It is also the wish list of a pater familias who had not yet been confronted with the thought that his family would not survive him for long. Among the thoughts for his son, one stands out: "If you have the misfortune to become king..."

Saint Denis: Visiting the Commune

The commune (township) of Saint Denis is home to a very diverse population, a cross-section of people from the metropole and France's former colonies. Parisians from the arrondissements further south often shy away from this suburb and riots in early 2016 contributed to worsen the reputation of Saint Denis. This is unfortunate as the surroundings of the basilica can be very lively and engaging.

The heart of the commune is easily accessible, a stone's throw away from the metro station. A large open space shared with the nearby Hotel de Ville allows for an undisturbed view of the façade of the basilica, the decorated portals and the single spire. The area is usually quiet, none of the bustling and buzzing that must have enlivened this space in the Middle Ages. The place can become animated at the end of a civil wedding when newlyweds of North African Algerian descent are surrounded by a party rocking to the sound of drums and flutes, *tbels* and *zornas* as the instruments are called. Saturday is market day, and the main street, stretching downhill from the basilica, is colorful and so is the food market housed in a nineteenth century metal and glass structure behind City Hall. There, stalls overflow with exotic staples, every manner of vegetable, spice and meat items meant to satisfy the culinary tastes of descendants of immigrants who have come to France in waves since the end of the nineteenth century.

Away from the lively place and busy main street, to the right of the basilica, is a stern building hidden behind a long wall. It houses the *Maison d'Education de la Legion d'Honneur*, a French secondary school founded by Napoleon. After the Revolution of 1789 the Abbey had stood empty and in 1809 the Emperor gifted it to the Order of the Legion d'Honneur with covenants to establish a school for daughters of legionnaires. He defined the type of education they should receive, one that would keep them modest and prepare them well to become efficient housewives. Things have changed since Napoleon. Discipline is still strict but the Maison d'Education delivers now a high level of education preparing girls for a variety of careers. Unfortunately, it can only be visited on rare occasions.

The *Marché aux Puces*, the Flea Market, the largest antique market in the world is within a (very) short taxi ride from the basilica. It is not administratively in the commune of Saint Denis but in the nearby commune of Saint Ouen. The Flea Market is a major tourist attraction, a heaven for seekers of collectibles as well as for connoisseurs of antiques and is probably on the "to do list" of most visitors to Paris.

The origins of this flea market can be traced to the thirteenth century when ragmen could first be seen in the streets of Paris. Many centuries later they became an eyesore for the burgeoning bourgeoisie and, in the 1860's, as Baron Haussmann was aggressively rebuilding Paris, were forced to resettle outside the walls surrounding the city. They congregated in fields north of Paris, in the area now known as Clignancourt and built the first dealers' stalls at the end of the nineteenth century. On weekends, they would crowd the *guingettes*, these outdoor cafes so ubiquitous on the outskirts of the city. Over time the dealers of collectibles and antiques replaced the ragmen; since the 1920's they have taken over an ever-increasing area and today have their shops in more than a dozen markets.

Countless stalls still crowd the sidewalks. They are colorful reminders that most of North and many West African countries were once French colonies. Leather belts made in Morocco and wooden masks carved in Mali compete with French berets. Foreign visitors negotiate prices in pidgin English sprinkled with French words and enlivened by an abundance of hand signs. The crowd is dense, the music blaring and the air rich in smells of French fries and cigarette smoke.

Serious second-hand and antique dealers belong in the numerous alleys off the *Rue des Rosiers*. This narrow road runs through the heart of the Flea Market and opens to at least fifteen subsidiary markets. Marché

Dauphine is a recent one, a brick building supported by a metallic structure reminiscent of les Halles.

For most marchés, for Dauphine, Paul Bert or the older Vernaison, the label *flea* is only a nod to their past. One-room stores filled with furniture, books, paintings or disparate objects invite the shopper to stroll in, touch and bargain. The regulars know where to look for rare books, prints or jewelry but they also stop and rummage through objects that used to fill a grandmother's attic.

The flea markets are best visited during lunchtime, the time of day when their Frenchness is most evident. The owners of neighboring stores congregate around make-shift dining tables and bring out bottles of wine, appetizing *saucissons* and, of course, crusty baguettes. Some of them are ensconced in antique armchairs, others perched on folding chairs and they chat, mostly oblivious to ambling prospective clients. The mood is unhurried. Even serious buyers seem to have time on their hands. In each alley the browsers are immersed in memories of times past. The objects they touch, feel, weigh or even wear represent a moment in the history of France.

Les Puces is worth a visit not only for those with an eye for antiques but for visitors ready to immerse themselves in a colorful crowd. It might be filled with tourists but the vendors give it a definite French touch. The markets are doing business only three days a week. They come alive on Saturday morning and all the wares are packed up again on Monday evening.

Notre-Dame de Chartres

The tradition started in 1935 and almost every year since, thousands of students from the Ile de France have gone on pilgrimage to Notre Dame de Chartres. They follow the example set by Charles Peguy, the poet, who twice walked from his home, south of Paris, to the cathedral. He had gone in June 1912 to pray to the Virgin for the recovery of his sick son and died shortly after his second journey; he was one of the first to fall during the First World War. Peguy inspired countless pilgrims to take the road to the home of Mary. During their long march they read his *Presentation de la Beauce a Notre Dame de Chartres* written in the mode of an ancient litany, well suited to a slow rhythmic walk. They will expect to catch sight of *la fleche irreprochable*, the south spire of the cathedral rising above an ocean of wheat in the plain of Beauce. After three or more days, as they reach the parvis, they will recite five prayers written by Peguy the poet-pilgrim.

The fleches of Notre Dame de Chartres

Charles le Chauve, Charlemagne's grandson, started Chartres on the road to fame when, in 876, he gifted the *sancta camisa,* the tunic worn by Mary at the time of the birth of Jesus, to what became known as Mary's cathedral. When the Marian cult flourished in the twelfth century the relic attracted large crowds and the town became a prominent destination for pilgrimages.

During the High Middle Ages Chartres housed a renowned school, the *école de Chartres.* Under the guidance of Fulbert, bishop between 1006 and 1028, the school's reputation spread throughout Europe. The école de Chartres flourished again during the twelfth century when it was influenced by platonician philosophers; one of their disciples was Jean de Salisbury, Thomas Becket's secretary and later bishop of Chartres.

Today's solid stone building, famous for its High Gothic style, stands on the site of a burned down wooden Romanesque cathedral. Its construction started during the last years of the twelfth century and lasted up to 1260. During the subsequent centuries there would be recurring additions and changes, the chancel in particular would go through a major remodeling in the eighteenth century.

Notre Dame de Chartres is the queen of all French Gothic cathedrals. An icon in the high spheres of art, culture and religion it inspired not only poets but also writers and philosophers. When Oswald Spengler compares culture epochs in *The Decline of the West* Chartres is there, at the peak of western culture around 1300.

Chartres, south transept rose and lancet windows

Chartres has the richest collection of stained-glass windows of any cathedral. Rose and lancet windows, all richly decorated, are walls of glass, unobstructed by pillars and columns. Arches transfer the weight to massive piers outside of the building. These flying buttresses surrounding the cathedral are distinctive features of Chartres and of other tall Gothic structures. Numerous sculptures adorn the facade and the north and south porches; Old Testament themes predominate in the north portals and the familiar Last Judgment is in the central south portal.

Chartres is said to be the best preserved example of Gothic architecture in France. Much work is ongoing to preserve the outside structure and the statuary. As to the interior and the stained-glass windows, a major renovation was started in 2009 and was still ongoing ten years later. The meticulous cleaning of the darkened stones has revealed the pale ochre tones of the original plaster; the painted stones are now bright and colorful. Their sight delivers a shock and is a reminder that the use of color was common in Antiquity and the Middle Ages, witness the color reconstruction of Roman marble statues and keystones of Gothic cathedrals, based on surviving traces of pigment.

While work was in process the surprising luminosity of the renovated nave stood in sharp contrast to the still somber transept. The stated purpose of this makeover, as it has been called, was to return the building to its original appearance. This goal as well as the decision-making process leading to the overall renovation have been questioned particularly by medievalists in the U.S. They do not doubt that the interior of the cathedral had become dark and the grime a distraction even when it enhanced the colors of the stained-glass windows but why, they ask, do more than cleaning? Layers of plaster and paint superposed over many centuries are hiding behind the grime, which ambiance should the restoration recreate?

The stained-glass windows also have been cleaned and repaired while the scaffoldings were in place. They are the *pieces de resistance* of Chartres, 175 overall of which 150 are originals, each one a composition of richly colored glass pictures arranged row by row, column by column, to tell a story. Most themes are religious, some are secular and a few recall events of the time; among those, the notable ones are the martyrdom of Thomas A Becket and the rose window donated by Blanche de Castille, mother of Saint Louis.

The Virgin and the
Three Queens

In *Mont Saint Michel and Chartres* Henry Adams makes the bold statement that the Virgin and three Queens ruled French taste and thought during the great period of Gothic architecture. The name of the Virgin, *Notre Dame*, is attached to many great Gothic cathedrals. The three queens are headed by Alienor, "Queen by the wrath of God" as she called herself. She was in Adams' eyes the greatest of all French queens. Her daughter, Marie de Champagne, was not a queen in title "but certainly a queen in social influence." She did, wrote Adams, create the literature of courtly love. The third queen was Blanche de Castille, one of Alienor's granddaughters and mother of Saint Louis.

"Notre Dame" and the Marian Century

The most admired cathedrals built during the High Middle Ages had been placed under the protection of Mary. The glorious cathedrals in Chartres, Paris, Amiens and Reims were dedicated to Mary, to *Notre Dame*, Our Lady. What does this say about the approach that people had to the sacred, especially the all-important role ascribed to the divine as a protector against the hazards of everyday life? The imposing cathedrals rising in the middle of towns in the Kingdom of the Franks were vessels reaching for the sky. These intricate stone compositions were conduits for messages of hope, and could be trusted to carry requests for life saving graces and expressions of boundless gratitude.

The need for divine assistance was ever-present in the lives of people in the High Middle Ages. Their land faced repeated devastations in the wake of invaders and warlords, their clans were decimated by plagues which they saw as a punishment for their sins and they were powerless in their struggle against a hostile nature. There was only faith to combat adversity; reason was not yet considered a potent weapon. Faith was in the God of the Church of Rome, His son Jesus and the Holy Ghost. This Trinity, though, was too overbearing, too out of reach and people were afraid that their prayers would not reach such heights. They needed someone closer to them, someone who would understand their pleas and carry them to their savior.

In special circumstances people had always called upon saints, the successors of sorts of the gods of the Romans, but Dante in his *Commedia*, renamed *The Divine Comedy* at the beginning of the fourteenth century, did not place familiar saints in the highest order of the Mystic Rose. Mary is the one sitting in the topmost tier of the *heavenly stadium*. During the High Middle Ages people put their faith in the Virgin Mary, the most approachable and reassuring intercessor. She was their Lady and they honored her by building and placing under her protection dozens of cathedrals as well as hundreds of churches and an even greater number of so-called Lady Chapels. The cathedrals and churches honoring Our Lady and the places where she was said to have performed miracles became the destination of pilgrimages, a focal point for people in search of communion and comfort.

In *Mont Saint Michel and Chartres* Henry Adams, in an effort to be convincing for the "religious American mind," introduces the dollars and cents side of the building of Lady Type of Churches. His computation leads him to conclude that the magnitude of the investments made in the Virgin during the High Middle Ages "expresses an intensity of conviction never again reached by any passion." He then writes,

> "Dragged by a Byzantine court, backed by popular insistence and impelled by overpowering self-interest, the Church accepted the Virgin throned and crowned…"

This faith in Mary has continued to flourish since the end of the Middle Ages even if it never again matched the extremes reached in the twelfth century. *Lumen gentium*, Light of nations, a fundamental document of the Second Vatican Council, Vatican II, convened in 1964, included a very delicately worded reminder that love for Mary is essentially different from the adoration due to God and His Son. The specificity of the Marian cult was not reaffirmed only to pacify the Protestant brethren but also truly reflected the historical moderation of the leaders of the Church in the face of intense popular veneration.

Devotion to Mary had started early in the life of the Church of Christ and spread most widely in the Eastern Church. Mary appears in only a few places in the New Testament but there was a long-standing practice of dwelling on the foreshadowing of Mary in the Old Testament. Reaching beyond the New Testament and connecting Mary to the House of David added depth to the Marian doctrine.

Mary is mentioned in the Gospel of Luke and in the Gospel of John; further references to Mary's life are found in apocryphal texts of the second century. Luke tells the story of the Annunciation and recalls how Mary, troubled by the message of the Angel Gabriel, expresses her faith in God with the words "be it done to me according to thy word." This theme of the Annunciation would capture the imagination of countless painters and sculptors. John mentions Mary twice in his Gospel. The apostle recounts how Mary is at the side of her Son when He performs His first miracle, the changing of water into fine wine at a wedding in Cana. There, for the first time, the Son called His mother *woman*. In the eyes of the disciples she became clearly the mother of humanity, the new Eve. Then, in John 19:25-27, Mary is at the foot of the cross and Jesus addresses her again "Woman, behold your Son," and to the apostle John "Behold your mother." Mary becomes the spiritual mother of all men.

In the Niceno-Constantinopolitan Credo she is referred to as the Virgin Mary and the Council in Ephesus in 431 affirmed that she is the *Theotokos* and not only the *Christotokos,* the mother of Christ. The etymology of Theotokos is *mother of God* but its deeper meaning is "the one who gave birth to the one who is God."

During the early Middle Ages, devotion to Mary was expressed mostly in the limited circle of the monastic orders. Starting in the eleventh century, these orders, the Cistercian in particular, would be the source of Mary's growing role in the doctrine of the church and the devotion of the faithful. The founders of monastic orders saw a clear parallel between the life of the Virgin and that of a monk, both reconciling action and contemplation. They set aside a special place for Mary in their spirituality and liturgy and dedicated their abbey churches to her. A long list of influential monks shared their affection, their intense admiration and their deep devotion to Mary in their writings and sermons. Alcuin, the English monk who joined the court of Charlemagne in *Aix la Chapelle* at the end of the eighth century, contributed considerably to Marian theology and piety; Fulbert of Chartres, who made the school of Chartres famous throughout Europe after the turn of the first millennium, recounted stories that witness the Virgin's intercession on behalf of men. Then came the twelfth century which Fr. Luigi Gambero in *Mary in the Middle Age* called "truly the Marian century, true in the doctrinal sense and in liturgical and popular devotion."

The dogma of the Assumption would be proclaimed only in 1950 but the creed of Mary taken up in body and soul to heaven after her life on earth, had been held since Antiquity and had grown in importance in the twelfth century. Mary was then seen sitting close to the Lord and in the best position to intercede for man. The Theotokos, the Mother of God, became the Mother of Mercy, *Mater Misericordiae* and *Mediatrix.* The Marian title of Mother of Mercy was disseminated from Cluny but the title Mediatrix had been introduced many centuries earlier. Already in the ninth century Mary was seen as closer to God than bishops and saints and had become the link between man and God. In the eleventh century, Peter Damian, a doctor of the church, formulated the motto *Ad Jesum per Mariam*, to Jesus through Mary. Mary-through-which-the-Savior-came was now also Mary-chosen-by God-to-plead-the-cause-of-humanity before her Son.

None other than Saint Bernard symbolizes this transition from Mary-giving-Jesus-His-humanity to Mary-the-way-to-God. The Cistercian monasteries were dedicated to the Virgin and Saint Bernard in particular is associated with her worship. He is said to have introduced the *Salve Regina*. The story was told of Bernard, still a young man, praying before a painting of the Virgin Mary and three drops of the milk that had nourished Jesus falling on his lips. The same miraculous and mystical event has been connected with other men deeply devoted to Mary but it fits well in the life of Bernard the so-called champion and proclaimer of the virtues of Mary.

Saint Bernard did not contribute much to the Marian theology and doctrine. The moving poems he wrote in her honor spoke to the heart more than to the mind. He thus became a major catalyst in the enormous *investment* made by people in Mary during the twelfth and thirteenth centuries. In *The Divine Comedy* Dante is guided through *Inferno* and *Purgatorio* by Virgil, as far as human reason can go. Then Beatrice, his earthly platonic love, the symbol of Divine love, leads him through *Paradiso*. When she returns to her throne among the blessed, Saint Bernard is the guide who takes Dante to the light of God. Bernard "her faithful one" calls on Mary to aid Dante and in the last canto of the Comedy offers his *Prayer to the Virgin*:

> "Lady thou art so near God's reckonings that who seeks grace and does not seek thee first would have his wish fly upward without wings."

Representations of a majestic Mary, draped in a long and enveloping *pallium*, mantle, held wide open by angels and protecting people huddled at her feet, started to appear in the eleventh century. In these iconographies the *personnages* are members of a monastic order, a confrérie or the community of men. Whichever case, the message is the same, Mary is Mother of Mercy. These representations of the Virgin of Mercy and her protective mantle find a visual echo in the facade of cathedrals. The *rose windows* crowning the *ogive shaped portals* recall the head of the Virgin held high above the welcoming folds of her mantle.

The Virgin of Mercy as a subject of Christian art remained popular long after the end of the twelfth century. In *Our Lady of the Navigators* Mary's cloak enfolds famous men of the sixteenth century and most presumably Columbus. It is one of the earliest paintings whose subject is the discovery of the Americas and has a place of honor in the Alcazar of Seville.

In the Footsteps of Alienor in Aquitaine

Walking in the footsteps of Alienor in Aquitaine opens a window in the life of the *Queen by the wrath of God* and also provides an introduction to the southwest of France.

Bordeaux

The town is better known for the *Chateaux* along the Gironde to the north of the city than for its medieval quarter. A drive through Saint Julien, Pauillac, Margaux and Saint Estephe does not need any recommendation. These and other communes are home to most of the *grands crus* and *premiers crus* listed in the Bordeaux Wine Official Classification of 1855. The ranking, established that year during the *Exposition Universelle* at the request of Emperor Napoleon III, is the reference for the red Bordeaux. *Chateau Latour*, to take but one example, has retained its name even though the wine maker and the owner of the property have changed many times. A wine tour is a most pleasant experience, easy to organize and not to be missed.

Recalling Alienor in Bordeaux gives a purpose to the visit of the downtown of a city which is one of the most engaging in France. The *Musée d'Aquitaine* is a good introduction and a reminder of the rich history of the town and the large expanse of territory called Aquitaine during the Middle Ages. The museum is in the old part of town, within walking distance of the Cathedral Saint Andre where Alienor was married to Louis VII. The cathedral is a fine example of gothic in the south of France and is on the UNESCO World Heritage List. The *Palais de l'Ombrière* where she spent her youth and where her wedding reception took place, used to rise nearby.

The medieval *Bordeu*, as the town once was called, is compact and rich in churches and, here and there, remains of a thirteenth century wall have been integrated into modern constructions. The medieval gateway called Porte Cailhau, built to honor a victory on the battlefield by the French king Charles VIII, offers a regal exit from Alienor's town and entrance into a more modern era. The best of what eighteenth century Bordeaux has to offer is there, along the Garonne: the *Place de la Bourse* flanked by the *Hotel des Fermes* and *Hotel de la Bourse,* all reminders that the town has long been a major trading center. A shallow water pool on the bank of the Garonne reflects the illuminated buildings after sundown and offers the most memorable postcard decor.

A ride in the tramway which runs parallel to the river allows a glimpse of other elegant buildings, *hotels particuliers* and landscaped gardens. Further up-river the waterfront is a long façade of residences built in the middle of the eighteenth century. This section of town, les

Chartrons, is proof that the aristocracy and bourgeoisie of the town have known periods of great financial success.

The era of prosperity for Bordeaux goes back as early as 1241 when it was granted a very valuable privilege by the king of England (or did the city council grant this privilege to itself?). The town, which controls the estuary of the Garonne, was allowed to sell the wine of its immediate region before giving the up-river producers access to the northern European markets. This was an extraordinary commercial asset at a time when wines did not age well and were drunk during the first year. This marks the beginning of quality wines in the nearby *Graves* region. The privilege survived the Hundred Years War and was only abolished in 1776. It did not benefit only the wine producers of the Bordeaux area but also the merchants, mostly foreign, who were transporting and selling the wine. The Dutch were the first to make their home in Bordeaux in the seventeenth century, then the British settled next to their warehouses in the Chartrons neighborhood and finally came the Germans. All were Protestants, did not commingle with the Catholics, made serious money and eventually bought vineyards. Some of the *Chateaux* still bear their names, Barton, Lawton or Lynch.

The Catholic aristocracy of Bordeaux had lost its monopoly but remained involved in the wine trade. It also derived considerable revenues from its investments in sugar plantations in the Antilles and in the boats transporting men and goods to and from the Americas. The slave trade, which gained in importance after the middle of the seventeenth century, allowed the labor-intense cultivation of sugarcane to expand rapidly in the French Antilles. Western Africa, the Antilles and the harbors along the Atlantic in southern France formed the three sides of a so-called *triangular trade*. Slaves were exchanged for trinkets along the coast of Africa in slave trade center such as Gorée, the small island off the beaches of Dakar in Senegal. Ships carrying their human cargo sailed to the Antilles and returned to Bordeaux loaded with raw sugar. This triangular trade was highly profitable, a bonanza for the aristocracy and bourgeoisie of many harbors and Bordeaux in particular.

Poitiers

Poitiers, the capital of Poitou, keeps watch over the northern entrance of Aquitaine. The medieval town was built on a tabletop surrounded by two rivers, the Boivre and the Clain. This was a strategic location on the path of the tribes from northern and eastern Europe moving to southwest Gaul. The site was protected by solid stonewalls built in late Antiquity; later, during Alienor's time, a long wall would be added beyond these Gallo-Roman ramparts. The town was well-positioned to become an important religious center in the early days of Christianity. In the middle of the sixth century, Radegund, the holy queen, wife of cruel Clothar, previously encountered in the chapter on *the Merovingian dynasty after Clovis*, was buried in one of the churches. Her body is said to be in a sarcophagus in the crypt of l'Eglise Sainte Radegonde. The saint's renown in Poitiers challenges that of Alienor.

During Alienor's days, the ensemble of highly esteemed religious institutions within its walls, and the fame of the dukes who controlled its destiny, caused the town to be held in high regard. Poitiers is where the dukes of Aquitaine, suzerains of the counts of Poitou, would receive the homage of their vassals. The character and tastes of one duke, Guillaume IX, Alienor's grandfather, a larger-than-life personality, greatly influenced this meridional court. He was undisciplined, always at odds with the church, parading his mistress, appropriately named Dangerosa, around Poitiers. When in Poitiers, the duke held court in a palace built in the eleventh century on the highest point of the tabletop. Excessive and unpredictable, he knew how to be charming and generous (see upcoming chapter on *Courtly Love* for more on Guillaume IX, le Troubadour)

Alienor's taste for poetry, music and dance, and her often irreverent humor were nurtured in the atmosphere of culture, poetry and debate of her grandfather's court. The ducal palace where she held her own court would later become a courthouse and is known today as the Palais de Justice. Its most noteworthy feature is the great hall where Jeanne d'Arc was interrogated in 1429.

The well-proportionated *Eglise Notre Dame la Grande* rises behind the palace, at one end of a small market place which allows an unobstructed view of its Romanesque façade. Today, yellow tinted stones give the church a peaceful, mellow appearance but in medieval times the same stones were painted and the façade polychromatic.

The episcopal section of town, on the east side of the plateau, is connected to the Palais by narrow, winding, cobblestone streets and houses Saint Peter's cathedral, a fourth century baptistery and Radegund's church. This is the medieval Poitiers where Baron Haussmann, the man who would rebuild Paris, resided in 1831, next to the cathedral. He stayed there for only a short time and complained bitterly about the steep, poorly lit streets on his side of town.

Abbey of Fontevraud

Alienor died in 1204 at the age of 82. She was survived by two of her ten children and a long list of crowned grand children. The duchess of Aquitaine, former queen of France and England, had retired in the Abbey and is buried in its church. Fontevraud, a place she often visited, meant much for her throughout her life. The future queen of England had travelled there a few days after her marriage to Henry to give thanks, and to confirm the pledge she and her first husband, Louis, had made. She had presumably given for the first time when she was barely twenty-five years old, shortly before leaving for the Crusade with Louis. This would have been the beginning of a long list of gifts to Fontevraud made at crucial moments in her life.

The large ensemble of buildings is an easy drive north of Poitiers, near the Loire River. Shortly after its founding, the Abbey benefited from the generosity and protection of royal families and earned its name *Abbaye Royale de Fontevraud*

Alienor's painted recumbent stone statue is one of four at the eastern end of the long nave of the church. Henry rests next to her and their son Richard the Lionheart is at the foot of his father. Richard's heart is buried in Rouen; Anjou and Normandy, not England, seemed the most appropriate places for the remains of the first Plantagenet kings. The fourth recumbent statue, in wood, is that of Isabelle of Angouleme, the second wife of King John, the youngest son of Henry and Alienor.

On most sunny days, light filters through the lightly stained-glass windows. The chancel is bare of any ornaments and long, smooth pillars accentuate its elevation. The slightly yellow tinted *tuffeau,* the stone of the Loire Valley used in many of the *Renaissance chateaux* along the valley, gives the church its gracious appearance.

Royal gisants at Fontevraud, Richard next to Isabelle.

Nothing in this sparsely decorated Romanesque church recalls the tormented history of the nearby Abbey. The order of Fontevraud was founded in 1099, a period rich in monastic initiatives, barely one year after Robert and twenty other monks had left the abbey of Molesme and settled in Citeaux. Fontevraud welcomed both monks and nuns but an abbess was to head the congregation and she had to be a widow. These unusual regulations written by the founder of the order, Robert d'Arbrissel, are symbolic of the importance given to women in the eleventh and twelfth century.

Fontevraud would become a refuge for women of noble birth rejected by their entourage. Several became abbesses—their portraits and those of other abbesses, line a long gallery adjoining the cloister, and illustrate the story of the Abbey. The property was pillaged during the Revolution and, as would be the case with several of the largest monasteries in

France, transformed into a prison in 1804. Since 1975 the complex of buildings and gardens houses cultural activities year-round and is one of the highlights of the western stretch of the Loire Valley.

Courtly Love and the Roman de la Rose

Guillaume IX, Duke of Aquitaine, Alienor of Aquitaine's irreverent grandfather, is also known as the poet *Guillaume le Troubadour.* He sang about love, the joy and torment brought by love, about eternal devotion to a lady. His poems were written in langue d'oc, the language familiar to the courtiers in Provence and Aquitaine, not in Latin. A lord praising love was a cultural novelty which would spread to other courts and be known as courtly love.

Guillaume is the first troubadour of whom we have any record but the origins of courtly love have been traced to the writings of Ovid. The Roman poet claimed that his poem *Ars Amatoria,* the Art of Love, caused him to be exiled by Emperor Augustus. Ovid's concept of love was realistic not romantic, he was openly sensual and spoke freely of extramarital affairs "the best partner in a love affair is another man's wife." When his poems had a revival in the twelfth century his love-as-warfare was transformed into the gentler art of courtly love, a code of the relationship between man and woman. The lover now owes the lady allegiance, he addresses her with humility and is submissive. Such pure love, was believed to be virtuous and ennobling.

The traditional roles of men and women were reversed and the domination of the women was professed. This is to be expected as the art of courtly love did develop during the twelfth century, the truly Marian century. Despite this new context, social norms were respected. This, too, is to be expected as courtly love was the domain of well-born men and women.

In *The Waning of the Middle Ages,* Huizinga writes about "unsatisfied desire placed by the troubadours of Provence in the center of the poetic conception of love." This was an uncommon concept which dealt with the feelings of a small elite concentrated in the great courts. There, the influence of the warrior mentality, so overbearing in small courts, was diluted within a more diverse community and women found opportunities to shine. Poetry was a vehicle which suited their education and sensibility. The relationships between men and women in these heterogeneous great courts needed to be restrained and courtly love introduced rules which favored the spiritual expression of love over the physical.

The game of courtly love was played with great formalism. In a typical scene, the actors are a lady, always a member of the upper class, possibly the wife of the suzerain, and the suitor of a lower rank, a troubadour, a knight most often unattached, sometimes a mere squire. She is the unattainable object of desire and courtly love allowed the suffering, unsatisfied lover to sublimate his sexual desire. The conventions, despite the novelty of love as a subject, still reflected the social structure of a feudal society; the lady received the prerogatives of the suzerain, the suitor the obligations of a vassal.

The game of love was also the theme of true competitions in the courts. While knights demonstrated courage and strength at tournaments, other jousted with words. The lady of the chateau would challenge them to debate on "What is true love?" "Can feelings between husband and wife ever be as strong as between lovers?" and scores of similar topics regarding proper manners and behavior. They would sing their poetic arguments and a crowd of ladies, clerics and knights would choose a winner. The lady would reward him with a silver crown, a finely chiseled dagger, a silk belt or other valuable trophies.

Alienor introduced the concept in Paris when she was queen of France, then in London after she married Henry II. She also established a court of love on a grand scale in Poitiers. Her daughters, Alix, Countess of Blois, and Marie, Countess of Champagne, were true disciples. The city of Troyes, under Marie, was home to a celebrated court poet known simply as Chretien de Troyes. Poems about eternal love originating in the entourage of Alienor and her daughters would be disseminated by troubadours and minnesingers to the other courts of Europe.

One of the highlights of courtly poetry was the *Roman de la Rose*, rich in allegories familiar to the readers of courtly poets. It most certainly influenced Chaucer's *Canterbury Tales*. The poem, begun by one author in 1240 and finished by another in 1280, attests to the changes in courtesy during the thirteenth century. By the end of that century, the unnatural formality of courtly love had been replaced by erotic poetry.

The first poem was written by Guillaume de Lorris in the tradition of the *fin'amor* sung by the troubadours. In a dream, a young courtier enters a garden, and while admiring a rosebud *si tres bel,* so very beautiful, is struck by the arrow of love. The arrow pierces his eye and enters his heart, and so begins his quest for the Rose. It was well understood at the time that the rose represented the sex of a woman. The young man will be helped by Love and distracted by Fear and Shame, and Jealousy will build a wall around the rosebush. When the poet writes the last of his 4,000 verses, he has not revealed what becomes of the Lover and the Rose.

Jean de Meun, the second poet, will add 18,000 verses several decades later, but the allegory now conveys a new message, and the symbolic meanings attributed to the pursuit of the rosebud are more naturalistic. When the action resumes, the young man in love meets Reason and the army of Love faces the protectors of the Rose. At the end of the poem, encouraged by Nature and helped by Ruse, the lover plucks the Rose.

The poem would be viewed as an initiation to the rules of the game of love. During the forty years separating the two parts of the poem, the ethic of courtly love had given way to the call of nature. The courtly conception of love, which makes unsatisfied desire its center motive, had been replaced by sexual pursuit, the glorification of pure love by the glorification of seduction.

The second part of the Roman de la Rose became the catalyst for the first French literary quarrel. In 1401 the poet Christine de Pizan reacted vehemently to a letter of praise of the *Roman*, written by the humanist Jean de Montreuil. She was siding with Jean de Gerson, the Chancellor of the University, while de Montreuil belonged to the Royal Chancery and heated exchanges between the two camps lasted for several years. The issues of the esthetic and moral values of de Meun's poem and, more generally, of proper literary norms, were at the heart of the debate. For Christine de Pizan, the quarrel was also more personal. She was outraged by the immorality, misogyny and indecency of de Meun's piece.

Why Jean de Montreuil praised the poem so long after its publication remains an unanswered question. Christine de Pizan claimed that fortuitous circumstances triggered the debate. History has retained that she intervened in the defense of women but Tracy Adams author of *Christine de Pizan and the fight for France* makes the point that Christine's active participation "suggests that she was moved at least as much by the desire for recognition among influential people as by moral indignation." De Pizan did indeed gain recognition which was an asset when she moved shortly after from love poetry to political allegories. One of her works in particular, written a few years later, *Livre des fais et bonnes meurs du sage roy Charles V,* became a mirror for princes. It would be one of the manuals used for the education of the Dauphin, the future King Louis XI. Christine de Pizan was truly an exceptional personage for her time and remains the most noted woman writer in the Middle Ages.

The Roman de la Rose would be immensely popular. It was copied numerous times (more than 320 total or partial versions have been recorded). The *Roman de la Rose digital library* available at roman-delarose.org has stored 130 versions. Among the most richly illustrated is the manuscript dated 1520 at the Morgan Library in New York; the first part of the late thirteenth century manuscript held at the *Bibliothèque Nationale de France* also has delightful illuminations in the margins.

How gallant relationships were conducted in some courts during the latter parts of the Middle Ages says something about self-control, restraint of emotions and drives and belongs in the history of the civilizing process of man. The standards of behavior set by courtly love were a step forward, a small step indeed but a step nevertheless, in the evolution of human behavior which led to civility and ultimately to what would be labeled *civilization.*

The concept of courtly love lost its relevance when fidelity and trust, homage and oaths no longer ruled human relationships. In other words, the game stopped being played when France was no longer a feudal society and when the Middle Ages came to an end.

Blanche, Queen of Queens

Blanche de Castille was only twelve years old when her grandmother chaperoned her across the Pyrenees to be married to Louis, the oldest son of Philippe Auguste. Twenty-four years later, Louis succeeded his father as Louis VIII and Blanche de Castille became Queen of France. Blanche and Louis had thirteen children and their oldest surviving son, the future Saint Louis, was only twelve years old when his father died after a reign of only three years. The heavy burden of the regency fell on Blanche's shoulders.

These would be difficult times for the young woman. The barons, bruised after Bouvines, thought their hour had come to carve out their share of a kingdom unified by Philippe Auguste. They plotted to push aside *the Spaniard* as the regent had been labelled but Blanche showed her political savvy and the autocratic genes in her blood. She preserved the political heritage of Philippe Auguste and successfully ended the Albigensian wars in Languedoc.

Blanche de Castille inculcated her son Louis, the future Saint Louis, with strong moral principles and a high sense of royal duty.

Saint Louis, who would become one of the most admired kings in the history of France, had a boundless admiration and love for his mother. She became the *old queen* when he married Marguerite, the oldest daughter of the Count of Provence, a few years before he came of age. There was not enough room at the side of Louis for two women and history has retained the portrait of an unforgiving mother-in-law drawn by Jean de Joinville, the great chronicler who lived at the royal court.

The *old queen* administered the affairs of the kingdom with energy and determination while the royal couple was in Egypt during the Seventh Crusade. This was a calamitous expedition, the French lost many men among which one of Louis's brothers, the count of Artois and the king himself, ill with dysentery, was taken prisoner. He was set free only after agreeing with the Mamelukes to a considerable ransom. Blanche shouldered the heavy burden of gathering the funds to honor her son's commitment.

Blanche de Castille died in November 1252 while Louis was in the Holy Land organizing the defense of the Kingdom of Jerusalem. She was buried on the grounds of the Abbey of Maubuisson. An English chronicler said of her: "she had the sex of a woman but the grip of a man." He could have added, "like her maternal grandmother."

Regent twice, queen consort and queen mother but never queen of France in her own right. There would be no reigning queens in the Kingdom of France, unlike the English Elizabeth or later Victoria, only regents, wives and mothers of kings. At the end of the fifteenth century, Anne de Beaujeu preserved the throne for her brother Charles VIII while he was underage, and a few decades later Louise de Savoie managed the affairs of the kingdom while her son Francois I was battling in Italy. Other mothers of kings were called to stand-in for an underage son. Catherine de Medicis from 1559 to her death thirty years later was the force behind the crown that three of her sons struggled to keep on their heads. At the beginning of the seventeenth century Marie de Medici, Louis XIII's mother, relied on the advice of Concini to quell a revolt by the lords and Louis XIV was still a child when his mother, Anne d'Autriche, in the middle of the same century, had to deal with *la Fronde,* a truly revolutionary movement which left a deep impression on the future Sun King. Anne d'Autriche, by her determination in the face of adversity, most closely resembles Blanche.

During the regency of these women the monarchy survived rebellions by powerful lords of the kingdom, religious wars and quasi-revolutions but when it comes to their place in history they must be judged by the standard of Blanche de Castille. Blanche had inherited the efficiency and authority in the conduct of public affairs of her grandmother Alienor. The wise and forceful policies she enforced and the high respect she held for the duties of the king set her in a league of her own.

Alienor and Blanche are symbols of the status of women in the twelfth and thirteenth century. They played a role in civil society which had been denied to women in Antiquity and would no longer be theirs when power became centralized in the hands of absolute monarchs. One other name belongs on the list of great women in the Middle Ages: Joan of Arc, the maiden that will make a short but glorious appearance in history two centuries later.

Women of high status in the Roman Empire had not been given access to public office and, as one might expect, nor to the army. They held one religious function, priestesses of Vesta, the Roman goddess of the hearth fire; the *vestal virgins* performed important rituals and were granted privileges otherwise reserved for men. Roman law, a form of civil law, gave all rights to fathers, the *pater familias.* Some women, nevertheless, did wield much power, influence fathers, husbands and lovers and became feared powerbrokers. Those of the Julian-Claudian dynasty had been among the most notable: Livia, Agrippina, and the one whose name has such a sinister resonance, Messalina. They tended to political connections but played their role behind the scene and were not expected to have a public life.

Christianity opened new horizons for women of all conditions and for slaves. They heeded the message that they were made in the image of God, that all human beings deserve the same respect. Many women made it their mission to evangelize, to preach the tenets of the new religion and some became the catalyst of major conversions. Two deserve a special mention in this context, Helena, the mother of Constantine and Clotilde, Clovis's wife. History has also remembered the names of women, Blandine and others, persecuted during Late Antiquity as they remained true to their faith and became martyrs. Monastic life was open to women and numerous abbesses led exemplary lives. It is fair to claim that women in the High Middle Ages played a role in religion that was disproportionate to their place in society.

Marilyn Yalom in *Birth of the Chess Queen* draws an intriguing parallel between the increase in female power after the eleventh century and the changing role of the queen in chess. In the game as played in Persia a vizier sat to the left of the king as befits the shah's closest advisor. The vizier was still on the board when the game was brought to Europe by the Arabs in the eighth century and played in Spain. A piece called queen was first mentioned at the beginning of the eleventh century at the time the game came to France from Spain. By the end of the twelfth century, the vizier had been replaced by the queen throughout Europe, a transition which might coincide with changes in the social role of women.

The chess queen had initially inherited the weak firing power of the vizier, allowed to move only one space at a time. She would have to wait for the reign of Isabella of Castille at the end of the fifteenth century to move in all directions and become the mightiest piece on the chessboard. The piece was called queen/ reine in some countries and dame/dama in others. Chess historians have noted that *queen* was used in protestant countries and *dame*, as in *notre dame*, in catholic ones.

The *investment* made to honor the Virgin Mary to quote Henry Adams, the power wielded by secular queens as exemplified by Alienor of Aquitaine and Blanche de Castille and the unique role played by the Lady in courtly love all enhanced the prestige of highborn women in the twelfth century. The chess queen is an icon of the power of women during that period. Chess queen and flesh and blood queens were the king's other half.

Crusades in the Middle East

"Deus Vult": The First Crusade

November 1095, in Clermont Ferrand, Pope Urban II, born in France, shaped by Cluny and a disciple of Gregory VII, delivers an unexpected message to an assembly of bishops, clerics and lay Christians: "Go help your Byzantine brethren who are being attacked by the Turks and free the Holy Land that has fallen into the hands of this vile race." The chronicles of the time gave various interpretations to the event but this was the pope's message. All those present were so moved that they cried out, *Deus vult*, God wants this.

In the days of Urban II, Christians living in the ex-Roman Empire of the East, later known as the Byzantine Empire, were more oppressed than ever by Turkish Muslims. In 1055, the Seljuk Turks had become masters of Bagdad, replacing the Arab Caliphate. A few years later, Alp Arslan, meaning Heroic Lion, a strict Turkish Muslim, defeated the Byzantines near Malazgerd in Armenia and paved the way for his descendants to conquer Asia Minor; they would be in Nicea, at the door of Constantinople, in 1078. Meanwhile, in 1071, other Turkish warriors had taken Jerusalem from the hands of the Fatimids, Arab Shiite Muslims, who controlled Egypt at the time. The survival of the Christians of the East, also called Greek Christians, was truly at stake.

The *fresh and vigorous life* which, later, will energize the Renaissance of the twelfth century, will stimulate adventurous knights. From various horizons in Europe, they answered the pope's call and went on military pilgrimages to the Middle East called Crusades. The Christian spirituality and vitality which will support the investment in cathedrals sustained these first European colonial expeditions.

Ordinary people in Western Europe were also stirred by Urban's call. They actually were the first to be on the move and crowd the roads to the Orient. Thousands, mostly poor and unarmed, left France in the wake of a charismatic donkey-riding leader known as Pierre l'Hermite; they were joined by even more pilgrims as they progressed through Germany on their way to Constantinople. These people of diverse backgrounds left a trail of destruction and crime and a sinister reputation among the local populations. Their worst deeds were against the Jews settled along the Rhine and in Prague who became the victims of these greedy fanatics.

The so-called *People's Crusade* reached Constantinople in August 1096 and the Byzantine emperor was quite happy to ferry them across the Bosphorus. They progressed inside Anatolia unconscious of the hardships awaiting them. A few months after setting foot in Asia, tens of thousands of these naive and unprepared pilgrims, were ambushed by the Turks in a narrow gorge a few miles from Civetot. Pierre l'Hermite, and the few who survived the massacre, joined the next Crusade, that of the barons, and eventually had an influence on its outcome but the People's Crusade was essentially over after Civetot. Eight months later, the ost of Godefroy de Bouillon would ride through the same Turkish countryside and be filled with fear and anger at the sight of fields of bones, a chilling reminder that they would need more than faith to free the Holy Land.

The barons were, at last, on the long and dangerous overland road to Jerusalem. Their first hurdle was not Sultan Kilij Arslan and his Turkish archers but Emperor Alexius Commenus and his Petcheneg mercenaries. (Note: Alp Arslan and Kilij Arslan came from competing branches of the Seljuk house). Four large armies reached the Byzantine Empire between late December 1096 and early May 1097 and negotiated their crossing to the Asian side of the Bosphorus. The first was led by Godefroy de Bouillon and his knights from the Ardennes, then came Bohemond's Normans from Sicily followed closely by Raymond IV, Comte de Toulouse, also known as Raymond de Saint Gilles. The last sizeable group came from Normandy and was headed by Robert

Curthose, oldest son of William the Conqueror. Within a short period of time, mostly crude knights and even cruder men on foot, accompanied by non-combatants, progressing at an average speed estimated at 15 miles a day, were crowding the roads leading to Constantinople. The relationship between the Crusaders, particularly the first three groups, and the Byzantines was tense, and bloody confrontations on the way to the capital and around the city became unavoidable. Matters grew worse when the Byzantine emperor requested that the leaders of these expeditions swear an oath of allegiance, in other words become his vassals, for any conquest they might make and agree to hand over any land that had previously been part of his empire. The barons protested vehemently but had to concede. They needed the cooperation of the emperor to secure access to food and fodder, not a small affair for large armies far away from their home bases. As to the emperor he could sense that the barons could be as much foes as friends and he was relieved when the last group was ferried to Asia. This first contact between the Crusaders and the Byzantine Empire did not augur well for their future cooperation.

The four armies which had come from different ends of Christian Europe were far from forming one homogeneous force. The pope could count on the leadership of Raymond de Saint Gilles and Bohemond. The first one had already fought the Muslims in Spain. He had taken part in the 1087 campaign led by French knights against the Arabs in Aragon, the Reconquista, a preparation of sorts for the Crusades. Bohemond de Tarente was another tested warrior. He was a son of Robert Guiscard, who, lacking opportunities in Normandy, had gone on the road, conquered Naples and chased the Arabs out of Palermo. Robert and Bohemond had also tried unsuccessfully to take Constantinople and there would be no lost love between Bohemond and the Byzantines.

The pope did not entrust the leadership of the Crusade to a warrior. He wanted to make it clear that this was an affair of the Church and called upon Adhemar de Monteil, Bishop of Le Puy. His decision was facilitated by the absence of a king; this First Crusade would be the only one without the presence of a king. The Byzantines would refer to this army of Crusaders composed mostly of Franks and Normans as *Celts*. Middle Eastern sources will generically refer to all those who participated in the Crusades as *Frankq*. This is also how the crusaders saw themselves, Franks from the old Carolingian empire.

The Crusaders would not face a united Muslim front. As they prepared their long march eastwards, the political landscape in the Middle East changed in their favor. The empire of the third Seljuk sultan, who had died a few years earlier, in 1092, had been shared among family members. Syria had fallen in the hands of two nephews who did not see eye to eye; one had taken residence in Aleppo and the other in Damascus. Later, in 1098, the Fatimids had regained control of Jerusalem.

Shortly after they joined forces on the Asian side of the Bosphorus, the Frankq victoriously battled the Turks at Dorylaeum, south of Nicea, and this first encounter gave Bishop Adhemar a chance to prove that he was an excellent leader on the battlefield. The skirmishes with the Byzantines and the first battles against the Turks were only the prologue to an arduous campaign that would test the military abilities and the resilience of the Crusaders. It also tested the commitment of the barons to pursue a common goal. Their quarrels over power and share of conquests did bring the military expedition to a standstill after the conquest of Antioch. It was the humble and the poor, the survivors of endless perils, who rebelled and forcefully reminded the barons that their pilgrimage was for the sake of God and not earthly possessions. The message was understood and Raymond de Toulouse, in a grand symbolic gesture, barefoot and dressed as a pilgrim, led his army out of Antioch.

The poor had saved the First Crusade and the barons were again on their way to Jerusalem. They fought during two long years before finally conquering the Holy City in June 1099; it has been estimated that between 100,000 and 150,000 men and women had left Europe and that not more than 12,000 entered Jerusalem. The initial number included the great mass of people who followed Pierre l'Hermite, the non-combatants who accompanied the knights, the infantry and the indispensable cavalry. Such impressive numbers are impossible to confirm. In *A History of the Crusades* Steven Runciman estimates that the People's Crusade had attracted 20,000 and that roughly 4,000 mounted knights and 30,000 infantry left Constantinople; he further assumes that the non-combatants could not have been more than a quarter of the whole force and, therefore, that the initial number must have been below 100,000.

The Christians were deeply moved as they walked in the footsteps of Jesus and then their seemingly successful expedition was marred forever by a bloodbath, the indiscriminate slaughter of tens of thousands of Muslims in the streets of Jerusalem; even the masses huddled in the Dome of the Rock and the *al Aqsa* mosque were not spared. This would be an indelible blemish on the First Crusade and a political mistake for its leaders.

There would be seven other so-called Crusades stretching over a period of 175 years. Most historians agree that the military expedition called by Pope Urban II in 1095 was the First Crusade even though French knights had already campaigned against Muslims in Spain in the mid-eleventh century. These earlier expeditions were never labelled Crusades mostly because the pope had played only a minor role. On the other hand, after the eighth Crusade in 1270, numerous military expeditions blessed by the popes would still be called Crusades. What, then, was a Crusade?

Armed Pilgrimage, Military Expedition or Crusade?

U rban II's sermon contains the essential elements of the definition of a Crusade. The tenor of his address leaves no doubt that he was calling for a new sort of pilgrimage, a military expedition for the glory of God and he offered those who would enlist an innovative *package*: the carrot of indulgences, a form of amnesty; the protection by the church of all their assets and those of their family while they were on this pilgrimage; and the cross in red cloth which symbolized their personal commitment, a signature of sorts. The *red cross* gave the participants a sense of belonging, an element of identity and was at the origin of the name *crusade* given to the great adventure preached by the pope. The blessing by a pope, the granting of indulgences and the vows taken by those who enlisted would remain the defining features of the military expeditions called Crusades.

The men, prelates and others, who stood at the foot of the pulpit listening intently to Urban II, and those who would be told about his sermon, could not imagine the extraordinary energy that would be released by his call to action, but they were familiar with the terms of his offer.

They knew about the armed pilgrimages that had taken place during the eleventh century. Individual pilgrims had learned to travel together and be accompanied by armed men to face the dangers of hostile lands. The church had acknowledged that the price of salvation was self-defense and that self-defense justified the use of arms.

They understood that he was calling for an expedition against the infidels in the Middle East. The first chronicle written around 1105 reported that the pope's primary purpose was to assist the Christians threatened by the Turks. Subsequent chronicles gave the pope's message another dimension, a call for an *expeditio Hierosolymitana*, a call to liberate the terrestrial Jerusalem, the Holy City where the passion of Jesus had taken place, where He had manifested His glory. Jerusalem was also the place where the predictions of the Apocalypse, the return of the Antichrist, and other events described in the apocryphal books, were to be realized. For some would-be Crusaders the Jerusalem of the Holy Land was the prefiguration of the celestial Jerusalem and they envisioned their armed pilgrimage as their last journey. For others, taking the terrestrial Jerusalem out of the hands of the infidels was a worthier proposition than fighting on the side of the Byzantines.

Those who heard about Urban II's call knew that he was recruiting for a *just war*. In the fifth century, Saint Augustine had defined a just war: the cause had to be just, the intention right and it must rest on the authority of the prince, that is, the pope. The men called to defend other Christians and to reconquer Jerusalem were assured that the Crusades fulfilled all these criteria.

When Urban II reached the climax of his sermon and the crowd joined him in chanting *Deus vult*, those who volunteered knew they were answering God's call. As newly enlisted soldiers of God they knew they deserved a reward, and they were familiar with the compensations given by the pope. Since the middle of the ninth century the forgiveness of sins had been granted to those fighting the so-called Saracens who controlled the Mediterranean and later the same benefit had been extended to all those who contributed directly or indirectly to the fight against the infidels. This *remuneratio* would be called indulgence and would become a powerful tool of medieval theocracy.

Why 1095?

Why did the defining features of a Crusade coalesce in 1095? The search for answers has led to many speculations. The danger-filled environment for the Christians in the Middle East was most certainly an important catalyst. Pragmatic minds, then and later, also read a political act in Urban's call. The time had come for the pope, as it would be for his immediate successor, to flex his muscles. Popes, emperors and kings were elbowing for a front seat on the political stage (recall the Canossa Incident in 1077). In calling the European Christians to volunteer for an expedition to the Middle East, Urban II was testing his political power.

There would also be sociological readings of the origins of the Crusades. In *The Civilizing Process* Norbert Elias refers to land becoming scarce in Europe by the middle of the eleventh century and the need for men to seek opportunities beyond their frontiers, and then speculates "it is probable that without the social pressure from within the Western Frankish region and then all the other regions of Christendom, the Crusades would not have taken place...the social pressure supplied the motive force...the Church steered this pre-existing force... it gave the struggle for new land an overreaching meaning and justification... it turned this into a struggle for the Christian faith." In his call Urban II referred to this need to release tension within society. He admonished the barons and their knights to go battle elsewhere than on his turf, to release their bellicose impulses in fights against the Muslims and not in their backyard. The Crusades would be an answer to the surplus of energy created in Europe by economic and demographic expansion. It would give a chance to the junior sons of the nobles and those who were landless to seek fortune in the Middle East. Seen in this light, Urban's Crusade could be called the first European colonial war.

The military expeditions against the Saracens during the previous centuries, the increasing popularity of pilgrimages, the growing attraction of Jerusalem and the reforms of the Church undertaken by Urban's predecessors had prepared people for his call. Then, in Clermont Ferrand in 1095, the pope had added enough enticements to hook those who heard his sermon.

A highly favorable environment does not in itself fully explain the immediate and marvelous popular adhesion to the idea of Crusade; a psychological catalyst was needed and it was undoubtedly provided by a powerful religious enthusiasm. The pope might have had the bellatores in mind when he made his call but his message resonated at first among ordinary people and many of them joined the People's Crusade. The poor were the most responsive, oblivious to the dangers that stood on their way to walking in the footsteps of Jesus and gaining their salvation. Barons and knights would be driven by a similar religious enthusiasm even if their departure was less spontaneous. Unfortunately, it would not be long before the People's Crusade became a sordid affair and the barons succumbed to the mirage of earthly glory.

It must be noted that French historians referring to the enthusiasm generated by the Crusades make frequent use of the word *merveilleux* with the meaning of "that could only come from God." The same word with the same meaning will appear centuries later to qualify the destiny of Joan of Arc.

As early as the Second Crusade, seeking victory over Muslim foes will be replaced by the search for personal salvation. Louis VII led this crusade to fulfill a vow made by his deceased brother Philippe and also in penance for the death of the one thousand people trapped in the flames of the church in Vitry-le-Francois during the burning of the town that he had ordered.

There were still preachers cum firebrands addressing crowds in apocalyptic terms and leading God's poor souls to wreak havoc among Jews but the true tone of the Second Crusade was set by Saint Bernard. He preached about penance and purification and on March 31st, 1146 in the presence of King Louis VII, rallied a huge crowd to the cause of the crusade.

The idea of Crusade would remain associated with Jerusalem but the Popes abused the concept of *just war* when they encouraged military expeditions to other parts of the world. These expeditions would also be called Crusades and those who volunteered benefited from the indulgences they would have received had they been on their way to the Holy Land. The Spaniards, who were fighting the Moors and had been dissuaded by the pope to join the first Crusade, received the same indulgences as the participants in a crusade to Jerusalem. These benefits were later extended to the Saxons who fought the Slavs east of the Elbe and to the Livonian crusaders in today's Latvia and Estonia during the last years of the twelfth century. Pope Innocent III, at the beginning of the thirteenth century, will declare the fight against the Cathar heretics to be a just war and bless the first Albigensian Crusade.

Muslims, also, extended their understanding of the Crusades in time and space. Islamic works about the Middle Ages treat the Crusades as just an extension of the aggressions began by the Normans when they conquered Islamic Sicily around year one thousand A.D. and which lasted up to 1492 when the last Muslims were driven out of Spain.

Despite all the deviances from the original spirit of a crusade, *to go on a Crusade* remained the highest political ideal of kings and great lords in Europe during the Middle Ages. In the words of Huizinga "The conquest of Jerusalem could not but present itself to the mind as a work of piety and heroism, that is to say, of chivalry."

Going on a crusade was perceived as a sacred duty, a *must* before facing one's creator even if, after the Eighth Crusade, the attraction of Jerusalem, strong as it still was, led to mostly unfulfilled dreams; there was much talk of wearing the cross but few took to the road. The English King Henry V, for one, did not. On his deathbed in 1422 he expressed regrets that God had not let him live long enough to go and conquer Jerusalem. A few decades earlier, in 1396, the house of Burgundy had answered a call for help from the king of Hungary to stop the invading Ottoman Turks. There was glory to be gained by going on a crusade and becoming the protector of Christendom but this military expedition ended in a disaster and a tragic defeat at *Nicopolis*. It was the last large-scale crusade.

The Kingdom of Jerusalem: A Feudal State in the Middle East

The first Crusade had one tangible achievement: the founding of the *Kingdom of Jerusalem*. Even though legend says that he refused to wear a gold crown in the very place where Jesus had worn a crown of thorns, Godfrey is considered to be the first king of the new kingdom.

Several of the great lords had not continued their march towards Jerusalem after fighting their way through Anatolia. They did not resist the lure of an exotic kingdom in the Middle East and stopped short of their avowed goal of freeing the Holy City.

As early as September 1097, Baudouin, Godfrey's brother, a born conqueror, had taken over the county of Edessa, north of today's border between Syria and Turkey. He had achieved this in the most unscrupulous manner and then married an Armenian princess to consolidate his conquest.

Bohemond de Tarente stayed behind after the conquest of Antioch and headed a principality there.

Raymond de Saint Gilles, Count of Toulouse, after contributing more than his fair share of the conquest of the Holy City, did not escape the temptation to add a county along the Lebanese coast to his possessions in southwest France. In 1102 he settled next to the peninsula of Tripoli and set siege to the town held by Fatimid Muslims. One by one he conquered the territories that would form the county of Tripoli; the town itself surrendered after his death to his oldest son Bertrand.

The Kingdom of Jerusalem

Godfrey's reign was short-lived, he died a year after having been one of the main actors during the capture of Jerusalem. As soon as Baudouin, in faraway Edessa, received news of the death of his brother, he led a small group of four hundred knights and one thousand foot soldiers towards the Holy City. It was a dangerous journey, and Baudouin knew that somewhere along the mountainous Lebanese coast, he would be under the menace of the deadly Turkish archers who controlled Damascus. He pressed forward after reaching Antioch and continued even after one half of his men abandoned him. Luck was on his side when a sworn enemy of the Turks came to him and offered information about a planned ambush lying in wait. Baudouin showed great skill, outmaneuvered the Turks and succeeded in reaching Jerusalem with a small group of survivors. He was crowned Baudouin I on Christmas day 1100. The courage of Baudouin and of his men impressed the Christian communities, raised their spirits and they rallied behind him after his coronation.

Baudouin, the warrior, had conquered the cities along the coastline and, despite numerous setbacks, gained control of a territory extending from southern Palestine to the north of present-day Syria.

When Baudouin was crowned king, he became head of a kingdom that was far from united and would have to contend with the powerful and ambitious lords in Edessa, Antioch and Tripoli. He successfully imposed his authority and became the acknowledged suzerain. In his role as feudal lord he answered pressing calls for assistance on the battlefield and resolved disputes between his vassals. He was the true founding father of the Kingdom of Jerusalem and established it as a solid military monarchy.

In 1118, during a daring expedition to Egypt, Baudouin became suddenly ill and by the end of April he was dead. Luckily for the kingdom, his cousin Baudouin du Bourg, who had succeeded him as count of Edessa, on a pilgrimage to Jerusalem, arrived on the day of the funeral. The great barons were duly impressed by his character and without hesitation elected him king. Baudouin II was a true knight, more calculating than his bold cousin. He would be a wise suzerain for thirteen years and consolidate the kingdom built by Baudouin I. During his reign, the Frank and Muslim leaders remained in a constant state of war but their relationship became more cordial. Weakened by years of battling in all corners of his kingdom, Baudoin surrendered the crown to his eldest daughter Melisande and her husband Fulk of Anjou. He then retired in a community of monks in Jerusalem and died shortly after.

Baudouin II had married a Cilician Armenian, and remaining

without male heir, had searched several years earlier for a proper husband for Melisande. At the instigation of the King of France, Louis VI, he had given her hand to Fulk. The count of Anjou and Maine was no adventurer in search of fortune. He was the head of a powerful house in Capetian France, had four children from a first marriage and one of his grandsons would become Henry II, first Plantagenet king of England. Fulk, after planting the seeds of a great house in Europe, managed his oriental kingdom wisely. He died in 1143, victim of one of those fatal horseback riding accidents that were so recurrent in the Middle Ages; while he was hunting, his horse tripped, fell on him and crushed his skull.

The death of their king came at the worst time for the Franks. Fulk's oldest son was too young to reign and the kingdom was governed by his wife, Melisande. She took her role most seriously and was feared by the great barons. After Baudouin III was crowned, her obstinacy at holding on to power was such that the new king had to use force against his mother. During her regency the danger for the kingdom came from the Turks in control of Aleppo. Zinki and then his son Nour ed-Din, the Atabegs, that is, the governors, drove the Franks out of Edessa, exterminated their Armenian allies and set their sights on Antioch. The Franks were at risk of losing major portions of the territories which they had patiently brought under their control during the previous half century.

Reinforcement from the homeland was dearly needed. Bernard de Clairvaux, with great conviction, preached a new crusade in March 1146 at Vezelay. A year later the German emperor Conrad III preceded Louis VII of France and his wife Alienor of Aquitaine on the road to the Holy Land by way of Constantinople. Before departing, in May 1147, Louis and Alienor had gone to the Abbey of Saint Denis and had been entrusted with the red and gold oriflamme, the battle standard of the French kings. The pope himself presented Louis with a pilgrim's bag and stick, a reminder that, in the eyes of the church, the Crusades remained foremost pilgrimages even though they had become military expeditions.

For reasons which might have more to do with domestic affairs than political necessity, the French king, ignoring the calls to fight Nour ed-Din and help the count of Antioch regain control over his county, set out for Jerusalem and then, unsuccessfully, besieged Damascus. This was a very unwise decision and the Second Crusade came to nothing more than military disappointments and petty infighting. Fortunately for historians, this lackluster endeavor was enlivened by a supposed affair between Alienor and her uncle Raymond de Poitiers. Raymond had been lured to the Holy Land a few years earlier to marry Constance, the very young heiress of the principality of Antioch and would be killed a few months after the French king departed from the Holy Land on Easter 1149. More would be heard in the years to come of the man who killed Raymond; his name was Chirkouh, a Kurdish emir, trusted companion of Nour ed-Din. Constance, intent on enjoying her widowhood, did not resist her attraction to a dashing newcomer to the Holy Land, Renaud de Chatillon, who would soon acquire a sinister reputation and become instrumental in the fall of the kingdom.

Baudouin III, who came of age in 1152, would be the model King of Jerusalem, the first to be born in the Holy Land. He was known for his virtues, battled Nour ed-Din successfully and began a charmed life when he married the beautiful young Theodora, the niece of the Byzantine Emperor Manuel Comnenus. The prospect of a close association between the Frankish Kingdom and the Byzantine emperor raised high hopes of decisively defeating the Turks and the Arabs. Unfortunately, the *Byzantine* politics of Manuel and, to the great despair of the Christian community, the death in 1162 of Baudouin III at the age of thirty-three (poisoned by his physician?) did not allow this promising policy to materialize. The young king was mourned by friends and foes throughout the kingdom.

The next feudal king, Amaury I, brother of Baudouin III, also died too young for the good of the kingdom. He had launched early in his reign a strategy which, if successful, would have consolidated the Christian presence in the Holy Land. The Shiite Fatimid Caliphate ruling Egypt was in full decadence and Amaury saw a great opportunity to establish a Frankish protectorate to the south of the Kingdom of Jerusalem. Nour el-din who had added Damascus to his conquests and was in full control of Muslim Syria, was also aware of the weakening hold of the Fatimids on Egypt. The Christian and the Muslim leaders fought to a standstill in Egypt neither gaining an advantage. Amaury thought he had tipped the scale in his favor when he married a Byzantine princess but he then made a strategic mistake which pushed the Egyptians in the arms of the Turks from Syria. By 1169, Chirkouh, Nour ed-Din's general and companion, was the new vizier of Egypt. Still, there was hope that with the collaboration of Byzantium the Franks could establish authority over Egypt and there was also hope that when Nour ed-Din died his son might see the benefit of an alliance with the Franks against the Syrian Turks. Amaury was putting the last touch to his strategy when he died of typhus in July 1174. This was one more terrible blow to the Kingdom of Jerusalem. All the while, the rise of a united Muslim monarchy announced the slow and inexorable decline of Frankish control in Palestine and Syria.

There had been no rest for the kings of Jerusalem and for the lords in Edessa, Antioch and Tripoli during the first seventy years of their rule in the Holy Land and greater Syria. The records show tragedies for the Franks but also debacles for the Turks, furious cavalry charges by the Crusaders matched by deadly whirlwinds of Muslim arrows. The territories occupied by the Franks remained in constant flux, controlled by a transitory and violent minority of Christian lords. Brave and *courtois* behavior was followed by the most cruel acts and demonic treasons.

More stability could have been gained if strategic alliances had been in place. The *poulains,* the hot-headed second-generation Franks, did not have the political savvy of their fathers and in their eyes any type of cooperation with the Muslims was treason. There should have been solid alliances with the Greek Christians and several were sealed but the Byzantines always remained distrustful of the Crusaders and rightly so. The hopes of a more lasting Frankish community in the kingdom also rested on substantial reinforcement from Europe but too many warrior-pilgrims ended up massacred in Anatolia on their way to the Holy Land.

Yusuf Salah-ud-Din ibn Ayyub

There is an often overlooked building behind the great Omayyad mosque in Damascus. A sign at the entrance reads "The Shrine of Saladin." Inside, in a mausoleum, two sarcophagi, side by side. The marble one donated by the German Emperor Wilhelm II is empty - the remains of the sultan rest in one made of carved wood.

A modest tomb in the shadow of a great mosque befits Saladin, a Kurdish Sunni, whose fame lies as much in his modesty as in his success in uniting the Muslims and defeating the Franks.

Saladin was a nephew of Chirkouh and had been at his side when the Muslims and the Franks battled in Egypt. He was still there when his uncle died two months after being named vizier of the Fatimid Caliphate; Chirkouh had been prone to excesses and suffocated after too copious a meal. The advisors to the caliph thought they had in Saladin a most suitable replacement. He was young, inexperienced, and they could manipulate him with ease. They would quickly be proven wrong.

The new vizier behaved as the real master of Egypt. He was not ambitious but good fortune had placed him in a powerful position. As vizier, he was under the authority of a young dying caliph but he truly owed his position to Nour ed-Din and Damascus was far from Cairo. For five years Saladin succeeded in keeping Nour ed-Din at bay, all the while showing respect for the atabeg.

In 1174, Nour ed-Din died and was succeeded by his underage son, as-Saleh. The time had come for Saladin to move beyond Egypt. With seven hundred warriors he dashed to Damascus and proclaimed himself king of Egypt and Syria. The chroniclers will call him sultan. He will claim to be the true successor to Nour ed-Din and the protector of his son. After the death of as-Saleh at the end of 1181, Saladin was the uncontested leader of Egypt and Muslim Syria.

While Saladin alternatively cajoled and threatened the Muslim believers and their emirs, his true enemy remained the Franks. He was determined to reconquer Jerusalem but waited to be in command of a united army of committed Muslim believers before moving aggressively into Palestine. Patience was a virtue that would serve him well, even though his detractors in the Muslim camp presented it as a weakness.

The Kingdom of Jerusalem had a new king. Amaury had died the same year as Nour ed-Din and had been replaced by his thirteen-year-old son, Baudouin IV. When he became king, the young man was already hopelessly weakened by leprosy. His tutor, Guillaume de Tyr, left moving portraits of his royal student. Guillaume, who would be elected archbishop, is the author of a *History of the Crusades* which has remained one of the greatest chronicles of the men who came to the Holy Land during the first Crusade and founded the Kingdom of Jerusalem. The future archbishop saw in the king a charming young man, gifted and attractive, and was the first to recognize the symptoms of the cruel disease that would afflict the prince.

For many years the young King of Jerusalem would hold his own against Saladin. In 1180, Baudouin and Saladin signed a quasi-peace treaty. This was a major achievement for the Franks and their king, but the fragile peace was broken by the inconsiderate and reckless behavior of one man, Renaud de Chatillon. Renaud was a magnificent warrior but without scruples and political sense, the true picture of a lawless adventurer who repeatedly broke the terms of the peace agreement. This played into the hand of Saladin and led to war.

The *Leper King*, one of the noblest figures of the Crusades, died in March 1185. His reign had been eleven years of physical agony, but he had never lost his dignity and had steadfastly exercised the responsibilities of a Christian king. As his end neared, and he could no longer ride, he would ask to be carried to the battlefield on a stretcher. This act of bravery and his very presence would galvanize the Frank knights and cause even the most battle-hardened warriors of Saladin to retreat.

A few months after Baudouin's death, his sister Sybille, despite her brother's warnings, had her husband, Guy de Lusignan, crowned as king. She had made a frivolous choice when she had married the young man from Poitou whose only asset was his *bella figura,* and she made an unconscionable mistake when she put her crown on his head in September 1186. Guy de Lusignan and a clique of supporters, who included the brutal, brigand-knight Renaud de Chatillon, soon put the Christian Kingdom of Jerusalem again on the verge of collapse.

Guy de Lusignan had been king for only a few months when Renaud breached the truce one more time. The state of war returned. Saladin called on his allies and thousands of Arab, Turk, and Kurdish warriors on horseback and on foot were soon on their way to Damascus. The sultan knew that such a formidable army would overwhelm the Franks if he could draw them into a major battle and he set his trap. The Muslim army besieged the citadel of Tiberius on the shores of Lake Tiberius, also known as Sea of Galilee, and waited. Raymond III of Tripoli begged de Lusignan for restraint even though Raymond's wife was prisoner in the citadel. The weak king, however, followed the selfish advice of several lords and, led by his own stubborn pride, set his armies on a deadly course against the Muslim forces. He assembled more than one thousand five hundred knights and twenty thousand men on foot near Sephora in Galilee and on July 3 left the safety of the wells and marched towards Tiberius. The knights were confident they could cross the arid plain in one day but had to endure a torrid sun and the constant attacks of swirling Muslim horsemen. At dusk they still had been kept from reaching the waters of the lake and were suffering from desperate thirst. They set up camp on a hill called *Hattin* and the first rays of dawn revealed a hopeless situation. They were surrounded and, later, despite heroic attempts to break through, were overwhelmed. The men who survived the massacre at Hattin were taken prisoner, and the Franks had no army left to defend their kingdom. Saladin spared the life of Guy de Lusignan —he was a king after all— but Renaud de Chatillon paid the price of his arrogance.

It was not long before Saladin and his allies were under the walls of Jerusalem. Balian d'Ibelin, one of the few knights who had been allowed to return to Jerusalem, had taken charge of the defense of the city. Everyone participated and there were numerous heroic acts but Balian wisely accepted the generous surrender terms offered by Saladin.

The respect shown by the Kurd for his enemies was lauded by the chroniclers of the time. In early October the sultan made his historic entry into Jerusalem and, in a symbolic gesture, toppled the gilded cross erected by the Christians almost a century earlier on the Mosque of Omar. By the end of the year, only a few fortresses in the mountain ranges and a handful of coastal towns were still in the hands of the Franks.

Richard's Crusade

Reports of the disastrous debacle at Hattin prompted Pope Gregory VIII to call for a new Crusade. Three sovereigns took the cross, Frederic I also known as Barbarossa, Henry II and Philippe Auguste. The German Emperor was the first on the road, with a superb army, maybe a hundred thousand strong. He left Ratisbonne in May 1189 and masterfully crossed perilous Anatolia, in the process sending fear through the ranks of Saladin's commanders. Then, a miracle saved the Muslims in Syria. While crossing a river in southern Anatolia, on horseback, Emperor Barbarossa fell and drowned, unable to stand because of the weight of his armor. The organizational strength of the German army became its weakness, leaderless it disintegrated.

It was only in April 1191 that Philippe Auguste landed in Saint Jean d'Acre. The English king, Richard I, reached Syria a few months later. Richard I had taken the cross after the death of his father Henry II in July

1189. The French king returned barely more than a year after reaching the Holy Land; always the realist, he saw an opportunity to take political advantage of Richard's absence from the Continent.

The King's Crusade turned out to be Richard's crusade and his battles against Saladin would be among the most epic of two centuries of expeditions to the Holy Land.

The English king will be in sight of the walls of Jerusalem on several occasions but will never try to conquer the city; he was well aware that the Franks only held the coast and Saladin, in control of most of the interior, was too much of a threat. Richard was formidable during battles and his bravery forced the admiration of the Muslims. In July 1192, Jaffa, surrounded by Saladin, was ready to surrender, when the sight of the English king on a nearby beach sent the besiegers in a panicked flight. The fierce fighting between Richard and Saladin continued up to the end of the summer when news came from Europe that John, Richard's brother, and Philippe Auguste were seizing control of Richard's kingdom. A peace agreement was hastily negotiated. It allowed the Franks to keep control of the coast from Tyre to Jaffa and granted access to Jerusalem to the Christian pilgrims.

There was dissension in both camps, the leaders had lost their drive to vanquish, and the time had come for the Franks and the Muslims to catch their breath. With a peace agreement in place Richard felt free to return to Europe. His journey would be adventurous, the kind that makes for enjoyable historical novels. As to Saladin, physically weakened, he knew his end was near. He had been in poor health for years and had consulted regularly with the judeo-arabic doctor Maimonides. He rode to Damascus where he would die peacefully on 2 March 1193 while listening to verses from the Koran.

His last military campaign had been a painful disappointment. His entourage had known that he had not pursued the Franks hard enough after his glorious victories at Hattin and Jerusalem. This had come to haunt him when, in August 1189, Guy de Lusignan, of all men, had gathered enough knights to set siege to Acre. Saladin had come to the rescue of the Muslims trapped in the city. The besiegers were now besieged! The Franks, though, were in the most favorable position; they were in control of the harbor and were well-supplied in men and goods from Europe. For two years neither side had been in a position to make decisive progress, and then, at long last, the Franks had entered Acre. This had been a blow to Saladin, a cruel reversal.

The concluding act of the siege of Acre should have been the negotiation of the release of prisoners but King Richard, for whatever reason, killed the three thousand men he had captured. The Muslim chroniclers always contrast the brutal act of the Christian king with the numerous cases of chivalrous behavior shown by Saladin during his feuding with the Franks.

A Pilgrimage without Faith

This is how the French historian Rene Grousset called the Sixth Crusade which is worth a special mention because of the role played by the German emperor Frederic II. The emperor, who had become king of Jerusalem by marriage, was fascinated by Islam, actually more by the culture than the religion, and intensely suspicious of Frankish nobility. He took advantage of divisions in Saladin's empire and succeeded in restoring the Kingdom of Jerusalem, obtaining through diplomacy and negotiations what the sword of King Richard had failed to achieve. The Christians kept Jerusalem for a few years only. After the Muslim Empire was reunited in the hands of one of Saladin's nephew, the Franks, once again, controlled only a narrow strip of coastal land and, by 1247, were at risk of being overwhelmed. This, as we shall see in the last chapter, is when Saint Louis led the Seventh Crusade.

A Complex Heritage

Although the Crusades have left memories of the exploits of Richard and Saladin, the heroism of the Leper King and the myths and legends of the monk-warriors, the massacres after the fall of Jerusalem and the sack of Constantinople have left even more lasting impressions. The judgment of history would be harsh on the Crusades, particularly during the Age of Reason when the Middle Ages were seen as infused with religious obscurantism.

Along the roads followed by the Crusaders, the Franks are still associated with excessive pride and cruelty. Among Muslims, the

Crusades have remained a source of resentment against Christians and, by extension, the West.

It is difficult for enlightened minds in the twenty-first century to see the Crusades in anything other than a negative light, all the while acknowledging that only an irrational force, faith, could have driven thousands of men and women to leave everything behind and start on the dangerous journey to Jerusalem. It is also presumptuous for the same enlightened minds to be critical of the people who participated in the military expeditions to the Middle East. They had the mentality of their time, capable of violence and cruelty and then, without discontinuity, accomplish great acts of generosity and devotion. They lived in a world where religion was omnipresent and modeled every aspect of their life. There was no separation between religious and profane. The Muslims, these other believers, had the same motivations and followed the precepts of the jihad codified several centuries earlier.

The Crusades were instrumental in molding a Christian West. Unfortunately, the Soldiers of Christ, as they are sometimes called, opened the gates to abuse of violence and intolerance under the cover of so-called just causes.

Crusades in Languedoc

A new heresy in Occitania.

Since the early days of Christianity, there had been various interpretations of the scriptures, and speculations on the nature of Christ and the Trinity. At the turn of the millennium, many Christians worshiped Christ mostly as a pure spirit and rejected his human nature. These believers were not in conformity with the thinking in Rome which, at that time, was reaffirming the physical presence of Christ in the Eucharist. These dissidents also preached a more spiritual life and were very critical of the Church as an institution and worldly power.

Catharism was one such heresy which found a favorable ground in the southwest of France. It might have been an avatar of *Bogomilism*, the dualist doctrine preached in the middle of the tenth century by the Bulgarian priest Bogomil and which had followers in various parts of western Europe during the next two centuries. The name *cathar* coined in 1163 by Eckbert von Schonau, a German monk, might be derived from a Greek word meaning pure. The Cathar did not survive persecutions in northern Europe but flourished in the north of Italy, Bosnia and Greece. In France, they found a home around Toulouse and Albi. In that region, by the end of the twelfth century, a loose federation of Cathar churches was competing with the Church of Rome.

The men and women who formed the clergy of the Cathar church became later known as *Perfects*. They had received the *consolament*, the imposition of hands by a Perfect, and the Holy Spirit was believed to have descended from heaven and inhabit the corporal body of the postulant. He/she had become *hereticus perfectus*, a perfect heretic. The consolament was administered to the *credentes*, believers, only in one other circumstance, on their death bed. The Perfects did not think themselves as Cathars but as *bons hommes* and *bonnes femmes*.

The Cathar religion flourished in the region sometimes called Occitania, the land where the *langue d'oc* was spoken. There, the people had lost their enthusiasm for the Catholic Church, the local Catholic bishops were not forceful in eradicating this heresy, and the dissident religion found a serious following among the local lords. The Catholics in Occitania were comfortable with their Cathar neighbors, whether they lived in a city or in a castrum, a fortified town where people mingled and different religions coexisted peacefully. One should not be surprised that beliefs coming from the Orient took root there, noted Michelet, as the region had seen the commingling of Gauls, Romans, Saracens, Visigoths and other peoples coming from Spain, and had been strongly influenced by three religions, Jewish, Christian and Muslim. Ever since the first Crusade, Occitania had looked towards the Mediterranean and been receptive to new doctrines.

Dualist Heretics or Mere Dissidents?

In the eyes of the great Church of Rome the Cathars were dualists alleged to believe in two gods, one good, one bad; *gnostic* and *Manichean* are terms often used as synonyms for dualist. On the eve of the thirteenth century, this was a very serious accusation. The Nicene Creed begins with "We believe in one God," and Saint Augustine in the fifth century had thoroughly discredited Manicheism, a dualist religion started in the third century by the Persian prophet Mani. Ever since, it had been convenient for the Church of Rome to label many doctrinal deviances as dualist in nature and so to accuse them of being heresies.

At the source of the dualist beliefs is the question of the origin of evil: *Unde malum*? Whence evil? Evil become a theological conundrum when it conflicted with beliefs in the existence of a benevolent, omniscient, and omnipotent God. This is how David Hume presents the questions as posed in the third century BC by Epicurus:

"Is he [God] willing to prevent evil but not able? Then he is impotent. Is he able but not willing? Then he is malevolent. Is he both able and willing? Whence then is evil?

The Gnostic dualists in the second century had offered a satisfying theodicy, an attempt to reconcile the existence of evil with a benevolent and omnipotent God: they argued that the world is not the work of God but of an inferior deity. When the Cathar religion took root in Occitania in the twelfth century, this was the one answer that could satisfy a believer. It was in sync with the rhythm of life, which had no room for atheism, and it offered a satisfying theodicy.

The Church looked for the answer to the threat of dualism in the theodicy of Saint Augustine (354-430) who believed in a perfect world ruined by the Fall. God created man free of evil, but he was betrayed by his creation. Evil was not in the nature of the created man; it was brought to him by the devil, a fallen angel. Evil is not a creation of God but a reckless product of free will gone bad. God is one, mighty, and good.

The Cathar reading of the ancient documents available to the Christians differed from Augustine's theodicy. Their interpretation was that God could not have anything to do, directly or indirectly, with the evil world in which we live. The Cathar in the southwest of France called their faith the *entendesa del Be,* a deep understanding of the Good.

They did not believe in two Gods but in one God who was good. As the existence of evil cannot be denied, however, they also believed that evil had its own primary cause. For a Cathar, everything bad or evil in this world emanates from this pre-existing principle, and humanity is bad by nature. The first man was not created good, and if the name of the evil creator is Satan, Satan was not a good angel who became evil. The evil human body holds prisoner a soul that needs to find its way back to God.

How will the soul find its way back to God? In another major departure from Christian orthodoxy, the Cathars believed that when the body dies, the freed soul enters another body—an animal if the dead has been a serious sinner, a human body otherwise—to do penance and then moves from body to body as long as it has not found a good home. It might take up to nine reincarnations to return to God. An eschatology that ignored purgatory and where hell is of this world was of course foreign to Rome. It must be noted that most of what is known about these beliefs comes from the examinations (i.e. the interrogations of Cathars) conducted by the inquisitor Jacques Fournier in the county of Foix around 1320.

It is evident that if flesh is evil, Jesus could not have become incarnate. Nor could there have been a Passion. Christ was sent by God to bring the Holy Spirit and show the souls the way out of the evil world. The Cathars were among the last Docetists, those who claimed that Jesus only *seemed* to be a man.

The dualist belief in an evil world not created by God led to irreconcilable differences with the Church of Rome. The two churches shared only one belief, the existence of a good God who had sent a savior. Otherwise, they diverged on other creeds and practices.

The dualist label did influence people's attitudes towards the Cathars, and their religion was positioned far outside orthodox Christianity. The label also fed the numerous myths surrounding their history.

The beliefs of the Cathars have been seen in a different light in more recent times, thanks to the publication in 1939 of abstracts of manuscripts going as far back as 1220. Up to then, only a few archives had been available, and most of what was known came from the archives of the Church of Rome which largely represented the views of the victors. The documents actually used by the Cathars that have been recently unearthed and analyzed show that their faith was grounded in the New Testament and in apocryphal texts. Modern scholars of the Cathars don't hesitate to call them Christians and label them dissidents not heretics.

The Church's War

In 1198, the cardinals unanimously selected Lothario Conti to be the new pope, Innocent III. He was still a young man, thirty-eight, well known in Rome and well-respected in the Church. Innocent would become the true representative of God on earth and never hesitate to remind kings and lords of the absolute supremacy of the spiritual over the temporal.

The new pope and his allies in Cluny could not let the Cathar dissidence/ heresy survive and prosper on the periphery of the Church of Rome. As he began his pontificate, Innocent III was confident that he could convert those who had lost their way, even though the preaching by Saint Bernard, the charismatic Cistercian, half a century earlier, had failed to change minds in Occitania. The legates launched a campaign of public theological debates which did not succeed in stirring much passion. After other unfruitful attempts at reaching out to the lost sheep the pope thought he had found the right missionary in the Spaniard Dominic de Guzman. The Occitans were taken aback by the young preacher's humility, which was in such sharp contrast with the pomp surrounding the legates and prelates. Although Dominic travelled throughout the countryside tirelessly preaching to the dissidents, his efforts achieved only limited success. His close contact with the Cathar heresy had one major outcome. Dominic was convinced of the need for informed preachers and, under Innocent III's successor, a new order of Mendicants would be created, the Dominicans.

Despite all the efforts of the Church of Rome, the Cathar dissidence kept gaining ground. Innocent III came to realize that this new religion could not be eradicated as long as it benefited from the protection, or at the very least the tolerance, of lords in Occitania. The most powerful was Raymond VI, Count of Toulouse, a direct descendant of Raymond IV who had such an influence on the outcome of the first Crusade. A holy war would be necessary and this is when an incident, most unfortunate for Occitania, changed the course of events: in January 1208, the legate Pierre de Castelnau was assassinated after leaving a stormy meeting with Raymond VI. The pope saw the hand of the Count behind this affair, and without further delay called for a crusade against the heretic Cathars.

Philippe Auguste could not be tempted to join the crusade, but did not discourage his barons and many took the cross with great enthusiasm. The largest body of what became known as the *Albigensian crusaders*, led by a legate, left Lyon in June 1209, while a second group followed the archbishop of Bordeaux, and a third one, the bishop of Le Puy. The three groups met at Casseneuil where the first burnings at the stake took place. A month later, the joint forces were in front of Beziers. This fortified town along the Mediterranean controlled a region that had been very welcoming to the Cathars. A foolish mistake by the burghers allowed the assailants to enter the city, and there followed one of the most cruel massacres of the Middle Ages. No one was spared. The event gave birth to the legend which says that, when asked in the heat of the battle, how the crusaders entering Beziers would recognize the heretics, the orthodox legate Amaury would have answered *kill them all... Novit enim Dominus qui sunt eius,* God will surely recognize his own.

In August, the crusaders laid siege to Carcassonne. Viscount Raymond-Roger Trencavel, known for his sympathies towards the Cathars, was hoping to negotiate an honorable surrender. He left the safety of the fortified *Cité,* rode to the camp of the assailants, then, in a treacherous move, the crusaders did not allow him to return. Carcassonne, left leaderless, surrendered. The people who had sought refuge behind the fortifications were allowed to leave, the Cité was spared destruction and the crusaders amassed an enormous bounty. Young Raymond-Roger Trencavel, only 24 years old, was thrown in a dungeon where he died three months later. His treatment by the French barons from the North is a sad demonstration of their contempt for their peers from Occitania.

Carcassonne

Carcassonne is both the *Cité Médiévale* at the top of a butte that has been occupied since the sixth century BC and, in the valley below, a fortified town built in the thirteenth century, the *Bastide Saint Louis.*

Carcassonne, Cité Médiévale

The Cité Médiévale is a massive ensemble of ramparts and conical towers, the largest remaining fortress in Europe, inscribed on the UNESCO World Heritage list. It was recognized by UNESCO as an excellent example of a medieval fortified town and the successful outcome of nineteenth century restoration work.

The Romans occupied an *oppidum* on top of the butte rising above the lowlands south of the river Aude. It was at the southern end of a territory they had annexed at the beginning of the second century BC known as *Gallia Narbonensis.* When barbarian tribes became threatening in the fourth century the settlement raised a defensive wall. These fortifications, rebuilt during the Middle Ages, still form the inner enclosure of the Cité.

In 1067 Carcassonne became the property of the Trencavels, the powerful vassals of the count of Toulouse. An age of prosperity ensued, work began on a Romanesque cathedral in 1096 and a chateau was built in the early twelfth century near the western part of the Roman wall. The Albigensian Crusades put an end to the town's Golden Age. In 1226, Carcassonne was annexed to the Royal domain and became the seat of a seneschal, the local representative of the king.

The town lost the strategic military role tied to its proximity to Spain when, in 1659, the Treaty of the Pyrenees handed the Roussillon over to the Kingdom of France, and the border between Spain and France moved much further south, to the Pyrenees Mountains. The Cité had lost its main *raison d'être* and military and civil servants relocated to the town below. The population declined steadily and the massive walls and dungeons fell into disrepair.

The Cité was mostly abandoned when, in the nineteenth century, members of the local elite campaigned for its safeguard. They gained the support of Prosper Mérimée, a man of multiple talents, best known as an archeologist and dramatist, who had been named Inspector General of Historical Monuments in May 1834. In 1840 the cathedral became a protected historical monument and a few years later the same consideration was extended to the fortress as a whole. Eugène Viollet-le-Duc, who had already been assigned the restoration of the cathedral, was entrusted with the renovation of the fortress. He began work on some of the towers in 1855 and, after his death in 1879, this gargantuan project was continued by Paul Boeswillwald and lasted up to 1910.

In an attempt to recreate the appearance given to the fortress by the royal engineers in the thirteenth century, Viollet-le-Duc did a meticulous reading of the ruins. His renovation was in the spirit of the original but did not attempt to preserve the historical buildings. This led his critics to claim that after Viollet-le-Duc's demolitions and rebuilding the end product was not authentic. The controversy died over time, his approach left its mark and he became the best known renovator of medieval religious and civil constructions. Today's visitor discovers the medieval fortress as Viollet-le-Duc imagined it.

One enters the Cité Médiévale at the Porte Narbonnaise. A guided tour starts at the Tourist Office located just to the right of the Porte, and continues through a maze of narrow streets to the chateau and the cathedral. On the way back to the Porte Narbonnaise, on rue du Plo, a modest sign indicates an *Occitan School,* one of several bilingual schools in the Pays d'Oc whose goal is the preservation of Occitan.

At the bottom of the northwest slope of the *oppidium*, the Pont Vieux connects the Cité to the *bastide* Saint Louis. The bastide, nestled between the river Aude and the Canal du Midi, is square shaped with streets crossing at perfect right angles. In the middle, the Place Carnot, former Place aux Herbes, comes to life every Saturday, on market day. This is where the people of Carcassonne dwell today. This new town was started by Saint Louis and was meant to counter the influence of the Cité Médiévale. Its fortifications were destroyed by the Black Prince during the Hundred Years War. The town was, at the time, still located near the border with Spain, it needed better protection, and sturdier walls were built. A bastion was placed at each corner and Bastion Montmorency, built in the middle of the sixteenth century, still seems to protect the entrance to the town from the southeast.

The bastide is *the* place to be on July 14 when the town celebrates the French *fête nationale* with the most stunning fireworks and illuminations.

Simon IV de Montfort: Saint or Devil?

The crusaders' uncontested military victory left the pope with a diplomatic conundrum: who should succeed Trencavel? The spiritual leaders of the Crusade decided to present the title of viscount of Beziers and of Carcassonne to a French baron. The duke of Burgundy, the count of Nevers and the count of Saint Pol, all turned their back on the offer made by the legate Arnaud-Amaury in the name of the pope. It would have been dishonorable to accept a proposition that went against secular custom and feudal rights. The suzerains of these lands were the king of Aragon and the count of Toulouse and the powerless Trencavels were still their honorbound vassal. It was not for the Church to dispose of the title. At last, the decision was entrusted to a commission of two men of the robe and three barons. They elected Simon IV de Montfort.

Who was this new actor in the fight against the Cathars? The de Montforts were minor lords who had settled at the beginning of the eleventh century in the Yvelines, a large plain bordered to the west by territories controlled by the king of England and to the east by the kingdom of the Franks. Several would be named Simon. Little is known about them, so little in fact that reputed historians still don't agree on the precise title of the newly elected viscount of Béziers. Some claim that Simon IV is actually Simon V.

Simon IV de Montfort had first appeared on the political stage at the side of Philippe Auguste while the French king was unsuccessfully fighting Richard I of England. Simon, then, had fallen under the spell of Thibaud de Champagne during the time the count was recruiting for a new crusade; going on a crusade to the Holy Land was a must for an ambitious knight. Simon had entrusted his fief to his wife, Alix, and joined friends and neighbors on the expedition which would be the notorious Fourth Crusade.

During the early stages of that Crusade, the Venetians had convinced the crusaders to set siege to Constantinople. The background of this diversion is to be found in the increasing hostility between Rome and Constantinople and the ambitions of Venice in the Orient. The immediate pretext was a plea of help by Alexis IV to reestablish his father on the throne of the Byzantine Empire and the crusaders' need of the Venitian fleet to reach Egypt. The doge had seen a potentially rewarding quid pro quo and had been more than happy to oblige the crusaders while enticing them to give a hand to the dispossessed emperor. A golden opportunity for His Serenity to intervene in the affairs of Byzantium.

The crusaders did enter the Byzantine capital in April 1204, and then, during three days, proceeded to savagely sack the city. The French contingent, to its credit, did not go further than the outskirts of the city and did not participate in this ignominious act which would have a disastrous long-term impact on the relationship between Greek and Latin Christians. Simon did not go as far as Constantinople but neither did he give up on his initial mission. He reached Jaffa and joined several raids against Muslims led by Amaury, King of Jerusalem, before returning home around 1204.

These adventurous days had established the credentials of Simon IV as an excellent warrior and a true leader. He was around fifty when he was elected viscount, a mature, courageous man, quick in making decisions on the field of battle and knowing how to be ruthless. The choice made by the commission might have seemed a stretch but Simon could be trusted to be loyal to his king and his church.

After the short and successful Albigensian Crusade the lords from the north had returned to their lands and Simon IV was left in Occitania with a hard core of trusted companions. The new viscount was the *Sword of the Church* but, in the eyes of the local lords, he was nothing more than the head of an occupying army. He had to battle ceaselessly, was forced to move swiftly from one corner of his land to the other, unable to trust any of these lords who were his vassals in name only. After the pope confirmed his rights over the land he conquered, the young warrior found more interest in colonizing than in eradicating heresy. Stunningly successfully, a legend in his own time, he also was surprisingly cruel, some will say out of necessity, others out of temperament. A saint for some, a devil for others. Wherever the truth, acts of chivalry would be noticeably absent during this war, one of the cruelest of the Middle Ages.

The military success of the crusade was a smoke screen. Simon IV de Montfort held his conquests only through terror while his powerful neighbor, Raymond VI, Count of Toulouse, controlled much of Occitania. As to the main goal of the crusade, the eradication of heresy, nothing much had been achieved. The Cathar believers were now dispersed throughout the land.

The church knew that it could not destroy the heresy as long as it did not control Raymond's territories. It could have given the *Sword of the Church* to the count of Toulouse but did not trust him to fight heresy. The relationship between Raymond VI and Rome had been tense for many years. The count had been excommunicated in 1207 for his lack of cooperation in fighting the Cathars and, shortly after, had been accused of masterminding the assassination of the legate Pierre de Castelnau. Subsequent attempts to prove his innocence and his willingness to fight the heresy had failed to convince Innocent III. The church trusted Simon

IV de Montfort to bring down Raymond VI and, in the spring of 1211, the second stage of the Crusade began.

Simon IV conducted another harsh military campaign. He conquered, lost and reconquered many towns and castles, slowly encircled Toulouse and his campaign culminated in a memorable encounter in September 1213. In front of Muret, a modest castle a short ride south of Toulouse, an outnumbered Simon faced the combined forces of Raymond VI Count of Toulouse and Peter II King of Aragon. The king had come from Barcelona with one thousand of his glorious knights to fight for the honor of Occitania. Brave but too impetuous, he joined the fray early in the encounter, was quickly surrounded by French knights, his *maynade*, knights from his House of Aragon, came to the rescue, but all succumbed and Peter II was killed. Simon was victorious once more.

The king of Aragon had been a formidable presence in the region. He was the brother-in-law of Raymond VI and controlled extensive territories in Languedoc. Montpellier had become his by marriage, Perpignan and the Roussillon, the county tucked in the most south-eastern corner of France, had belonged to the Aragonese crown since 1172 and the counts of Foix and Comminges were his vassals. At the beginning of 1213, Peter II had pleaded for an end to the Albigensian crusade but, unable to convince the Pope, had sided with the people of his culture, the Occitan. At the time of the battle of Muret, he was fresh from a victorious crusade in Spain against the Maures and a brilliant success at the battle of *Las Navas de Tolosa*. He had always hoped to play a major role in the Crusades and his dramatic death at Muret came too soon to allow him to influence the final outcome of this clash of cultures.

This had added one more chapter in the history of the relationship between Spain, Catalonia in particular, and France. The count-kings of Aragon (count of Barcelona and king of Aragon) will control land north of the Pyrenees long after the defeat at Muret. A border between the French and Aragonese territories would be negotiated in 1258. The Spanish possessions, sometimes called North Catalonia, would change hands several times during the coming centuries and would be definitely annexed by the Kingdom of France only under Louis XIV in 1659.

The death of Peter II of Aragon and the disaster of Muret seemed a mortal blow to the enemies of the Church of Rome. Toulouse was their ultimate stronghold but it remained such an intimidating symbol of the power of the count that Simon waited up to May 1215, and turned his entrance into a very symbolic affair. The legate was at the side of Simon of course, but most importantly, so was the son of the king of France—a reminder that the king was the victor's suzerain.

During these troubled years in Occitania the Sword of the Church had been held by de Montfort and Philippe Auguste had stayed out of sight. The time for the king of France to be personally involved had not yet come, the Church was leading the fight against heresy and that played into the hands of the secular powers.

Innocent III used the forum of the Fourth Lateran Council in 1215 to remind the 483 prelates, archbishops and bishops assembled in the ancient Basilica Saint John Lateran on the morning of November eleven of the importance of fighting heresy. Dissidence was spreading in the south of France, becoming a growing threat to the Church of Rome and the spiritual and secular powers, jointly, needed to restore orthodoxy. The council heeded the warnings and made it an obligation for the secular powers to combat heresy; those who opposed the church ran the risk of being declared heretic and see the pope dispose of their lands. This is when Simon IV de Montfort, the knight from the faraway Yvelines, was granted all the fruit of his conquests over heretic lords.

Raymond VI had resigned during the council and transferred his assets to his son but to no avail, the Raymonds were dispossessed of all the land they had lost during their war against de Montfort. A few months after the end of the council, the king confirmed Simon's title of Comte de Toulouse.

The old Count Raymond was not a man to accept this state of affairs. As Provence had not been colonized by the crusaders, he retreated there with his young son, and prepared his reconquest. The Raymonds could count on strong support in Occitania where the decisions of the council had been perceived as unduly punitive. Civil war was unavoidable.

Toulouse was the key to the success of this new campaign. Raymond VI, benefiting from the complicity of the people in the city, entered his (former) capital in September 1217 and forced de Montfort's garrison and the members of the de Montfort clan to find refuge in the citadel, the so-called Chateau Narbonnais. Simon, who was battling somewhere in Provence, returned in great haste. The ensuing siege was long and frustrating for the French. The Occitans started the rumor that the men of the king were punished by God. As the siege entered its ninth month, a rock fired by a stone-throwing machine crushed Simon IV de

Montfort's skull, and so died a great soldier. Amaury de Montfort, his oldest son, could not protect the de Montfort holdings, he did not have his father's genius in the field and the lackluster help he received from the future Louis VIII was of no avail. He lacked the strength to be the temporal sword of the Church.

While the saga of the de Montfort in Languedoc was coming to an end, the Raymonds remained very present. When Raymond VI died in 1222, Raymond VII had regained the lost territories and the Cathars were again conspicuous. Unsurprisingly, the young count was not more successful than his father in convincing the church that he would put substantial pressure on the Cathars, and the pope needed to turn to another champion in his fight against heresy in Occitania.

The King's War

When Honorius III replaced Innocent III he set his mind on crushing the heresy. This called for another crusade and this one could only be led by the king of France. After much bargaining, and only after the legate had affirmed the rights of Louis VIII to Raymond's land, did the young king take the cross. The date was January 30, 1226, the campaign against heretics had clearly shifted to a war of conquest; the king could claim he was, after all, simply doing his duty as monarch.

Neither side had made significant progress when Louis VIII succumbed from a case of dysentery. His reign had been short, not even four years, and his successor, the future Saint Louis, was only thirteen years old. After a period of unproductive stalemate, the Count, the Church and the mother of the king acting as regent, thought it wise to make peace. The Occitans were spent and did not hold high hopes of ultimately defeating the king. As to Blanche de Castille, a peace treaty presented her with a tempting opportunity to bring a southern province into the fold of the kingdom.

The Paris Peace Treaty, also called Treaty of Meaux, was signed in 1229 (there will be another Paris Peace Treaty thirty years later between Louis IX and the English king Henry III). One of the cornerstones of the treaty was the marriage of Blanche's second son, Alphonse de Poitiers, with Raymond VII's daughter Jeanne, his only child; both children were nine years old.

This would be a great coup for the Kingdom of France. Raymond never had any other children and, when Jeanne and Alphonse both died without heir in 1271 while returning from the eighth Crusade, the county of Toulouse and other territories in Languedoc became a significant addition to the kingdom.

Thus, the descendants of Philippe Auguste became the main beneficiaries of the Albigensian crusades which he had only reluctantly endorsed. The crown gained a large window on the Mediterranean Sea and, even though the kingdom will remain anchored in the Ile de France, over time, southern traits will balance its northern temperament.

As to Languedoc, it became *provincial* in the old sense of the word, at the fringes of its powerful neighbors of the north. It lost its independence and its new masters, the Capetian kings, lived far away, in the Ile de France. At a time when information was circulating at the speed of messengers on horseback, the worlds of Paris and Toulouse remained far apart. The Occitan kept their *langue d'oc* but it was now a dialect. They also kept the spirit of religious dissent born with the Cathars. The revolutionary teachings of Calvin and Luther will find great receptivity in Languedoc in the middle of the sixteenth century. Calvinist churches will find homes along a Huguenot Crescent from La Rochelle to the foot of the Alps by way of Cahors and Montpellier. The Occitan, shaped by the preaching of the Cathars, easily grasped the Protestant concepts of justification by faith, the emphasis on scripture and the rejection of the bad, wealthy Church of Rome. They also kept seeking answers to the question at the heart of the Cathar heresy, how to reconcile the existence of God with the presence of evil in the world

Another cornerstone of the Paris Peace Treaty was a quid pro quo: in exchange for giving his daughter to Blanche's son, Raymond VII was again acknowledged as Count of Toulouse. He was also reconciled with the Church but not before a very humiliating rite of penance. The count was led inside a church barefoot, a rope around his neck and flogged in front of the altar. The church where the ceremony took place was no other than Notre Dame de Paris.

In *Before Church and State,* Andrew Willard Jones argues that the heretics had been in violation of the laws of the king as much as those of the church. The people from Languedoc became men of the king and men of the Roman church in the same act of submission. The temporal and spiritual worlds were united in their fight against dissidence and in the promotion of orthodoxy. In this social order there was no room for Cathars.

The heretics remained as present in Occitania as they had been when the first crusaders entered the southwest some twenty years earlier. While the king had done well, the church had not reached its goal. A special institution devoted to fighting heresy was needed. It would be instituted by Pope Gregory IX in April 1233, called *Inquisition* and entrusted to the Mendicant orders, mostly the Dominicans.

The Ultimate Sacrifice: Montsegur (1244)

Pierre Seila and Guillaume Arnaud were the first two inquisitors; Pierre stayed in Toulouse and Guillaume went on a grand tour southeast of the city where he left a trail of fear and suspicion. His zeal and disregard of customary court procedures unnerved the civil authorities, city councils and others. The count of Toulouse complained to the pope but to no avail. The Inquisitors methodically pursued their mission, and the so-called heretics who held to their beliefs were forced into a clandestine life. They still had enough supporters and money to move from one hiding place to another but the noose inexorably tightened.

The hardcore of the resistance sought refuge in the Pyrenees Mountains. Earlier, in 1204, Cathars seeking a haven in these troubled and dangerous times, had built a castle on top of a *pog*, a peak in the Pyrenees. They had found refuge there during the worst of Simon IV de Montfort's persecutions and now, harassed again, this time by the Inquisitors, many had returned to the safety of this mountain hideout. More than 200 would live there in what became the home base of the Cathar Church, Montsegur.

In 1242, Guillaume Arnaud went on another grand tour. He had been assigned a travel companion by the pope, a Franciscan, and they were accompanied by a retinue of nine. On May 28, the party rested in the castle of Avignonet, a small relay town between Toulouse and Carcassonne. Their travel plans had been widely known and the viguier, provost, of Raymond VII, had approached Pierre Roger de Mirepoix, the commander of the garrison at Montsegur, with specific instructions to kill the Inquisitors. A group of more than sixty, all local gentry, rode the seventy miles separating Montsegur from Avignonet and waited outside the town. At nightfall, they were led to Guillaume Arnaud's room and the dreaded Inquisitor and his companions had barely time to kneel in prayer before being pierced by the swords of several assailants.

The message delivered by the viguier to de Mirepoix could only have come from Raymond. The count had not abandoned the fight after the Treaty of Meaux of 1229 but would not have wanted his men to be seen committing such a criminal act. He had failed to forge alliances with foreign sovereigns and this daring coup was meant to awaken Languedoc—but few in Occitania were ready for another war against the barons from the north. Whatever revolt ensued aborted quickly. Raymond went to Paris to renew his homage to the king, signed a new peace agreement in October 1242 and returned to Occitania having promised one more time to fight the heretics.

The Church did not forget its dead, and in the spring of 1243 prepared for the destruction of Montsegur, the Synagogue of Satan. The king's seneschal recruited men from all corners of the province and one year to the day after the Avignonet coup, laid siege to Montsegur.

It seemed an impregnable position. Towards the end of the year the royal recruits became increasingly frustrated and the Perfects were biding their time. Then, a daring team of Basques, at considerable risk, reached a rocky platform on the other side of the keep. Prodded by the bishop of Albi, they lugged heavy wood beams to the top and built a trebuchet, a medieval stone throwing machine. The besieged, at first, survived this new threat but, as the assailants kept closing in, and as their position was becoming desperate, they began surrender negotiations. The representatives of the king, in a generous spirit, granted amnesty to everybody, even to de Mirepoix. The pardon was extended to the Perfects who would renounce their faith, but none took the offer. During a moving ceremony, twenty one *credentes*, believers, asked to be given the *consolamentum*, the sacrament that would make them Perfects. Two hundred and twenty Cathars were led down to a clearing at the foot of hill where they were tied to tall stakes and died in the blaze of a bonfire.

It was March 1244 and the Cathar movement had been decapitated. The fall of Montsegur was the end of any serious dissent by the Cathars from the laws of the king and the Church of Rome.

By 1252 fewer than a hundred Perfects were left when the Church of Rome intensified once again its efforts and began using torture to obtain names and confessions. It will take many more years for all traces of the heresy/dissent to disappear from Occitania and the last known Perfect will be burnt at the stake in 1321.

Montsegur: the "Pog" and its Legends

Pog of Montsegur

The *pog* of Montsegur, the low mountain shaped as a sugarloaf, is an eerie sight. At its top, precariously balanced, is the refuge of the Cathars, barely visible from the road winding through the deep valley. Now and then the ruins emerge from the shadow of the Pyrenees Mountains. At the base of the western slope of the pog, near the *prat dels cremas*, the field where the bonfires were most presumably built, is a simple stele, the only memorial to the tragic events of March 1244.

The ruins, at the end of a treacherous climb, are those of a fortress built around 1280, one of many outposts along the border between France and Spain. The hideout of the Cathars was most presumably a castrum, a fortified village and a keep but any vestige of a Cathar presence has long disappeared.

The tragedy of the Perfects at Montsegur has been recollected time and again. The mystery surrounding the faith of the Cathars, the austerity of their sanctuary, high above a hidden valley in the Pyrenees, the abnegation of men and women singing and praying together as they entered the bonfire, are ingredients that have been kneaded into captivating stories and tales.

The records left by the Inquisitors who interrogated the survivors of the capture of Montsegur indicate that on the eve of the bonfire a handful of Perfects escaped, carrying gold, silver and other valuables. The plot thickened when word spread during the nineteenth century that the valuables also included sacred texts. One of the originators of this myth was Napoleon Peyrat, an anticlerical poet-turned-historian who wrote a *History of the Albigensians* in 1870. No treasure or secret texts ever surfaced.

The pog in the Pyrenees inspired occultists in Paris. They fancied that Montsegur was no other than Montsalvat, the chateau where the Knights of the Holy Grail had safekept the holy cup held by Jesus during the last supper. This was actually not wildly esoteric as the Montsalvat mentioned in Wolfram von Eschenbach's poem, *Parzifal*, and on which Richard Wagner's opera *Parsifal* is loosely based, had been said to be in the wilderness of the Pyrenees.

Another chapter in the mystique of Montsegur came courtesy of a young German, Otto Rahn. He became entranced with the Cathars and in 1933 wrote *Kreuzzug gegen den Gral*, Crusade against the Grail, which places the Cathars in the center of esoteric Grail studies. A few years later, Rahn joined the NAZI party, published *Luzifer Hofgesind*, Lucifer's Court, and redefined the Cathars as southerners of Nordic blood. In the wake of Otto Rahn, a coterie of novelists found inspiration in the mysteries surrounding the beliefs and deeds of the Cathars.

The Inquisition: Arbitrary and Efficient

A judicial process dealing with heretics was already in place when Gregory IX instituted a Special Inquisition. The fight against heresies had mattered to both kings and popes. It had been their creed, ever since Emperor Constantine, that anyone not adhering to the orthodoxy of the church was undermining the foundations of society and opening the door to anarchy.

Since the middle of the twelfth century, the popes had directed the bishops to be at the forefront of the preservation of faith. The Episcopal Inquisition, though, had not been efficient. It was limited geographically and lacked conviction. The secular powers outside of Languedoc had been more active. Frederick II, the Holy Roman Emperor, had even been anxious to take the leadership of the fight.

The need for a fundamentally different approach had led Gregory IX in 1233 to entrust the process to a dedicated cadre of dignitaries of the church reporting to none other than him. The spirit of the institution required them to co-operate with the bishops but, in practice, the considerable authority they wielded put them a step above. Gregory IX paid great attention to the selection of the first inquisitors and could not place his trust in better hands than those of the Mendicants, and primarily the Dominican friars. The *Order of Preachers,* more commonly known as the Dominicans, was new. It had been recognized by Pope Honorius III in 1218 and had quickly spread throughout Europe. Dominic de Guzman, the founder of the Order, had fought heresy in the southwest of France during the previous decade, and his disciples were true combatants of the faith and soldiers of the Church of Rome.

The Dominicans and the other Mendicants conducted their new mission with fanatical zeal. Well-educated and well-coached, they proceeded very systematically, and their novel approach to inquiry would remain the hallmark of all inquisitions. These men must not be confused with the Spanish inquisitors who appeared on the scene much later, at the very end of the fifteen century, the infamous, dark, cruel and fanatic inquisitors whose most notorious model was Torquemada.

The techniques used in the repression of heresy up to Gregory IX (such as the accusatory process and the adversarial procedure) having failed, the new inquisitors had to innovate. The new approach, approved by the pope, took shape slowly and its main attributes would be secrecy and arbitrariness.

The initial inquiries conducted by the inquisitors in Languedoc were general inquiries, the individual ones came later. The inquisitors followed various routines but typically traveled from town to town, village to village, accompanied by a retinue of clerks and gaolers and protected by a few soldiers commissioned by the king. The party was usually small, never more than twenty-four people. Whenever they had reasons to believe that the crop of heretics would be good, they settled in some monastery or maybe in the residence of the bishop, and let it be known that they would soon start their inquiries. This opened a grace period, up to a week, which allowed anyone to come forth and confess his/her sins against the Church of Rome. Those who volunteered avoided the most painful forms of punishment: confiscation of assets, imprisonment or death. They were imposed only canonical penances such as the wearing of a distinctive sign and pilgrimages. The mere confession and penance, though, was not the ultimate goal of the process. A true confession had to include the denunciation of other offenders, and before releasing their prey, the inquisitors kept probing: Who? Where? When? They kept meticulous records which allowed them to crosscheck information from various sources, and slowly build other cases. The inquisitors would be more lenient in their sentencing when they collected a list rich in promising names.

The presumed heretics who had not taken advantage of the grace period were instructed to appear in front of the inquisitors. Those who did not present themselves were temporarily excommunicated, those who did were interrogated. The opening words of the inquisitor always were "I know you have sinned" but nothing more would be said. Guilty of what? Based on whose denunciation? The accused never really knew. He was expected to confess whatever he thought the inquisitor wanted to hear and, most importantly, had to implicate others. This process built on secrecy, denunciation and threats was one of the Machiavellian innovations introduced by the Dominicans. Those who did not volunteer what the inquisitor wanted to hear, or were too honorable to denounce others, were thrown in jail.

There were no defense lawyers and the roles of judge, prosecutor and investigating judge were all played by one person, the inquisitor. One person alone rendered the judgment and decided on the sentence and that was, of course, the inquisitor.

Torture was an efficient means of obtaining crucial information or accelerating a confession. It will be explicitly allowed by the bull *Ad extirpand*a issued in 1252 by Pope Innocent IV. Before or after the bull, the records of those who confessed will never mention that they had been tied to a rack or their feet had been in the stocks.

Those who refused to acknowledge their mistakes and those who recanted had de facto excluded themselves from the Church of Rome. As they were heretics, they could not be allowed to reintegrate society, and the only outcome was death. The sentence of death for heretics was condoned by the Church. In his great classic *Summa Theologica*, left unfinished when he died in 1274, Saint Thomas Aquinas will address the question whether heretics ought to be tolerated and argue that "On the side of the heretic, there is sin, whereby he deserves…to be severed from the world by death", "On the side of the Church, however, there is mercy which looks to the conversion of the wanderer" "If after the first and second admonition...the Church can no longer hope for his conversion...the heretic should be delivered to the secular tribunal to be condemned to death."

The church did entrust the execution of the death sentence to the men of the king or the feudal lords. Burning was the verdict willed by the Holy Roman emperor and the king of France; fire was the ultimate purifier. For their contribution to the arrest and execution of the sentence, the secular powers' reward was the right to confiscate the assets of the victims. The church excommunicated, the secular powers confiscated.

In their drive for efficiency, the Dominicans had devised a clinical approach which gave the prosecutor no room for empathy and created such fear and suspicion in the prosecuted that it inexorably tore apart their humanity. The fundamental tenet of this diabolical mental construct was that heretics did not belong with the creatures of God true to the Church of Rome and, therefore, did not deserve the consideration given to their fellow Christian brothers. Such a construct will have long-lasting implications and resorting to class identification will become a hallmark of the treatment of dissent in Western societies.

Centuries after the first inquisitors perfected their process, Eric Hoffer in *"The True Believer"* dissected the motivations of people who join mass movements and become fanatics. Hoffer was a man of the twentieth century and his thinking was colored by the study of the followers of Stalin and Hitler. Members of the Gestapo were true believers, they never doubted the infallibility of Hitler and the utopian world they had been sold on. People who ran death camps dehumanized their victims by identifying them as members of inferior classes of humans, by throwing away their identities and replacing them with tattooed numbers on their forearms. Eichmann was proud of his obedience, irrespective of what had been asked of him. During their trials after the war, men like him showed no remorse at having followed orders, even when these led to mass murder.

Inquisitors and members of the Gestapo are of all ages. Barbara Tuchman notes in *A Distant Mirror* that because people in the Middle Ages existed under circumstances so different from our own, "qualities of conduct that we recognize as familiar amid these alien surroundings are revealed as permanent in human nature."

Cathar Country in the Twenty-First Century

The Cathars were most at home in the urban centers, villages or small fortified towns, scattered in the area demarcated by Albi, Carcassonne, Foix and Toulouse. Today, their memory is alive alongside any road and in any village and town in that part of France. One sign will read "Vous êtes en pays Cathare," You are in Cathar country, another calls the area "Terre Cathare," Cathar land. Visitors are encouraged to visit *les Chateaux Cathares*, perched on buttes in the Pyrenees Mountains and local tourist offices give out pamphlets in English offering "Holidays in Cathar Land". A butcher in Albi, with dark humor, even calls his shop "Boucherie Cathare," Cathar butcher shop.

The region advertises its pride in a past long gone. The Cathar religion disappeared from that corner of Europe seven hundred years ago when the last heretic was burned at the stake leaving no one to perform the consolamentum. They left scant traces, a small number of documents scattered in various libraries in Europe and a few vestiges, Montsegur and a handful of ruins.

Hikers will enjoy trekking along the *Sentier Cathare*, the Cathar path, from Port-la-Nouvelle on the Mediterranean coast to Foix. The path is sometimes arduous but nature can be generous and the warm fragrances of the garrigue, the scrubland growing in the rocks, are rejuvenating. The trail will take hikers to several citadels where Cathars have lived, preached and sought refuge. The local Tourist Office calls these *Chateaux Cathares* but most are actually ruins of royal fortresses built at the end of the thirteenth century. Regardless of the history of these ruins, the walker can always hope that his musings will conjure the spirit of the Perfects.

The Cathars fitted well in Occitania, a region that had built its own civilization, borrowing much from an early Roman colonization and enriched by contact with Muslim and Jewish communities. The people of Occitania were protective of their independence, had their own language (the *langue d'oc*) and a taste for art, beauty and music. During the Middle Ages, Occitania nurtured the most inspired poets in Europe and troubadours sang the virtues of the Lady, object of courtly love, sublime but inaccessible. The Languedoc has retained some of this *joie de vivre*; people are welcoming and, when they converse in langue d'oi, the language forced on them by their northern compatriots, their speech comes out like a song.

Langue d'oc, Occitania and Cathar have deeply branded the identity of the south of France, west of the Rhone valley.

Albi

Bernard de Clairvaux started his mission to convert the Cathar dissidents in *Albi*, in 1145. Thereafter, these heretics would be called *Albigensians* and so would the 1209 Crusade. The word Cathar became more commonly used only after the second half of the nineteenth century. Despite this connection with the Cathar heretics, the town of Albi was faithful to the Church of Rome and a supporter of the Crusade.

After the eradication of the Cathar religion in Languedoc, the bishops of Albi undertook the construction of an imposing and austere cathedral. This was not a memorial but a demonstration of power should anyone intend to rebel again against the Church of Rome.

Cathédrale Sainte Cecile was consecrated in 1480. Its choir is separated from the nave by a magnificent rod screen, a late Gothic work in carved wood, with all the finesse of stone lacework. There are dazzling paintings by Italian artists on the vaults, the largest mural of the Last Judgment painted in the Middle Ages and more; the richly ornate interior stands in sharp contrast to the austere exterior.

The charming laid-back provincial town of Albi shared in the wealth created during the Middle Ages by the dye trade. A plant, *isatis tinctoria,* commonly known as woad, found a favorable terrain in the Laurageais, south of Albi. In the warm months of the year, its tall stalks would be capped by numerous rosettes of soft yellow leaves. These leaves crushed, dried and turned into a paste were the source of a colorfast blue dye. The Laurageais was the main producer of pastel (called *guede* in the north of France); the region became known as the *Pays de Cocagne,* Land of Plenty, and wealthy merchants built opulent Renaissance mansions in Albi and Toulouse. The bounty provided by the wild plant came to an end in the middle of the sixteenth century when indigo shipped from India became a cheaper source of blue dye (the name *indigo* is derived from the word India). Natural indigo, in turn, was replaced by the synthetic indigotine discovered in 1878 by the German chemist von Baeyer.

Albi has two famous sons, Toulouse-Lautrec and Jean-Francois de Galaup, Comte de Laperouse, and has dedicated a museum to each.

Henri de Toulouse-Lautrec's family left the most important public collection of his works to the city of Albi after Parisian museums refused, to their shame, to accept any painting depicting what they labeled *le monde vulgaire* of prostitutes, bohemian Montmartre and the seedy underside of Paris. The works are exhibited in the *Palais de la Berbie,* the former residence of the bishops, next to the cathedral. The medieval building, as imposing as a fortress, a true symbol of the power of the Church, was thoroughly remodeled in the early 2010's to specifically accommodate Lautrec's masterpieces. It was an ambitious project, an exemplary attempt to match the mood of a site to that of a collection. Throughout the various rooms the visitor will discover the mastery of Lautrec in his use of different mediums, lithographs, drawings, posters and paintings.

The *Musée Laperouse* honors the explorer who set off with two ships, Boussole and Astrolabe, on a voyage of discovery in 1785. Comte de Laperouse, born in Albi in 1741, had been commissioned by King Louis XVI to survey the Pacific. The two ships left Brest, headed for South America, entered the Pacific at Cape Horn, sailed from Hawaii to Alaska then down the Californian coast before crossing to the Philippines. The expedition is known to have gone north and must have left the Sea of Japan through the strait between Sakhalin and Hokkaido which still bears the name *La Perouse Strait.* What happened next will forever remain a mystery. Three years into the expedition the two ships vanished. In 1826 items from the ships were found on Vanikoro Island, south of the Solomon Islands, then, in 1964 wreckage of the ships was recovered on the same island and the wreck of the Boussole was formally identified in 2005.

The museum exhibits memorabilia from the great explorer and his ill-fated expedition and also houses eighteenth century navigational instruments, maps and scale models of ships.

In 2010 Albi was admitted into the exclusive *UNESCO World Heritage List.* The selection committee noted the "coherent and homogeneous ensemble of monuments and quartiers that has remained largely unchanged over the centuries…a complete ensemble representative of a type of urban development in Europe from the Middle Ages to the present day."

Mirepoix

Mirepoix is a quaint provincial town on the route to Montsegur. The family name Mirepoix was well-respected by the Cathars in the thirteenth century; Pierre-Roger de Mirepoix le Jeune had been in charge of Montsegur when the keep surrendered to men enlisted by the king of France.

Today, the name is familiar mostly to cooks for whom *Mirepoix* is a melange of diced onions, carrots and celery added to soups and stews.

The town is quiet during most of the year but it can be overrun by tourists from mid-July to mid-August, especially on market day. Its main attraction is a spacious square surrounded by thirteenth to fifteenth century houses whose first floors juts out to form covered arcades. The best known of the half-timbered houses is the Maison des Consuls. The end of the joists framing the arcade in front of the maison are decorated with carved wooden heads conveying humor and mischief. There are grotesque faces, heads of boars or even turtles and they all survived the historic fire that destroyed most of the town in the fourteenth century. On the other side of the square, a Gothic cathedral has one of the largest naves of any cathedral in Europe.

The Maison des Consuls is also a boutique hotel and several of its rooms overlook the square. In the evening, hotel guests can enjoy a *cassoulet* in one of the nearby restaurants, then, from the window of their room peek at the locals enjoying the last moments of the day at a terrace de café. In the morning they will wake up to the sound of the bells of the cathedral.

Toulouse

The flag of Occitania

The former capital of Occitania, seat of the Saint-Gilles' dynasty, whose numbers counted several illustrious Raymonds, had the most magnificent and liberal court in all of Europe in the thirteenth century. It was administered by the *capitouls,* consuls, chosen from the merchant class. The count of Toulouse was required to consult them before deciding on important affairs of the city. This spirit of independence was under serious attack after 1214 when Simon IV became Count of Toulouse and was crushed in 1271 when the county became part of the royal domain of the Kingdom of the Franks.

The *place du Capitole,* a majestic plaza, has remained the heart of the town and of the county. The flag of Occitania, a yellow occitan cross on a red background, is proudly flown next to the French flag on the façade of the *Hotel de Ville.* On the other side of the Plaza, elegant outdoor cafes welcome a diverse crowd of shoppers and business executives at all times of day. They enjoy the Mediterranean light which bathes a meridional city said to be pink at dawn, mauve at midday and red at twilight.

Basilique Saint Sernin, which contains many relics donated by Charlemagne, is the best-known Romanesque pilgrimage church in the south of France. Begun in 1080, the basilica was not finished until the fourteenth century but has no Gothic features. Its stylistic purity and massive size make it an extraordinary monument.

The Old Town is a labyrinth of narrow streets in the shadow of *les Jacobins*, the first Dominican monastery founded in 1215. Its red brick exterior has the solid and imposing presence of an impregnable fortress but the interior is spacious; light shines through brilliant red and blue stained-glass windows. Six columns support the roof vault and, at the eastern end, one column alone bears the weight of the vaulting of the apse. Its ribs fan out in the shape of a palm tree and the ensemble creates the feeling of a stone celestial oasis. Saint Thomas Aquinas (1225-1274), the great Dominican philosopher, author of the encyclopedic work on Catholic Theology known as *Summa Theologica*, rests here under a grey marble altar in the center of the nave.

Toulouse, a powerful medieval town, became a rich bourgeois city when it benefited from the dye trade. This very sought-after commodity enriched many bourgeois families in Toulouse as it did around the Pays de Cocagne. Some of these families used their newly acquired wealth to construct palatial Renaissance mansions and the town took on an Italianate architectural style.

Since the later years of the twentieth century the city has benefited from a much different industry. It became the most important complex of Airbus assembly lines and now also houses some of the aircraft manufacturer's research centers and renowned training facilities.

The rose city of Toulouse is one of France's most dynamic towns, well-known in the British Isles as one of Europe's major rugby centers.

Shortly after leaving Toulouse, the highway leading to the Mediterranean Sea crosses the *Seuil de Naurouze*, the watershed where a shift in the wind can cause a rain drop to end in the Atlantic Ocean instead of the Mediterranean Sea.

"The Good Days of Monseigneur Saint Louis"

The "Sacre," Anointing, of Louis IX (1226)

After the death of her husband, Blanche de Castille wasted no time escorting her eldest son to Reims to be crowned Louis IX.

It would be a very elaborate ceremony. The *ordo* for the sacre, the liturgical manuscript kept at the Bibliothèque Nationale in Paris, presents the rites, prayers and chants that had been carefully scripted. The same script would be used for the coronation of future French kings. Each stage of the ceremony was rich in symbolic meaning and conveyed the message that the power of the king and his aura were multidimensional, secular, sacred and religious.

In *Un long Moyen Age*, Jacques Le Goff, the French medievalist, gives a detailed account of the anointing of the future Saint. During the first phase of his rite of passage, the king-to-be sheds his old clothes and is handed shoes adorned with fleurs de lis, gilded spurs and a sword, all previously placed on the altar by the Abbot of Saint Denis, the guardian of the regalia. These objects are a reminder that the king is the secular arm of the church. He is then anointed. The gentle rubbing by the bishop of the sacred oil on the sources of power of his body: head, chest, shoulders and hands, elevate the king to a sacred link between God and his people. He now has supernatural powers and becomes the conduit for the divine protection of his kingdom. After the anointing, the king is draped in a cape sprinkled with fleur-de-lis and the bishop of Reims entrusts him with more insignias of his secular authority: a ring and, for the first time in such a ceremony, a unique scepter called *la main de justice*, the hand of justice.

During the last phase of the ceremony the king is crowned and installed on an elevated throne. Then, *coram Deo, clero et populo*, in front of God, the clergy and the people, he repeats the oaths he took previously to protect the Church, defend the Catholic faith and fight heresy.

The rites introduced by the Carolingians, Pepin le Bref in 751 and later Louis le Pieux in 816, had been used for the sacre of Louis IX. King by right of primogeniture he had become God's choice in the eyes of all. This did not make him a God, neither did following some of the rites used in the ordination of bishops make him a man of the Church, a king–priest, but after his anointing and coronation, the French king was much more than a simple link in a bloodline. He was a successor to David and the other kings of Israel.

Fleur-de-Lis

A *fleur-de-lis* decorated the azure mantle draping Louis IX. The motif had appeared at the time of Suger. Its origin is uncertain. It could be a stylized iris, a flower familiar to the Franks; a more esoteric theory sees it as the last avatar of a symbol known to the Merovingians as *crista*, crest, a representation of the rising sun found on their coins, a marker of divine protection. The fleur-de-lis decorated a piece of royal clothing for the first time at the wedding of Alienor and Louis VII in 1137. Louis IX made it widely popular and French royalty owes its emblem, three fleur-de-lis, to his modesty; no lions or eagles for the future saint, only a simple iris.

The name Suger is often associated with another emblem of French royalty: the *oriflamme,* the standard signaling the presence of the king on the battlefield. It was adopted at the beginning of the twelfth century along with the battle cry *Montjoie- Saint Denis* (the various etymologies of Montjoie are all unconvincing). The red (ori) jagged (flamme) flag had been the banner of the Abbey of Saint Denis and its shape might be derived either from a pagan emblem or have been inspired by the labarum, the military standard adopted by Constantine; in any case it kept its strong ties with Saint Denis where it was safeguarded (see page 5).

Sainte Chapelle

Saint Louis left his mark on a symbol of the close ties of royalty with religion in France: the magnificient Sainte Chapelle on the Ile de la Cité in Paris. It was commissioned by the king to house the alleged crown of thorns he bought in 1239 from the Byzantine emperor; unfortunately for today's visitor, the relic disappeared during the French revolution.

Sainte Chapelle

The second level of the Chapelle is a Rayonnant Gothic style gem. The walls are an ensemble of lancet stained-glass windows, some as high as fifty feet, and no central columns obstruct the view. These lancet-windows were restored in time to celebrate, in 2014, the eight hundredth anniversary of the birth of Saint Louis.

The ceiling is a star-studded azure sky. In Saint Louis's time, the warm colors of the rays of the sun, filtered by the stained-glass windows, shimmered on a white marble floor. The floor is not of marble anymore but the atmosphere is still ethereal.

The stained-glass panels tell stories mostly from the Old Testament and one panel in the lower right corner shows Helena, Emperor Constantine's mother, in Jerusalem, holding the true cross. Three crosses had been found on Golgotha and tradition says that the true cross was manifested by a miracle.

The entrance to the Sainte Chapelle is on the left of the imposing gates on the Boulevard du Palais. It is wise to buy tickets ahead of time and expect waiting time. A better option is to go to the Chapelle for a concert and combine the enjoyment of sights and sounds.

At the time of Saint Louis, the Chapelle was adjacent to the royal palace. The Romans had made the Ile de la Cité their base in Lutetia, Clovis had his royal residence there, and the Capetians had followed suit. The kings had felt safe surrounded by the Seine and, later, by the thick stone walls built by Philippe Auguste. From his chambers, Saint Louis had direct access to the second floor of the Chapelle.

In the middle of the fourteenth century, while King Jean II was held prisoner in England, and his son Charles was *Dauphin*, heir apparent, a popular revolt broke out in Paris led by Etienne Marcel, the Provost of Merchants. It reached a turning point in early 1358 when Marcel and his men chased two Marshals up to the Dauphin's chamber in the palace and slew them in his very presence. Thereafter the Dauphin never felt safe in the heart of Paris, and when he became King Charles V in 1364 he moved to the Hotel Saint Pol. (The Hotel located south of the Arsenal in the fourth arrondissement in Paris had been built in 1361; after 1418 the kings no longer used the *domaine royal de Saint Pol* as their residence in Paris; the Hotel was destroyed around 1520). The palace on the Ile de la Cité was left in the care of a *concierge* and it would later be known as *conciergerie* and became the seat of the Parliament of Paris, the highest court in the kingdom. During the Revolution of 1789 the prestigious building was home to the Revolutionary Tribunal. Between April 1793 and July 1794 close to 2,600 people were dragged from their cells in the Conciergerie to the tumbrels that would take them to the guillotine. Queen Marie-Antoinette was one of them on October 16, 1793.

The only remains of the royal palace are three towers and the so-called medieval halls. The current Palais de Justice, which houses several of the highest courts in France, including the Supreme Court of Appeal, was rebuilt at the end of the eighteenth century.

The visitor's entrance to the Conciergerie is on the Boulevard du Palais. A guided tour of the Conciergerie can comfortably be done in one hour and starts with the medieval halls, a fine example of Gothic secular architecture and continues with the revolutionary halls; particularly moving are Marie Antoinette's cell and her Chapel.

Victory at Taillebourg: The Seed of Future Wars

Louis IX remained under the tutelage of Blanche de Castille after his *sacre* and their relationship with the barons soon turned sour. The great lords had too much pride to be led by a twelve-year-old child and a woman. Their rebellion started shortly after the ceremony and Blanche and Louis IX confronted several coalitions. The king led his ost to battle in the west and in Champagne and proved to be a valorous warrior despite his age. One more feudal rebellion gave him a chance in 1242 to truly enter French military history.

At the origin of the rebellion was an appanage given to Louis IX's brother Alphonse de Poitiers by their father. In 1240, as Alphonse had come of age to take possession of his fief, one of the great local barons refused to acknowledge his authority. The Lord was Hugues X of Lusignan, a vassal of Louis IX, who belonged to a family made illustrious by their exploits in the Holy Land and by their ties with the English crown; Hughes X was wedded to Isabelle of Angouleme, King John's widow.

The French king brought his military strength to bear on his brother's side in this fight against an unruly vassal. As to Henry III, the English King, he joined the side of the Lusignans at the request of his mother Isabelle.

The unavoidable confrontation between the two coalitions took place at the foot of the Chateau de Taillebourg, a strategic location between Poitou and Aquitaine. The charge of the French king's cavalry won the day.

Bataille de Taillebourg, Eugene Delacroix

Eugene Delacroix has immortalized this event in a painting which now belongs in the collection devoted to the glory of French military history exhibited in the Galerie des Batailles in Versailles. The *Bataille de Taillebourg* is a powerful composition dominated by the silhouette of the king draped in a surcoat studded with fleurs de lis, and riding a white stallion. The warrior king is in the center of the action, wielding his mace, and creating an opening in the ranks of the enemy for his army to follow. This romantic painting is a tribute to Louis' military prowess and personal bravery, a sharp contrast to his traditional representations as a saint, champion of peace and justice. Eugene Delacroix would use his romantic style in the depiction of other battle scenes and do for Hundred Years War battles what some of his contemporary painters had done for Napoleonic victories.

The defeated Henry III signed a truce with Louis IX and then left for England by way of Bordeaux. A comprehensive peace treaty would be signed in Paris much later, in May 1258, and bring an end to the so-called First Hundred Years War. Louis IX returned the two provinces of Guyenne and Gascony to the English crown; in exchange, the king of England renounced all claims to Normandy and Anjou and acknowledged the suzerainty of the king of France in his two southwestern provinces. Louis IX had been generous in agreeing to the terms of the Paris treaty. To his baffled barons he preached love: there is no peace without love he declared, and referring to Henry, "the land I gave him was to tighten the ties between my children and his" (his mother was the cousin of Henry).

The seat of the English monarchy would now be at Westminster and the Plantagenets' focus would shift from the Continent to the building of an empire on the island.

The Paris Treaty would leave the English kings in the intolerable position of having to pay homage to the king of France for whatever land they controlled in the southwest. Despite Louis' good intentions, this was bound to poison the relationship between the two royal families. Decades later it would be one of the causes of the second, the calamitous, Hundred Years War.

In Search of Salvation

Hundreds of heteroclite documents dating from the thirteenth century remained stored, first in the *Trésor des Chartes*, the Royal Archives, then, after the Revolution, in the *Archives Nationales*, where they gathered dust. They were unearthed only in the nineteenth century and then, circa two thousand ten, minutely analyzed by the young French medievalist Dejoux. These are the handwritten notes and the documents gathered by the *enquêteurs*. These *enquêteurs* were itinerant judges commissioned by Saint Louis and formed a specific juridical institution.

In 1247, as he prepared to go on a crusade, the king had mandated enquêteurs to uncover and repair the abuses committed by his agents, *baillis* mostly, and by himself. Dangerous times were ahead and Louis needed to be ready to face his savior. The first step was to make restitution for ill-gotten gains.

Clerks of the king and Mendicants, predominantly Dominicans, were sent throughout the kingdom to listen to grievances against the king and his men, gather sworn testimonies and deliver a sentence. These enquêteurs recorded only griefs with quantifiable damage and would make restitution whenever one was called for. There was no punishment if the king's officer was at fault—just redress. Each step of the process was recorded in writing and translated into Latin. The notes of the plaintiffs and those of the enquêteurs are the bulk of the documents recently analyzed.

The files were closed on the spot, no report was sent to the king. This was not a step towards greater centralization or input for further legislation. The ultimate goal was only to make things right again, an exercise in accountability.

There had been enquêteur-type envoys before and the best known might be Charlemagne's missi dominici but Louis IX's were the first to conduct inquiries over the entire kingdom. This exercise whose purpose was the redress of past mistakes proved also beneficial for the king. It spread the image of a *just king* and helped consolidate his power in the newly conquered territories, mostly Languedoc. Prior to the general inquiry, the king had been mainly known in Ile de France, around Paris. After that, people in the kingdom knew that justice and peace were concerns of their distant king.

No other *enquête de reparation* will be conducted after Saint Louis. His successors in the fourteenth century will keep the idea of *enquêtes* but their objective by then will be to reform not to redress.

Saint Louis and the Seventh Crusade

Louis IX did go on a crusade in 1248. It would be called the Seventh Crusade. He had sworn four years earlier to take the cross if he recovered from a very serious illness which he had thought fatal. It would have been easy for him to be dispensed from his oath but neither his mother nor his kin were successful in dissuading him.

No other sovereign joined him so he left in August with a solely French party. The expedition was set to depart from *Aigues-Mortes*, a harbor along the Mediterranean, recently built to accommodate Louis' Crusade. It must have been an unusual sight when one thousand eight hundred vessels of various sizes, loaded with men and horses, sailed in the wake of the *La Montjoye*, the big circular hull sailboat carrying the king. Not much is actually known about these ships displaying triangular Latin sails and round hulls and called *nefs* at the time. This was the very beginning of a *royal navy*, the first sizeable French naval operation, called French even though Genoa had supplied the boats and the sailors. The fleet made for Cyprus, waited for favorable weather and sailed for Damietta in Egypt.

Close to fifty years after King Richard had left the Holy Land, only a small strip of the Syrian coastline was left in the hands of the Franks, and Louis IX had chosen to attack the weak link of the territories previously held by Saladin. In June 1249 he planted his oriflamme in Egyptian soil. The Crusaders waited out the flooding of the Nile in Damietta before marching towards Cairo. The next obstacle they faced was the stronghold of *Mansoura* protected by the Bahr es-Seghir canal. Only after a Copt revealed the existence of a ford were they able to continue their progression.

Robert d'Artois, the king's brother, took the vanguard across the canal and engaged in one of those acts of bravado that would cost the French knights so dearly in the coming centuries. Disregarding the instructions of the king he led his knights and the Templars in a foolish cavalry charge through the camp of the Egyptian emir and, without waiting for reinforcement, down the streets of the fortified town of Mansoura. There, the French were trapped and exterminated by the Mamelukes; Robert d'Artois and all the lords who had followed him in his supreme folly lost their lives. After this tragedy only the heroics of Saint Louis avoided a bigger disaster but he gained only a short reprieve. A few months later, weakened by typhus and cholera, the French had to surrender. The king himself was taken prisoner and freed against payment of a substantial ransom.

Going against the aspirations of the French lords, Louis IX then decided to postpone his return to France and reorganize the French presence in Syria. He stayed four more years in the kingdom of Jerusalem, and when he left, the Frankish contingent in the Holy Land seemed reasonably cohesive.

During their years away from the kingdom Louis created a bond with Jean de Joinville, the Seneschal of Champagne. Joinville, respectful of a family tradition, had taken the cross when the king had called for a new crusade. He had been in the heat of the battle at the time of Mansoura, captured and freed at the same time as the king. Despite his young age, at twenty-three he was eleven years Louis' junior, he had been of great comfort to the king during moments of danger and solitude. After his return from the Holy Land he stayed close to Louis, never a true advisor but a man the king could trust.

Late in his life, when he was already in his eighties, Joinville agreed to the request of Jeanne de Navarre to set down his memories of Saint Louis. Jeanne was the wife of Saint Louis' grandson, Philippe le Bel, and the memoire was for the benefit of her son the future Louis X. Joinville dictated what he called "the book of holy words and good deeds of our Saintly King Louis" presumably between 1305 and 1309, long after the events. The king's companion used his sense of observation to compose one of the great contemporary records of the Middle Ages. The *Life of Saint Louis,* as it was later called, is a sincere recollection of what the young seneschal had heard and seen from the king, an invaluable, even if often too flattering, source of information on the king. It is also a detailed account of the Seventh Crusade; more than seventy percent of the book is devoted to the six year expedition of Louis in Egypt and the Holy Land.

The "Grande Ordonnance" of 1254

Louis IX landed in Languedoc upon his return from the Holy Land. There, he met Gui Foucois, a brilliant jurist who would become Pope Clement IV. Gui came into the king's service and had a hand in drafting possibly the most important document of the reign, the *Grande Ordonnance.*

The crusade had been a turning point in Louis' life. He had seen a sign of God in the collapse of his army in Egypt, and become convinced that his kingdom was not virtuous enough to be granted the honor of freeing the Holy Land. God had not been at the side of the king and of his companions because they were sinners, or so Louis thought. After his return in 1254, and during the last sixteen years of his reign, he made it his mission to reform his officials and cleanse the kingdom of sin. The first major act was the so-called Grande Ordonnance.

The enquêtes of 1247 had shown the extent of the abuses committed by royal officers, in particular the baillis. It was now time to make just rulership a reality. The *Grande Ordonnance de Reformation* of 1254 was seeking fairness, honesty and justice in the kingdom. Royal officials had to take an oath to respect the rights of their constituents, refrain from engaging in graft, corruption, the selling of offices and, more generally, taking advantage of their position. The ordonnance went even further and included measures concerning public morality such as banning dice and *femmes de mauvaise vie,* loose women.

The king himself was not excluded from the search for justice. The mandate of the enquêteurs in 1254 was broader than it had been in 1247 and extended to claims against the king. Many cases were brought against him, mostly in Languedoc. One source of grievance was the requisition of land at Aigues-Mortes for the construction of the harbor. These cases took a long time to be settled but, when called for, restitution would be granted by the king.

"Les Enseignements": The Teachings of the King to his Son

Louis would go on another crusade. Before leaving he wrote a letter known as *Les Enseignements*, which was advice to his son Philippe, the future King Philippe III le Hardi. He wrote a similar letter to his daughter Isabelle who was to become Queen of Navarre. These were testaments of sorts.

The first exhortation in the letter to Philippe is "Love God with all your heart and all your power; without love of God a person has no worth." The next thirty or so counsels focus on how to lead a Christian life and behave as a good king: be devoted to the Church of Rome and the pope, be good to the poor, do not rush into war and should you become king, be fair and just.

Well-educated and respected clerics had written extensively about what makes a good king, the virtues he should cultivate and the proper equilibrium he should keep between the Church and the secular powers in his kingdom. In the thirteenth century two concepts became key: justice and moderation. Of all a king's virtues, be it humility, prudence or wisdom, the greatest must be justice and he must practice moderation. Louis IX was known to seek justice in the legal as well as moral sense and he was a man of *juste milieu*, aiming at the golden mean so dear to Aristotle. The image of Louis IX sitting under an oak tree in the forest of Vincennes, rendering justice to his subjects, is a *lieu de memoire*.

Saint Louis rendering justice under an oak tree

"Dit d'Amiens": Louis' Verdict in Henry III vs Simon de Montfort

Louis symbolized justice not only within but also outside of his kingdom. In 1264, he was solicited to arbitrate a dispute between the English King Henry III and barons led by Simon de Montfort, Earl of Leicester. The choice of Louis had been a tribute to his preeminence on the European regal stage. His verdict would be called Dit d'Amiens.

Simon was no other than the youngest son of Simon IV de Montfort, one of the main protagonists of the first Albigensian crusade. Simon IV had inherited the title of Earl of Leicester from his mother but had never benefited from his fief as it had been confiscated by King John. Many others had known the same misfortune. They were descendants of Normand lords who had followed William during his conquest, been rewarded with fiefdoms in England and at the beginning of the thirteenth century were forced to entrust their fiefs to trusteeships. Philippe Auguste and King John had wanted them to pay homage to one king and one king only.

At the end of a circuitous process, the English titles of the de Montforts ended up in the hands of young Simon who moved to England and became truly Simon the English; he is sometimes referred to as Simon V de Montfort. He was admitted in the close circle of advisors to King Henry III, and in 1239 the king returned their feudal estates and the title of Earl of Leicester to the de Montforts. Simon V climbed another rung in English society when he married one of the king's sisters,

264

Eleanor. From then on, his relationship with Henry III blew hot and cold. Around 1250 he was leading the opposition seeking to gain some level of direct control over the governance of the kingdom at the expense of the king. By 1258 Simon V and the barons had succeeded in forcing the king into signing the Provisions of Oxford. Pope Alexander IV did not wait long to condemn the Provisions in the name of the defense of the fullness of royal power and the preservation of peace. This is when Henry and the barons had asked Louis to intervene. The future Saint Louis was an obvious choice and Simon V trusted the French king.

Louis was unable to achieve reconciliation between the claimants and in January 1264 rendered the same judgment as the pope, ruling in favor of the English king. "The honor of the king had been greatly harmed, the realm disturbed, churches oppressed; the Provisions had caused violence…." and so Louis quashed them. Simon V should have known that the two kings belonged in the same network of friends. As Andrew Willard Jones discusses in the opus previously cited, the essence of royal power is the power to preserve peace and for Henry and Louis this implied the liberty to choose one's council and ministers, to rule through one's friends.

Simon V was excommunicated, the barons did not accept Louis' judgment and civil war broke out. The rebels were successful at first and de Montfort became the uncrowned king of England. His brilliant rise then became a tragedy. The barons were defeated by the king's son, the future Edward I, and Simon V was killed at the battle of Evesham.

An Anti-Semitic King?

In *Les Enseignements* Louis exhorts his son to banish heretics and other wicked people from his land "as much as he can with the counsel of good people". He makes no specific mention of the Jews. This is surprising coming from a man whose personal distaste for Jews is well-documented and whose legacy has been tarnished by the anti-Jewish policies he implemented. Records show that he took more discriminatory measures than any of his predecessors or successors on the throne. During his reign, the Jews were labelled *servus* for the first time, they were forced to wear a distinctive sign on their clothes, the Talmud was burned in Paris around 1241, usury was prohibited, and Louis might have considered chasing all Jews out of his kingdom.

Despite this impressive list of discriminatory measures, Louis did not have a general anti-Jewish policy. Each measure reflects his need to consolidate his control over his kingdom and Rome's obsession with orthodoxy. Each measure must also be seen in the context of the time and reflects his pragmatism as much as his obsessive search for salvation.

The wearing of a distinctive sign is a case in point. The need for a *signum* is found in canon 68 of The Fourth Lateran Council of 1215. The first part of this canon forced Jews (and Muslims) "to be distinguished in public from other people by the character of their dress." The stated goal was to "avoid accidental unions with Christians."

This was an infamous decree that came to be at a time when Church and king were truly afraid of Jewish proselytism. Joinville reports that Louis forbade Christians to debate with Jews unless the Christian was a learned cleric.

The nature of the sign was left in the hands of provincial councils. In the Kingdom of France, the first to take action were councils in Languedoc, a region that had most recently fallen under the control of the king. The councils paved the way for the *rota*, the safran and/or red wheel, which will later be imposed throughout the kingdom.

The secular powers were slow in implementing the prescription of canon 68 and in 1258 Pope Alexander IV had to remind Louis IX that most Jews in his kingdom still did not wear a signum. It would seem that secular powers were motivated more by the control of populations than by anti Semitism. The policies of the French monarchy on this issue would not crystallize until late in the reign of Louis IX.

The Tragic Crusade (1270)

By 1268, Christians, once again, controlled only a few coastal cities in the so-called Orient. Political bickering and the pursuit of commercial interests, mostly by Italians, had led to anarchy. When Antioch fell to the Mamelukes who followed the banner of Baibars, the sultan who had brutally eliminated the descendants of Saladin, emotions ran high in Europe.

A few years earlier the pope had called for a new Crusade and Louis IX had asked to have the honor of leading this military expedition.

The king and his three sons received the cross but few in the kingdom followed their lead. Joinville, for one, firmly refused to join the king on another crusade. His duty, he claimed, was to protect his people in Champagne and he recalled that they had been mistreated while he was away campaigning in Egypt during the previous Crusade. He also argued that it was the king's duty to stay in his kingdom.

Louis did not follow this advice. Neither his poor health nor the pleading by his beloved mother would dissuade him from leaving.

In July 1270, knights, mostly French, sailed from Aigues-Mortes. The first port of call was *Tunis*, not a harbor in the Holy Land as the knights had expected. The king was answering the request from his brother Charles d'Anjou, king of Sicily, to bring the Sultan of Tunis to submission. This detour should have been eventless but heat, lack of water and sickness quickly overcame the Crusaders. The first to die was the king's last child and a few days later Louis IX himself was victim of dysentery or typhus under the walls of Tunis. After lying penitently on a bed of ashes for long hours, he died on August 25, 1270 at 3:00 in the afternoon.

The Man, the King, the Saint

It has been written that after the disastrous Seventh Crusade, Louis IX had given serious thought to becoming a monk. He was too much of a king for that but he would have been comfortable with a life of charity and humility. The story is being told that to do penance he was drinking his wine diluted, three quarters water and one quarter wine. To live the life of a monk would have catered to his appetite for dialogue, teaching and sharing his thoughts.

Much of what he said is known to us thanks to his reliable biographers led by the most widely known, Jean de Joinville. Other official biographies were written by the confessor of the king, the confessor of the queen, a chaplain of the king and the chroniclers of Saint Denis, altogether a rich corpus of what the king did and most importantly what he said. Historians have found in these texts more than they could reasonably expect about the public personae of a king who lived in the middle of the thirteenth century. They got an intimate understanding of his vision of what it meant to be a king, how he saw it as a calling, an embodiment of the will of God. They also gained a glimpse at the person behind the king and what they found was a complex man. Psychoanalysts would have much to say about his close relationship with his mother, the strong-willed Blanche, and his bouts of anger which were signs of a man who was "struggling with his body" as Le Goff wrote. He could be cruel and was so with the Jews.

In *Vie de Saint Louis*, Joinville confides that the king devoted surprisingly little time to his children and his wife, and then concludes that being a stranger to one's wife was "not a good thing." This did not stop the king from having a very active sex life with his wife, and to father presumably more than eleven children.

Louis had been a good king but not an enlightened king. He was a man of the thirteenth century, a time when the individual was still trumped by his *tribe,* when every step in life was guided by firm rules and when each rule had to conform to the scriptures.

In the eyes of the Church, Louis IX had been true to the mission given to him by God, and worthy to be recognized as a saint. He was canonized in 1297, twenty-seven years after his death, at the end of a relatively short process, and is the only French king who is also a saint. The same honor had previously been bestowed on members of other royal families in Europe, all honoring a political tradition. There can be no doubt that Boniface VIII canonized Louis IX to show goodwill towards France at a time when his relationship with King Philippe le Bel was strained. It is nevertheless true that this honor was bestowed on a king who had led what was considered at the time a truly exemplary life, and had placed justice and morality at the foundation of his government.

After his canonization Saint Louis became the object of a true cult. In 1297 his grandson King Philippe le Bel had a chapel built in his honor in a section of Compiegne called Royallieu. It would be endowed with precious relics, in particular a piece of the true cross. This was most certainly the first place of worship dedicated to Saint Louis. There would be many more in the royal domain of Ile de France. Centuries later and mostly at the time of Louis XIV and Louis XV (Saint Louis was the patron saint of Louis XV) a large number of parish churches throughout France became *église Saint Louis.* A census in 1960 located 172 such places honoring the saintly king in France. On the American side of the

Atlantic, the City of Saint Louis, founded in 1764, would become the Gateway to the West and in the Catholic Church, the Rome of the West.

When Louis IX died in Cartagena outside of Tunis nobody knew how to embalm his body and so his remains were parceled out. The flesh went to Sicily, the kingdom of his brother, to be kept at the cathedral of Monreale and the heart and the bones were brought back to France. These remains would be solemnly buried at Saint Denis on May 22, 1271. The fate of Saint Louis' tomb at Saint Denis remains shrouded in mystery. It was, at first, a simple gravestone and said to have been the site of several miracles. By 1282 it was known to be magnificent, richly decorated with motifs carved in gold and silver but no actual rendering of this masterpiece has survived. The remains of the king quickly became treasured relics and his canonization only made them more valuable. His bones were dispersed, entrusted to members of royal families and religious institutions; Notre Dame de Paris welcomed its share and, noblesse oblige, the heart was safeguarded at the Sainte Chapelle. The elaborate tomb at Saint Denis was destroyed presumably around 1420, during the Hundred Years War. When the Revolutionaries came to Saint Denis in 1793 there was nothing much left for them to desecrate and throw into the common grave, the ultimate resting place of all the royals buried at the basilica.

Louis IX became the best known and most beloved French king in the Middle Ages, a true Christian and a man close to his people. Philippe le Bel, his grandson, considered him to be the model king. The thirteenth century had been Saint Louis' century. Philippe Auguste and Louis VIII, his grandfather and father, had added several feathers to the cap of the Capetian kings; they had been wise politically and successful militarily. Louis IX had added *moral authority* to the persona of the king.

The End of "The Good Days..."

After the Renaissance of the twelfth century, France had known what was later called with nostalgia "the good days of Monseigneur Saint Louis." The metamorphosis of the Kingdom of the Franks into the Kingdom of France had made great strides during that period. When the good days came to an end there was still much work to be done. The authority of the king was fragile and contested by many constituencies. Large segments of Caesar's Gaul were beyond his control. Besançon, for one, was the object of constant battles pitting the German emperors and the bishops against the citizens of the town who called on the duke of Burgundy to be their white knight! As the century came to an end, the town was a pseudo-republic.

The fourteenth century held the promise of a consolidation of France's preeminence in Europe. Who could foresee that it would be, paraphrasing Barbara Tuchman, *the Calamitous Century?*

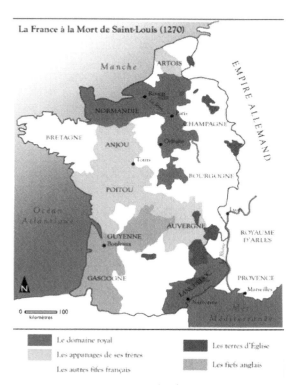

France at the death of Saint Louis

Photo credits

Sculpture of Saint Denis	Brian Kenney
Gisants at Saint Denis	Isogood Patrick
Caesar	Craig Code
Baptism Clovis	Boris 15
Coronation of Charlemagne	Viacheslav Lopatin
Viking Drakkar	Parry Suwanitch
Abbey of Fontenay	Massimo Santi
Bayeux Tapestry	Jorisvo
Chartres rose window	Valery Egorov
Sainte Chapelle	Ikmerc
Saint Louis	Chatsam

Special Thanks:

Jean-Benoit Bouron

Derek Boggs

Alex Swanson/ "The Map Archive"

Justin Weigold

Main Rivers of France

Bataille de Taillebourg

Treaty of Verdun, 843

Early Capetian France

Tower of Saint Denis

About the Author

Pierre Bognon is French born and educated in France and the United States. After retiring from a long career in business, love of country and love of history led him to become a passionate medievalist. "A tour of French History, from a Province of Rome to the Kingdom of France" on the early centuries of France, is the fruit of years of touring the country and learning from friends with deep roots in the soil of France. Pierre Bognon had previously published "The Anatomy of Sports fans, Reflections on Fans and Fanatics" in English and "Passion Supporter" in French.

Volume two of *A tour of French History* entitled
The Very Long Hundred Years War, is in preparation
and will be published in the autumn of 2020.

Index

expeditio Hierosolymitana 211

Robertians 96, 97, 100
Robert II 102
Robert I of Normandy 141
Robert le Fort 96
Roland 71
Rollo 91, 93, 94
Romana lingua 86, 87
Roman de la Rose 199, 200, 201, 202
Roncevaux 63, 71
Rose windows 187
royal fisc 107
royal navy 260
Rubicon 19
Runciman 209
rustica lingua romana 88

S

sacre 67, 253, 254
sacred oil 4, 53, 75, 253
Saint Augustin 75, 211
Saint Augustine 228
Saint Benedict 102, 121, 125
Saint-Clair-sur-Epte 93
Saint Dominic 176
Sainte Chapelle 255, 256, 269
Saint-Germain-en-Laye 64, 65
Saint Louis 7, 65, 82, 166, 181, 202,
    203, 231, 233, 238, 255, 256,
    260, 261, 265, 268, 269, 270.
    See Louis IX
Saint Martin 98
Saint Thomas Aquinas 245, 252
Saladin 160, 219, 220, 221, 222, 223,
    224, 261
Salian 38, 46, 48, 50, 53
Saracens 64, 72, 135, 211, 212, 227
Saxons 70, 91, 95, 142, 147, 213
Sentier Cathare 247
Sequani 16
Seuil de Naurouze 252
Sicily 94, 160, 174, 207, 214, 267, 269

signum 266
Simon IV de Montfort 234, 235, 236,
    237, 238, 264
Simon V de Montfort 264
simony 75, 120
Soissons 50
Sol Invictus 26
Spengler 187
Stamford Bridge 147
Stephen 4, 67, 125, 152, 154
Stilicho 37
Suetonius 70, 74
Suger 6, 8, 103, 110, 128, 152, 178,
    180, 254, 255
Syagrius 48, 50, 51
Sybille 221
Syria 26, 115, 209, 215, 216, 218, 219,
    220, 222, 261

T

Taillebourg 257, 258
Taizé 138
Tancrede 94
Teudisca lingua 86, 87
Teutons 12, 13
Theodokos 191, 192
Thomas Becket 156, 157, 186
Tiberius 20, 21, 58
Tolbiac 50
Tostig 144, 146, 147
Toulouse 133, 207, 209, 215, 226,
    230, 232, 234, 235, 236, 237,
    239, 240, 247, 248, 251, 252
Toulouse-Lautrec 249
tours philippiennes 112
Tower of London 111
Trencavel 231
triangular trade 195
Tripoli 215, 216, 219, 221
Tuchman 246, 270
Tunis 267